Classic Thinkers Series

J. M. Fritzman, *Hegel*
Bernard Gert, *Hobbes*
Dale E. Miller, *J. S. Mill*
A. J. Pyle, *Locke*
Andrew Ward, *Kant*

Berkeley

Daniel E. Flage

polity

Copyright © Daniel Flage 2014

The right of Daniel Flage to be identified as Author of this Work has been asserted in accordance with the UK Copyright, Designs and Patents Act 1988.

First published in 2014 by Polity Press

Polity Press
65 Bridge Street
Cambridge CB2 1UR, UK

Polity Press
350 Main Street
Malden, MA 02148, USA

All rights reserved. Except for the quotation of short passages for the purpose of criticism and review, no part of this publication may be reproduced, stored in a retrieval system, or transmitted, in any form or by any means, electronic, mechanical, photocopying, recording or otherwise, without the prior permission of the publisher.

ISBN-13: 978-0-7456-5633-5
ISBN-13: 978-0-7456-5634-2(pb)

A catalogue record for this book is available from the British Library.

Typeset in 10.5 on 12 pt Palatino
by Toppan Best-set Premedia Limited
Printed and bound in Great Britain by Clays Ltd, St Ives PLC

The publisher has used its best endeavours to ensure that the URLs for external websites referred to in this book are correct and active at the time of going to press. However, the publisher has no responsibility for the websites and can make no guarantee that a site will remain live or that the content is or will remain appropriate.

Every effort has been made to trace all copyright holders, but if any have been inadvertently overlooked the publisher will be pleased to include any necessary credits in any subsequent reprint or edition.

For further information on Polity, visit our website: www.politybooks.com

To Ronald J. Glass

I am not without some hopes, upon the consideration that the largest views are not always the clearest, and that he who is short-sighted will be obliged to draw the object nearer, and may, perhaps, by a close and narrow survey discern that which had escaped far better eyes.

— George Berkeley

Contents

Acknowledgements ix
Abbreviations xi

Chapter 1: Berkeley's Life and Writings 1
Why Study Berkeley Today? 1
Early Life 3
Bermuda and Rhode Island 7
Bishop of Cloyne 12
On Reading Berkeley 17
Further Reading 21

Chapter 2: Vision 22
The Historical Context: Methods of Inquiry and
 Theories of Vision 23
Berkeley on Seeing Distance (*NTV* §§2–51) 26
Perception of Magnitude (*NTV* §§52–87) 31
Situation and Numerical Heterogeneity (*NTV* §§88–120) 33
Heterogeneity and the Universal Language of Vision
 (*NTV* §§121–158) 36
A Look Back; A Look Ahead 39
Further Reading 41

Chapter 3: Abstraction 42
Historical Context 43
The Principal Arguments 48
Language 53
A Look Back; A Look Ahead 54
Further Reading 55

Chapter 4: The Case for Idealism and Immaterialism in the *Principles* — 56
The Case for Idealism (Sections 1–7) — 58
The Attack on Matter (Sections 8–24) — 70
Onward to Ordinary Objects (Sections 25–33) — 86
A Look Back; A Look Ahead — 94
Further Reading — 95

Chapter 5: *Three Dialogues between Hylas and Philonous* — 97
Background — 98
Dialogue One — 99
Dialogue Two — 105
Dialogue Three — 108
A Look Back; A Look Ahead — 112
Further Reading — 113

Chapter 6: Minds: Yours, Mine, and God's — 114
The *Principles* — 116
Knowing Minds: Dialogue Three — 124
Your Mind and God's — 131
A Look Back; A Look Ahead — 136
Further Reading — 136

Chapter 7: Moral Philosophy — 137
Moral Theories — 138
The Egoistic Notebooks — 142
Passive Obedience — 147
Alciphron — 158
A Look Back; A Look Ahead — 162
Further Reading — 163

Chapter 8: Economics and the Irish Condition — 164
Eighteenth-Century Ireland and the South Sea Bubble — 164
An Essay towards Preventing of the Ruin of Great Britain — 166
The Querist — 169
Further Reading — 176

Chapter 9: Concluding Remarks — 177

Endnotes — 182
Bibliography — 189
Index — 197

Acknowledgements

Books seldom leap fully grown from the head of Zeus. Typically authors work on them piecemeal, often before the thought of a book comes into mind. These bits and pieces are published as articles or read as conference papers. Eventually the author—or someone wiser than he—suggests that the dots posed by the articles be connected to form a unified whole, and a book is conceived. At least, that's how this book happened.

"Analysis in Berkeley's *Theory of Vision*," in *Berkeley's Lasting Legacy: 300 Years Later*, edited by Timo Airaksinen and Bertil Belfrage (Newcastle upon Tyne: Cambridge Scholars, 2011) anticipates the discussion of analysis in Chapter 2. It is published with the permission of Cambridge Scholars Publishing. Chapter 3 follows "Berkeley on Abstraction," copyright © 1986 Journal of the History of Philosophy, Inc. This article first appeared in *Journal of the History of Philosophy* 24:4 (1986), 483–501. Reprinted with permission by The Johns Hopkins University Press. Chapter 4 is a reworking of "Berkeley's Epistemic Ontology: The *Principles*," *Canadian Journal of Philosophy* 34 (2004): 25–60. Chapter 5 is closely associated with "Berkeley's Epistemic Ontology: The *Three Dialogues*," in Stephen Daniel, editor, *New Interpretations of Berkeley's Thought*, Journal of the History of Philosophy Books (Amherst, NY: Humanity Books, 2008), pp. 45–75. The discussion of Berkeley's argument for the existence of God in the *Principles* in Chapter 6 is a condensation of a paper I wrote with Ekaterina Ksenjek, "Berkeley, the Author of Nature, and the Judeo-Christian God," *History of Philosophy Quarterly* 29 (2012): 281–99, copyright 2012 by the Board of Trustees of the University of Illinois. Used with permission of the University of Illinois Press. The discussion of ethical egoism in Chapter 7 is based on "Was Berkeley an Ethical Egoist?" *Berkeley Studies* 19 (2008): 3–18. The discussion of the natural law theory found in *Passive Obedience* is based upon a paper I presented at a Workshop on Berkeley's Social and Moral Philosophy at the University of Helsinki, Helsinki, Finland in August 2010. The discussion of Berkeley's moral theory in *Alciphron* is based on a paper I presented at the International Berkeley Society Conference at L'Université de Sherbrooke, Longueuil, Quebec in June 2012. I wish to thank the publishers of these articles for permission to include modified versions of them in this book.

I wish to thank Phil Cummins, Ron Glass, Bertil Belfrage, Marc Hight, and the members of the International Berkeley Society for numerous discussions that helped clear some of the fog surrounding my understanding of Berkeley.

I am indebted to Emma Hutchinson of Polity Press, who suggested that I write this book. Without her encouragement, this book would not have been written. I wish to thank Emma, Pascal Porcheron, and David Winters for their editorial hand-holding during the writing. And I wish to thank Polity Press's readers for their comments on the original project and an early version of the manuscript.

Finally, I wish to thank my family for their continued love and encouragement.

Abbreviations

References to Berkeley's writings will be made parenthetically using the following set of abbreviations:

A *x:y* **p.** *z*	*Alciphron, or the Minute Philosopher*, Dialogue *x*, section *y*, page *z* in *The Works of George Berkeley, Bishop of Cloyne*, volume 3.
B-J *x* §*y*	Correspondence with Samuel Johnson, letter *x*, section y.
Cor. *x*	*The Correspondence of George Berkeley*, page *x*.
DHP *x*	*Three Dialogues between Hylas and Philonous*, in *The Works of George Berkeley, Bishop of Cloyne*, volume 2, page *x*.
DM *x*	*De Motu* section *x*.
Guardian *x:y*	*Guardian* number *x*, page *y* in *Works*, volume 7.
Intro. §*x*	Introduction to *A Treatise Concerning the Principles of Human Knowledge*, section *x*.
N *x*	1707–1708 notebooks (sometimes known as *Philosophical Commentaries*), entry number *x*.
NTV §*x*	*An Essay towards a New Theory of Vision*, section *x*.
PHK §*x*	*A Treatise Concerning the Principles of Human Knowledge*, Part I, section *x*.
Q *x*	*The Querist* (1750 edition), query *x*.
RGB *x*	*An Essay towards preventing the Ruin of Great Britain*, in *The Works of George Berkeley, Bishop of Cloyne*, volume 6, page *x*.

Abbreviations

SER *x*:*y* — Sermon number *x*, page *y* in *Works*, volume 7.

Siris §*x* — *Siris: A Chain of Philosophical Reflexions and Inquiries concerning the Virtues of Tar-water and divers other Subjects connected together and arising One from Another*, section *x*.

TVV §*x* — *The Theory of Vision, or Visual Language shewing the immediate Presence and Providence of a Deity Vindicated and Explained*, section *x*.

Works *x*:*y* — *The Works of George Berkeley, Bishop of Cloyne*, edited by A. A. Luce and T. E. Jessop, 9 volumes, volume *x*:page *y*.

Since we shall cite John Locke's *Essay* and the works of René Descartes with some regularity, we shall also make the following citations parenthetically:

CSM *x*:*y* — René Descartes, *The Philosophical Writings of Descartes*, translated by John Cottingham, Robert Stoothoff, and Dugald Murdoch; correspondence translated in part by Anthony Kenny, three volumes, volume *x*:page *y*.

Locke, Essay *x*.*y*.*z* — John Locke, *An Essay concerning Human Understanding*, Book *x*, Chapter *y*, Section *z*.

1
Berkeley's Life and Writings

George Berkeley (pronounced **Bark**-lee) was the second head of the eighteenth-century philosophical trinity known as the British Empiricists.[1] As the middle figure in time, Berkeley is often treated as the least significant of the three. He could not claim the great philosophical insight of John Locke (1632–1704), who argued that experience and reasoning based upon experience were sufficient to justify the new sciences of Galileo and Isaac Newton. Nor, we are told, could he claim the rigid consistency of David Hume (1711–1776), who argued that our claims to knowledge based on experience alone lead to skepticism and that there are no better grounds for claiming the existence of immaterial substance than there are for claiming the existence of material substance. One of the purposes of this book is to show that, even if taken as a halfway point in the development of British Empiricism, Berkeley's philosophy is interesting and significant in its own right.

Why Study Berkeley Today?

"But," you might say, "Berkeley died in 1753. That's more than 260 years ago. Why read him today?"

Historical texts—anything written before you write—are the data that philosophers use to develop their own positions. Philosophers examine these texts carefully and critically. They mine these texts for arguments and develop their own positions either by developing the arguments further or showing that the arguments fail. For example, if you wanted to defend the claim that everything that exists either is a mind or depends for its existence upon a mind—idealism—you would want to read the great idealists of the past. If their arguments are successful, you might incorporate similar arguments into your defense of idealism. If those arguments fail, you'll want to show why they fail and show why your arguments are stronger. Berkeley was an idealist. The only way to discover what arguments he presented is by carefully reading his texts.

Idealism is not popular in the twenty-first century. Materialism—the philosophical theory that everything that exists is material or depends upon matter for its existence[2]—is more often proposed now. Berkeley provided criticisms of the doctrine of material substance. So, if you want to defend philosophical materialism, it is incumbent upon you to show that Berkeley's arguments fail.

Historians of philosophy and historians of ideas read Berkeley for different reasons. Historians might be fascinated by a particular issue, or a particular period, or a particular figure. Just as a military historian might find the development and use of particular weapons fascinating, a historian of ideas might be interested in the development of utilitarian theories in ethics. Such a one might read Berkeley to see whether he is part of that tradition, and if he is not, how the natural law tradition of Aristotle (384–322 B.C.E.) and Aquinas (1225–1274) evolved into the utilitarian tradition of Jeremy Bentham (1748–1821) and John Stuart Mill (1806–1873).

Some people find Berkeley or his era fascinating in the same way that they may be fascinated by the Battle of Hastings or the First World War.

Some of us are intrigued by conceptual puzzles. As we shall see, many scholars believe Berkeley's arguments are weak or inconsistent. Assuming Berkeley was a serious philosopher, the challenge is to tease out a consistent and philosophically plausible reading of his writings.

And some people like to read great literature. Berkeley's *Three Dialogues between Hylas and Philonous* are generally recognized for their literary quality.

Those are among the reasons people still read Berkeley. But who was he?

Early Life

Berkeley was born on March 12, 1685 in the townland of Kilcrene, about a mile outside the city of Kilkenny, Ireland. He was raised on the grounds of Dysart Castle near Thomastown.

While the young Berkeley considered himself Irish (*N* 392–394), his ancestors were English. His father, William Berkeley, was a tax collector, landlord, and a military officer. Berkeley's mother hailed from Dublin and was related to the Wolfes of British military fame.

Berkeley entered Kilkenny College on July 17, 1696. This school was established in 1666 by James, the First Duke of Ormonde, as a Church of Ireland (Anglican) secondary school. When Berkeley entered, it already listed Jonathan Swift (1667–1745) among its illustrious alumni. Six months later Berkeley was joined by Thomas Prior, who was one of Berkeley's lifelong friends and correspondents. It is from Berkeley's letters to Prior and John Percival, who he met and befriended in 1708, that we know many facts about Berkeley's life.

Berkeley entered Trinity College, Dublin on March 21, 1700. This was the beginning of a twenty-four-year association with the College, first as a student and then as a fellow. Trinity was established in 1592 by a charter from Queen Elizabeth as part of the English attempt to establish Protestantism (Anglicanism) in Ireland. Due in part to the influence of William Molyneux (1656–1698), the Trinity College philosophy curriculum included the study of such recent philosophers as René Descartes (1596–1651), Nicholas Malebranche (1638–1715), and John Locke. In philosophical circles, Molyneux is best known for a question he posed to Locke (Locke, *Essay* 2.9.8).

Berkeley received his B.A. in the spring of 1704. He remained at Trinity and prepared for a competitive fellowship that became open in 1706. He became a junior fellow of Trinity College on June 9, 1707. Fellows were not allowed to marry and were required to take holy orders; this was common practice at many universities at the time. Berkeley was ordained as a deacon of the Church of Ireland in the college chapel on February 19, 1709, by St. George Ashe, Bishop of Clogher and ex-Provost of Trinity College. In the spring of 1710, Bishop Ashe, then Vice-Chancellor of the university, ordained Berkeley a priest. This act drew the ire of William King, Archbishop of Dublin, who deemed the ordination irregular: the Bishop of Clogher, King claimed, did not have ordination rights within the diocese of Dublin. Berkeley wrote an apologetic letter to Archbishop King, explaining his need to fulfill the terms of his fellowship and his lack of knowledge that the Bishop of Clogher had no right to ordain within the diocese of Dublin (*Works* 8:33; *Cor.* 37–38). The complaint was dropped.

The years between 1707 and 1713 are sometimes called Berkeley's "heroic period," since it was during this time that he wrote the philosophical works for which he is best known. In 1709 he published *An Essay towards a New Theory of Vision*. The work challenged the received views on how distance is perceived by sight (see Chapter 2). In 1710 he published the *A Treatise concerning the Principles of Human Knowledge*, Part I, which presents Berkeley's principal case for immaterialism, the thesis that matter does not exist (see Chapters 3–4). In 1712, he published *Passive Obedience*, which contains moral and political theory (see Chapter 7). In 1713, he published *Three Dialogues between Hylas and Philonous*, which is generally seen as a popular reworking of the arguments in the *Principles* (see Chapter 5). In addition to this, we have a set of private notebooks Berkeley kept between 1707 and 1708, in which he worked through some of the arguments he developed in the *New Theory of Vision* and the *Principles*.

In January 1713 Berkeley traveled to London. His objective was to publish the *Three Dialogues between Hylas and Philonous*, which was accomplished in May of that year (*Works* 8:65 and 67; *Cor.* 88 and 95). He originally intended to spend a relatively short time in England, but in fact he was absent from his position at Trinity College for almost eight years. He even obtained a license from Queen Anne to extend his absence from the College (*Works* 8:72 and 90; *Cor.* 104 and 127). While in London he became good friends with some of the major literary lights of the time, including Jonathan Swift, Alexander Pope, Joseph Addison, and Richard Steele. His association with Steele led to several articles in Steele's *Guardian*, a daily essay paper published between March and October 1713. None of the essays is signed, and there is some dispute regarding which essays Berkeley contributed. Several years after Berkeley's death, Berkeley's son George attributed numbers 3, 27, 35, 39, 49, 55, 62, 70, 77, and 126 to his father, although scholars have challenged some of the numbers the younger Berkeley included and have argued that other numbers were authored by Berkeley.[3] The principal topic of Berkeley's essays was "free-thinking," a philosophical and popular movement that challenged religious orthodoxy. It was a topic to which Berkeley returned in his *Alciphron*

(1732). He also edited the three-volume *Ladies Library*—primarily a collection of religious writings—for Steele.

In October 1713, Berkeley was named chaplain to Lord Peterborough, who had been made ambassador extraordinary to attend the coronation of the king of Sicily. This allowed him to tour continental Europe. He traveled through France and, during the winter, crossed the Alps into Italy (see *Works* 8:77–78; *Cor.* 109). While in Paris, he is believed to have talked with the philosopher Nicholas Malebranche. On November 24, 1713, Berkeley wrote John Percival that the Monsignor l'abbé d'Abigune was to introduce him to Malebranche that day. On November 25 he wrote Thomas Prior, "Tomorrow I intend to visit Father Malebranche, and discourse him on certain points" (*Works* 8:76; *Cor.* 108). No records of the meeting with Malebranche exist, although an apocryphal story claims that Malebranche was so astounded by Berkeley's immaterialism that he died shortly after the visit. Since Malebranche died in 1715, Berkeley should be exonerated of all charges of homicide by philosophical argument. His trip through France and Italy exposed Berkeley to a wide range of art and architecture, architecture being one of his early and prevailing interests. On his return trip, he arranged to travel from Paris to London with an Irish acquaintance, who was making the trip by way of Flanders and Holland (*Works* 8:85; *Cor.* 119). Berkeley returned to London on August 1, 1714.

Shortly after his return, Queen Anne died. The second daughter of James II (Queen Mary, wife of William of Orange, was James's first daughter), she was the last of the Protestant Stuarts at a time when British monarchs were required by law to be Protestants. Queen Anne was succeeded by George I of the House of Hanover, her second cousin and closest Protestant relative. Members of Parliament swore oaths of loyalty to King George and his descendants. In 1715, James Edward Stuart, son of James II and a Catholic, led a revolt of Scottish and English troops in an attempt to reclaim the British throne for the Stuarts. Many of the Tories were sympathetic with the revolt, since they had opposed the Glorious Revolution (1688) on grounds of the right to succession of the eldest son of the monarch. Although Berkeley himself had Tory sympathies and his *Passive Obedience* was viewed by some as expressing a central ideology of the Tory Party, he was opposed to the rebellion (*Works* 8:86–98, *passim*; *Cor.* 120–37, *passim*). In his *Advice to the Tories who have Taken the Oath* (*Works* 6:54–60) he argues that those who took an oath to George I have an irrevocable duty to abide by it and that to violate the oath would be injurious to the Church of England.

In 1717 Berkeley was awarded the Bachelor of Divinity and Doctor of Divinity degrees, and he was promoted to Senior Lecturer.

In the fall of 1716 Berkeley was offered a tutorship by St. George Ashe, the Bishop of Clogher. Berkeley became the traveling companion of Ashe's son George, who was taking a continental tour, which lasted until 1721. Much of their time was spent in Italy. Berkeley kept a record of the trip in his 1717–1718 journals (*Works* 7:246–335). The focus of the tour was on art, architecture, and, to a lesser extent, music. As Berkeley wrote to Percival from Rome, "I have got eyes but not ears. I would say that I am a judge of painting though not of music. . . . Prince Rospoli is that man who now gives music every week to strangers, where I am sure to fall asleep as constantly as I go" (*Works* 8:102; *Cor.* 142). In Naples, he observed the eruption of Mount Vesuvius, a description of which he sent to the Royal Society (*Works* 4:248–51). He experienced an earthquake in Messina, which was the basis for a discussion he published in 1750 (*Works* 4:256–57). On their trip back to London in 1721, they stopped in Lyon, France, where Berkeley wrote *De Motu* (*On Motion*) for a contest by the French Academy of Sciences.

He was back in Dublin in September, and was appointed Divinity Lecturer on November 20, 1721, Senior Proctor on October 27, 1722, and Hebrew Lecturer on November 20, 1723. Thereafter, his activities moved in a different direction.

Before turning to the second phase of Berkeley's life, a word should be said about *De Motu* and its relation to the *Principles of Human Knowledge*. When Berkeley published the *Principles* in 1710, it was marked "Part I." When the second edition was published in 1734, the part designation was dropped. As we learn from his 1707–08 Notebooks, Berkeley had originally envisioned the *Principles* as a work in at least three books: The first presents his case for idealism and immaterialism; the second was to focus on mind and morality (*N* 508, 807, 878). In 1729 Berkeley wrote his American correspondent, Samuel Johnson, "As to the Second Part of my treatise concerning the *Principles of Human Knowledge*, the fact is that I had made considerable progress in it; but the manuscript was lost about fourteen years ago, during my travels in Italy, and I never had leisure since to do so disagreeable a thing as writing twice on the same subject" (B-J 2, §6; *Cor.* 305). He has little to say about the projected third part beyond, "That which extremely strengthens us in prejudice is that we think we see an empty space. which I shall Demonstrate to be false in the 3rd Book" (*N* 583). This *suggests* that the third part would concern immaterialism and the physical sciences. Insofar as *De Motu* is a discussion of physical science on immaterialist principles, it might approximate what Berkeley had intended to include in *Principles*, Part III.

Bermuda and Rhode Island

Berkeley was a cleric as well as a philosopher. As early as 1716, he was looking for advancement (preferment) in the Church of Ireland (*Works* 8:98; *Cor.* 137). Upon his return from his second continental tour, he was nominated for Dean of Dromore (in the Church of Ireland, a dean is the chief resident cleric at a cathedral). Berkeley found the deanery desirable because it provided an income of £500 per year but carried no duties with it: it would have allowed him to retain his fellowship at Trinity College. Since the Church of Ireland is a state church, religious appointments are not free from politics. Berkeley was appointed to the deanery by the Duke of Grafton, Lord Lieutenant of Ireland, but the Bishop of Dromore challenged the right of the Crown to appoint deans, and made his own appointment. The result was an extended lawsuit. While the suit was progressing, with Berkeley becoming increasingly pessimistic about his chances of appointment, the Deanery of Derry (Londonderry), became vacant. Again there were several candidates for the post, but through the intervention of Trinity College, Berkeley ultimately prevailed. He received the official appointment (patent) on May 4, 1724, traveled to Londonderry to be installed, and that month resigned his Senior Fellowship at Trinity College. On June 8 he wrote Percival, "I am now on my return from Derry, where I have taken possession of my Deanery, and farmed out my tithe lands, &c. for £1250 a year" (*Works* 8:134; *Cor.* 196).

Berkeley was Dean of Derry for ten years. There is no evidence that he was ever dean-in-residence. Why is that? Beginning in about May 1722 (*Works* 8:127; *Cor.* 185) Berkeley developed a plan to found a college on the island of Bermuda. Indeed, one of the reasons he was happy to have been appointed Dean of Derry is that he believed being "possessed of so great a Deanery" would improve his chances for support for the college in Bermuda (*Works* 8:133; *Cor.* 195). But why did he propose to build this college?

Berkeley seems to have lost faith in the prospect of a Christian civilization continuing in Europe. When Berkeley returned from his second continental tour, Britain was in the throes of the South Sea

Bubble. The South Sea Company was a trading company; it focused on the slave trade, and was moderately successful initially. When King George I became governor of the company in 1718 confidence in the company increased, and in 1720 it offered to take over the British national debt. Prices of the stock soared briefly—and then the market collapsed. In 1721 Berkeley wrote *An Essay towards Preventing the Ruin of Great Britain*, in which he called for a return to religion, industry, frugality, and public spirit. It opposes economic speculation on moral and religious grounds, suggesting that the South Sea Bubble was evidence of the decay of civilization in Europe. Further evidence that Berkeley believed Europe was in decline and that the American colonies were the best chance for the continuation of civilization is found in the poem he wrote and sent to Percival in February 1726. Its last and most famous verse reads:

> Westward the course of Empire takes its way,
> The four first acts already past,
> A fifth shall close the drama with the day,
> The world's great effort is the last.
> (*Works* 8:153; *Cor.* 220; also *Works* 7:370)

But why Bermuda?

In the popular mind of the early eighteenth century, Bermuda was seen as something near paradise. It was the scene of Shakespeare's *The Tempest*. Sir George Somers had been shipwrecked on the islands in 1609, and they became popular due to tales of his adventures there. It was the subject of poet Edmund Waller's *Battle of the Summer-Islands*, which depicted it as a paradise. And Berkeley considered it the ideal place for a college that would cater to the sons of plantation owners and Native Americans, both of whom would be trained as missionaries for the Church of England. In his *A Proposal for the Better Supplying of Churches in our Foreign Plantations*, Berkeley makes his case for Bermuda. First, he indicates what would be required in choosing the location for a college:

> Many Things ought to be considered in the Choice of a Situation. It should be in a good Air; in a place where Provisions are cheap and plenty; where an Intercourse might easily be kept up with all Parts of *America* and the Islands; in a Place of Security, not exposed to the Insults of Pirates, Savages, or other Enemies; where there is no great Trade, which might tempt the Readers or Fellows of the College to become Merchants, to the neglect of their proper Business; where

there are neither Riches nor Luxury to divert, or lessen their Application, or to make them uneasy and dissatisfied with a homely frugal Subsistence; lastly, where the Inhabitants, if such a Place may be found, are noted for Innocence and Simplicity of Manners. I need not say of how great Importance this Point would be toward forming the Morals of young Students, and what mighty Influence it must have on the Mission. (*Works* 7:348–49; cf. *Works* 8:127–29; *Cor.* 185–87)

Each of these virtues, Berkeley claimed, is found in Bermuda. It was equidistant from most of the colonies (about 600 nautical miles), and poor conditions on the American continent—ranging from moral turpitude to poor roads (*Works* 7:449)—meant that any location on the mainland would be problematic for some potential users. These facts strengthen the case for Bermuda.

It was a period of missionary zeal, furthered and supported by the Society for the Promotion of Christian Knowledge (with which Berkeley was originally associated) and the Society for the Propagation of the Gospel (to which Berkeley was admitted in 1732). Berkeley's plan engendered great enthusiasm at Trinity College. His *Proposal* was published in 1724. A royal charter for St. Paul's College was granted in June 1725. Initially, funding for the college was by donations and pledges of support. By February 1726, Berkeley tells Percival that "The subscriptions amount to about four thousand pounds" (*Works* 8:152; *Cor.* 219). In April 1726, the House of Commons agreed to give a grant of £20,000 to fund the college, which was signed by King George II in July 1727; the signing had been delayed by the death of George I. The money for this grant was to come from the sale of some of the island of St. Christopher (now St. Kitts), which was ceded to Great Britain by France under the terms of the Treaty of Utrecht (1713). The wording of the grant ultimately proved to be to Berkeley's disadvantage, since it did not specify a date on which the monies would be paid. In addition to this, in 1723 Berkeley had inherited what he initially estimated to be more than £3,000 from Hester Van Homrigh (*Works* 8:130; *Cor.* 188), a legacy that was both a blessing and a curse. It was a blessing insofar as it provided funding for his college; it was a curse insofar as the estate was so encumbered with debts that they were not cleared before May 1727 (*Works* 8:180; *Cor.* 250–51). Berkeley was still involved in dealings with Van Homrigh's brother as late as May 1741 (*Works* 8:252; *Cor.* 422).

A problem with having charitable subscribers to a project is that they eventually wish to see their contributions bear fruit. But it is unwise to act on the basis of a government grant until the grant monies are paid. In 1728 Berkeley was caught between these two problems and decided to sail for the colonies. In August he married Anne Foster, daughter of the late Chief Justice of Ireland, and in early September they sailed for Newport, Rhode Island. Because the grant had not been paid, Berkeley attempted to shroud his departure in secrecy.

Why Newport? The terms of the grant required that the building of the college commence within eighteen months of Berkeley's landing in Bermuda, and without the money, the future of the college was in limbo. Further, Henry Newman, secretary of the Society for the Promotion of Christian Knowledge, had many contacts in New England. Finally, there is some reason to believe that Berkeley was questioning the wisdom of building the college in Bermuda, since he told his correspondents shortly after his arrival in Newport that Newport would be a fine place for the college (*Works* 8:190, 195, 199, 200; *Cor*. 265, 271, 283, 284). In June 1729 he wrote to Prior:

> I find it hath been reported in Ireland that we propose settling here. I must desire you to discountenance any such report. The truth is, if the King's bounty were paid in, and the charter could be removed hither, I should like it better than Bermuda: but if this were mentioned before the payment of said money, it may perhaps hinder it, and defeat all our designs. (*Works* 8:198; *Cor*. 277)

Berkeley settled in to wait for the royal grant. He bought a ninety-six-acre farm for £2,500, ostensibly to provide provisions for the college. He built a house, which he named Whitehall probably in honor of the "Chapel Royal, Whitehall," which was presided over by Berkeley's friend Edmund Gibson, bishop of London and bishop of the colonial plantations.

Rhode Island, like most of New England, was not a stronghold of the Church of England. Berkeley worked closely with James Honeyman, "the only Episcopal clergyman of this island" (*Works* 8:194; *Cor*. 267), and preached at Trinity Church, Newport. He befriended Samuel Johnson, who had been a tutor at Yale before converting to Anglicanism. Johnson was a philosopher, and their correspondence during Berkeley's time in Newport provides insight into some elements of Berkeley's philosophy. (Johnson was later the first president of King's College—now Columbia University—and he dedicated his *Elementa Philosophica* to Berkeley.) Whitehall became a center for both religious and philosophical discussions.

But the grant for the college was not to be. While Berkeley was waiting in Newport, critics of the project were circling in London. The money promised by the king and Parliament would not be paid unless it was available—the lands in St. Christopher were not sold until 1733—and the payment was approved by Prime Minister Sir Robert Walpole. While Walpole had contributed to the project, he was not an ardent supporter. Some politicians argued that the college was undesirable because it would make the colonies less dependent upon the mother country. People who were familiar with the colonies deemed Berkeley's proposal impractical. Thomas Bray was founder of both the Society for the Promotion of Christian Knowledge and the Society for the Propagation of the Gospel, and he had traveled in the colonies. In 1727 Bray was openly critical of Berkeley's *Proposal* in his *Missionalia: Or, A Collection of Missionary Pieces Relating to the Conversion of the Heathen; Both the African Negroes and the American Indians*. William Byrd, a Virginia planter, assured Walpole that the absence of food on Bermuda and the frequency of hurricanes made it an unfit place for a college and that prospects for recruiting Native Americans were slim. When the Bishop of London asked Walpole when or whether Berkeley could expect to receive the grant, Walpole replied, "If you put this question to me as a Minister, I must and can assure you that the money shall most undoubtedly be paid as soon as suits with public convenience; but if you ask me as a friend whether Dean Berkeley should continue in America, expecting the payment of £20,000, I advise him by all means to return home to Europe, and give up his present expectations."[4]

The Bermuda project failed. Berkeley left Newport in early September 1731, shortly after the death of his infant daughter Lucia (who is buried in the Trinity Church cemetery). He went to Boston, where he visited Harvard, and from which he sailed for London, arriving there on October 30.

While the Bermuda project failed, Berkeley's American sojourn was not without an impact on the American educational system. He sold his farm—the only home Berkeley ever owned—to Yale University for five shillings. The rent and proceeds from the farm supported graduate scholarships for Yale students. In 1900 the Society of Colonial Dames of Rhode Island purchased a long-term lease of Whitehall, which they maintain as a museum to Berkeley's visit. Berkeley gave many of the books from his Rhode Island library to Yale. While he attempted to return the funds that had been contributed toward the college, many contributors requested that the funds be used to further education in the Americas. In 1733, eight cases of books were sent to Yale and a case of books was sent to Harvard. In the nineteenth century, a number of Yale alumni were responsible for establishing a university and town in California named "Berkeley."

Bishop of Cloyne

The return to London was again a period of waiting. This time the waiting was for advancement in the Church of Ireland. His Bermuda–Rhode Island adventure had not endeared him to the Archbishop of Dublin, who described Berkeley as "a madman" when he was seeking the deanery of Down shortly after his return to London. But Berkeley also had friends in high places, including Queen Caroline. In early January 1734, he was offered the Diocese of Cloyne in southeastern Ireland. As he wrote Prior:

> On the sixth instant the Duke sent over his plan, wherein I was recommended to the Bishopric of Cloyne. On the fourteenth I received a letter from the secretary's office, signifying his Majesty's having immediately complied therewith, and containing the Duke of Newcastle's very obliging compliments thereupon. In all this I was nothing surprised; his Grace the Lord Lieutenant having declared, on this side the water, that he intended to serve me the first opportunity, though at the same time he desired me to say nothing of it. As to the A. B. D. [Archbishop of Dublin] I readily believe he gave no opposition. He knew it would be to no purpose; and the Queen herself had expressly enjoined him not to oppose me. (*Works* 8:225; *Cor.* 362)

He sent Baron Wainwright a formal resignation from the deanery of Derry on February 19 (*Works* 8:228; *Cor.* 366), and was consecrated bishop on May 19, 1734 at St. Paul's Church, Dublin. In early summer, Berkeley and his family moved to Cloyne. Except for attending a session of the Irish House of Lords in 1737–38, he remained continually in residence at Cloyne until August 1752.

Before discussing his years at Cloyne, we should say a few words about his literary activities between 1732 and 1735. Upon returning to London, Berkeley arranged for the publication of *Alciphron or the Minute Philosopher*, which was published in early 1732. *Alciphron* is a defense of Christianity against its critics, the free-thinkers. It is a work in seven dialogues. It was written while Berkeley was in

Rhode Island, which is where the dialogues are set. Dialogues two and three attack the moral writings of Bernard Mandeville (1670–1733), and Anthony Ashley Cooper, Third Earl of Shaftesbury (1671–1713; see Chapter 7). The remainder defends Christianity against charges of intellectual naiveté and unintelligibility. The work was originally published with a slight revision of the *New Theory of Vision* as an appendix, since *Alciphron* develops the divine-language argument that Berkeley championed in that work. It develops the arguments against free-thinking that Berkeley had first upheld in his *Guardian* essays (1713), a topic to which he returned in *A Discourse addressed to Magistrates and Men in Authority* (1738). On September 9, 1732, an anonymous criticism of his theory of vision was published in the *Daily Post-Boy*. Berkeley replied in 1733 with his *The Theory of Vision . . . Vindicated and Explained*. He published revised editions of the *Principles* and the *Three Dialogues between Hylas and Philonous* in 1734. These editions include brief discussions of "notions" and one's knowledge of minds, discussions he originally intended to include in the second part of the *Principles* (see Chapter 6). In 1734 he also published *The Analyst or a Discourse Addressed to an Infidel Mathematician*, which is a criticism of the Newtonian notion of fluxions (infinitesimals) and an indirect argument for Christianity. This was followed by *A Defense of Free-thinking in Mathematics* and *Reasons for Not Replying to Mr. Walton's Full Answer in a Letter to P.T.P.* in 1735, which are replies to critics of the *Analyst*.

Berkeley was an Anglican bishop in a country that was predominantly Roman Catholic: he once told Isaac Gervais that the ratio was approximately eight Catholics per Protestant (*Works* 8:270; *Cor.* 466). The British government's objective, to convert the Catholics to Anglicanism, is reflected in Berkeley's *Primary Visitation Charge* (*Works* 7:161–67), a work from his early years at Cloyne. Berkeley's approach was more open and reconciling than was common in the period. (On Berkeley's views on Catholicism see also his *Letter to Sir John James, Works* 7:143–55; *Cor.* 422–33.) Berkeley's work had a strong social orientation: he was concerned with the day-to-day welfare of the people in his community, whether Protestant or Catholic. He established a spinning school for the production of linen and a workhouse for the production of rope (*Works* 8:245; *Cor.* 398). He denied that he had established a hospital, while granting that he provided limited care for the sick (*Works* 8:289–90; *Cor.* 523).

His writings from the period were predominantly practical. Between 1735 and 1737 he published a book on economics and monetary theory, publishing one part in each of those years. The *Querist* is a book composed solely of questions. Through those questions Berkeley argued for the establishment of a Bank of Ireland, the use of more goods produced in Ireland by the Irish, and the virtues of labor (see Chapter 8). During the famine of 1740–41 Berkeley showed his solidarity with those suffering by refusing to powder his wig. Flour was used to powder wigs; it had more important uses at the time. It was also the occasion for his public foray into medicine. He published the following letter in Faulkner's *Dublin Journal* on 17 February 1741:

> Mr Faulkner,
> The following being a very safe and successful cure of the bloody flux, which at this time is become so general, you will do well to make it publick. Take a heaped spoonful of common rosin, powdered, in a little fresh broath, every five or six hours, till the bloody flux is stopt; which I always found to have happened before a farthing's worth of rosin was spent. If, after the blood is staunched, there remain a little looseness, this is soon carried off by milk and water boiled with a little chalk in it. This cheap and easy method I have tried of late, and never knew it fail. I am your humble servant, A. B. (*Works* 8:250; *Cor*. 419)

While this was his first, it was not his most famous medical prescription. In a letter to Prior, he also prescribed tar-water as a preventative or cure of the flux (*Works* 8:249; *Cor*. 418). Tar-water is the "medicine" Berkeley made famous.

In early 1744 Berkeley published *Siris: A Chain of Philosophical Reflexions and Inquiries concerning the Virtues of Tar-water and divers other Subjects connected together and arising One from Another*. Berkeley prefaces the first section by assuring "that nothing could, in my present situation, have induced me to be at the pains of writing it but a firm belief that it would prove a valuable present to the public. . . . that anything which greatly contributes to preserve or recover the health of the body is well worth the attention of the mind. These considerations have moved me to communicate to the public the salutary values of tar-water." The work proper begins with a recipe:

> In certain parts of America, tar-water is made by putting a quart of cold water to a quart of tar, and stirring them well together in a vessel, which is left standing till the tar sinks to the bottom. A glass of clear water, being poured off for a draught, is replaced by the same quantity of fresh water, the vessel being shaken and left to stand as

before. And this is repeated for every glass, so long as the tar continues to impregnate the water sufficiently, which will appear by the smell and taste. But, as this method produceth tar-water of different degrees of strength, I choose to make it in the following manner: Pour a gallon of cold water on a quart of tar, and stir and mix them thoroughly with a ladle or flat stick, for the space of three or four minutes, after which the vessel must stand eight and forty hours, that the tar may have time to subside; when the clear water is to be poured off and kept covered for use, no more being made from the same tar, which may still serve for common purposes. (*Siris* §1)

Siris was Berkeley's most successful publication. Tar-water, he said, prevents or cures smallpox (*Siris* §§2–3; cf. *Works* 8:273; *Cor.* 473), ulcers and distempers of the blood (*Siris* §4), coughs, pleurisy, pneumonia, erysipelas, indigestion, asthma (*Siris* §§4–6), and even hysteria (*Siris* §§99–104; cf. *Works* 8:294–95; *Cor.* 529). Most of the first 120 sections of the work are devoted to the medicinal virtues of tar. Additional sections are devoted to medical issues before Berkeley develops an elaborate metaphysics that concludes with a discussion of the Holy Trinity (*Siris* §§363–68).

Tar-water became a medical craze; it was treated as a panacea. A story goes that when a pharmacist was asked whether he sold tar-water, his reply was, "We sell nothing else!" Berkeley published three public letters to Thomas Prior discussing the virtues of tar-water (*Works* 5:171–99; *Cor*, 455–63, 495–502, 512–21), and his last work was *Farther Thoughts on Tar-Water* (*Works* 5:207–20). In 1746 Prior published *An Authentic Narrative of the Success of Tar-Water*. What accounts for the alleged medical virtue of tar-water? Perhaps in an age when the most commonly consumed potables were beer and whiskey—few people drank water—tar–water was a less poisonous alternative. That it was no panacea should be suggested by the fact that throughout the last decade of his life Berkeley suffered from chronic colic, regular bouts of gout, and sciatica.

1745 was a nervous year. Charles Edward Stuart ("Bonnie Prince Charlie") led an attempt to overthrow the Hanoverian monarchy. Since Stuart was a Roman Catholic, there was some sympathy for his cause among the Irish Catholic majority. Berkeley published two letters in the *Dublin Journal* addressed to the clergy. The first, published on Tuesday, October 15, 1745, was addressed to the Protestant clergy (*Works* 6:228–29). Harkening back to the Jacobite rebellion of 1715, Berkeley claims "from a very credible and unsuspected authority" that Stuart's plan was to leave the Church of England, but not the Church of Ireland, intact (*Works* 6:228). Berkeley was worried about what the actions of the "infidels" (free-thinkers, the nonreligious) would be if the rebellion were successful, since "how clamorous and vehement soever they may seem against Popery, may yet be presumed ready for a temporal interest to embrace it" (*Works* 6:229). Since the south of Ireland was vulnerable to attack and not well-protected by the military, Berkeley entreated the Protestant clergy to "provide ourselves with spiritual weapons—humiliation, repentance, prayer, and trust in God" (*Works* 6:228).

Berkeley's second letter, published on Saturday, October 19, 1745, was addressed to the Roman Catholic majority (*Works* 6:230–31). Berkeley was the only Protestant Irish bishop to make an appeal to the Roman Catholics. It was a call to prudence, reminding the Catholics that they had fared well under English Protestant rule, "that your persons have been protected and your properties secured by equal laws" (*Works* 6:230). He appealed to their interests:

> Is it not evident that your true interest consists in lying still and waiting the event, since Ireland must necessarily follow the fate of England; and that therefore prudence and policy prescribe quiet to the Roman Catholics of this kingdom, who, in case a change of hands should not succeed after your attempting to bring it about, must then expect to be on a worse foot than ever? (*Works* 6:230)

A change of government could result in a change of laws, which could entail that debts would go unpaid and land would be lost to the detriment of all concerned. Catholics had lived under rulers who did not share their religious views, yet they had obligations to those rulers. So, as long as George II remained on the throne, they were obligated to obey him. The success of Berkeley's letter can be judged by the fact that it was reprinted in the next issue of the *Dublin Journal* at the request of both Protestants and Catholics.

In August 1752, Berkeley traveled to Oxford, England, to oversee the education of his son George. On Sunday, January 14, 1753, while his wife Anne was reading to him from I Corinthians 15, Berkeley died. In accordance with the provisions of his will, his burial was not rushed:

> Item, that my Body, before it is buried, be kept five days above ground, or longer, even till it grow offensive by the cadaverous smell, and that during the said time it lye unwashed, undisturbed, and covered by the same bed clothes, in the same bed, the head being raised upon pillows: (*Works* 7:381)

If this seems like an unusual provision, you should remember that these were the days before embalming: Berkeley wanted to avoid a premature burial. He was buried in the chapel of Christ Church, Oxford, on January 20.

Berkeley had a lasting impact on philosophy, education in America, and the Churches of England and Ireland, not to mention the Irish people of his time. But his legacy to the Episcopal Church in America goes beyond attempts to establish an Episcopal seminary and gifts to Yale and Harvard. During his sojourn in Newport, he joined with all other missionaries of the Church of England in calling for the appointment of a bishop to the Americas. That would have allowed Americans to be ordained without undergoing a long and dangerous trip to England. It was not to be. Indeed, at the conclusion of the American Revolution, American Anglicans had no bishop. Obtaining a bishop was not easy: to be ordained a bishop in England required an oath of allegiance to George III. In 1784, Berkeley's son, George, appealed to Bishop John Skinner of Aberdeen, Scotland, to ordain Samuel Seabury of Connecticut as the first American bishop. Young George's appeals included allusions to his father's work in Newport. Skinner agreed to the ordination. This allowed the Anglicans in New England to reorganize themselves in 1789 as the Protestant Episcopal Church. So Berkeley was indirectly involved in the establishment of the Episcopal Church in America.

On Reading Berkeley

This book provides an introduction to Berkeley's philosophy. We examine his discussions of vision, his arguments for idealism and immaterialism, his moral philosophy, and his social philosophy. The approach is historical rather than critical, that is, we shall attempt to develop philosophically plausible interpretations of Berkeley's writings rather than finding fault with his views. This requires that we very carefully read what Berkeley wrote, that we pay attention to the historical context in which he wrote, and that we sometimes question some of our presuppositions. For example, does the fact that Berkeley was a Christian cleric entail that whenever he uses the terms *God* or *the Author of Nature* he is concerned with the Judeo-Christian God? Does he use those words consistently in all of his works? (See Chapter 6.) Did Berkeley hold the same views throughout his forty-year career as a philosopher—from the completion of his Notebooks in 1708 onward—or did his views change? Does a new edition of a work indicate that Berkeley changed his views? Or clarified his views? Or responded to political pressures? How are we to decide? Is Berkeley concerned with the same issues in the same ways as philosophers in the twenty-first century?

In much of the secondary literature, commentators jump from passages in the *Principles* to remarks in the *Three Dialogues* to entries in the Notebooks to *De Motu*, perhaps even to *Siris*, to find texts that support the conclusions of their arguments. These great displays of erudition used to mean that the author knew the primary texts well enough to find corresponding passages in many disparate works; now it might mean little more than that she is very good at word-searches through electronic editions of the texts. Sometimes this look-everywhere approach is not unreasonable: if you are concerned with Berkeley's view or views on a certain *topic*, for example, his use of the word *notion* in the 1734 editions of the *Principles* and the *Three Dialogues*, you should look at all the places where Berkeley uses the word. But if this is your first encounter with Berkeley, you're probably reading either sections of the *Principles* or the *Three Dialogues* and flights of erudition are not terribly helpful; indeed, they might beg some of the questions raised in the last paragraph. So our approach will focus on the arguments in the individual works in relative isolation.

Chapter 2 examines Berkeley's works on vision, primarily the *Essay towards a New Theory of Vision*. In the *Theory of Vision . . . Vindicated*, Berkeley claims that in his first work he had used the method of analysis (*TVV* §38). The method of analysis is a method for discovering explanatory principles that was widely practiced in the seventeenth and eighteenth centuries. I present an account of analysis and show how Berkeley uses it to criticize the geometrical account of vision that was prevalent at the time and to develop and defend his empirical account.

Chapter 3 examines the discussion of abstract ideas in the Introduction to the *Principles*. I argue that Berkeley attacks the abstractionists on three fronts: First, after giving an overview of the abstractionists' views in Introduction, Section 7, Berkeley argues that insofar as they also accept a conceivability criterion of possibility, their views are inconsistent. Second, insofar as abstract ideas were introduced to provide the meaning of general terms, they are not needed. And third, even Locke, the best of the abstractionists, claimed that abstract ideas are inconsistent, and therefore impossible.

Chapter 4 examines Berkeley's principal arguments for idealism—the doctrine that all existents are minds or mental dependents—and immaterialism—the doctrine that matter does not exist—in the opening thirty-three sections of *Principles*, Part I. Idealism and immaterialism are metaphysical doctrines: they are concerned with what exists and how it exists. Most scholars assume that Berkeley presents metaphysical arguments for his position and find his arguments wanting. I argue that he bases his metaphysics on epistemological foundations: he is willing to grant the existence of something only if it can be known. I show that Berkeley's argument is careful and systematic.

Chapter 5 examines the case for idealism and immaterialism in the *Three Dialogues between Hylas and Philonous*. Most scholars mine the *Three Dialogues* for arguments to supplement or reinforce those in the *Principles*. Our approach is different: rather than examining the argumentative trees, we'll look at the forest. I show that the dialogue is set as a contest between the immaterialist and the proponent of material substance. Whichever doctrine entails fewer skeptical consequences is taken to be correct.

Chapter 6 examines Berkeley's discussions of our knowledge of minds and arguments for the existence of God. Mind is central to Berkeley's philosophy, but he says very little about how it is known. In the 1734 editions of the *Principles* and the *Three Dialogues* he introduces a technical sense of the word *notion* with regard to one's knowledge of minds, acts of minds, and relations. Berkeley's mantra is you have a notion of the mind to the extent that you know the meaning of the word *mind* (PHK §27; DHP 234; A 7:5, p. 292). In the *Principles*, Berkeley's focus is on the difference between minds and ideas, stressing that one cannot properly have an idea of mind. A passage in the *Three Dialogues* suggests minds are known "immediately or intuitively" (DHP 231). We explore what that could mean. The chapter closes with a brief discussion of our knowledge of minds other than our own and an argument for the existence of God in the *Principles*.

Chapter 7 focuses on Berkeley's moral philosophy. The three major sources for discussions of moral philosophy in Berkeley are the entries marked *Mo* in his 1707–08 Notebooks, *Passive Obedience*, and *Alciphron*; minor sources include a sermon preached in 1708 and his *Guardian* essays. I argue that the position in the Notebooks is consistent with ethical egoism. I argue that in *Passive Obedience* and *Alciphron* Berkeley defends a natural-law theory and show how such a theory is an outgrowth of the egoism in the Notebooks.

Chapter 8 examines Berkeley's social philosophy. The three principal sources are the *Essay towards Preventing the Ruin of Great Britain*, the *Querist*, and *A Word to the Wise*. Berkeley's social theory is primarily economic and was developed in response to an economic crisis in Great Britain and the economic situation in Ireland.

We examine Berkeley's works in the order in which they were published. When *Berkeley* explicitly claims there are conceptual connections between his works—as he does between his immaterialism and his works on vision—we examine the connections. We shall examine the historical contexts in which Berkeley wrote. For example, Berkeley's discussions of vision make little sense apart from similar discussions in Descartes, Malebranche, and others, and he adopts or adapts their technical vocabulary. When Berkeley writes:

> It is, I think, agreed by all, that distance, of it self and immediately, cannot be seen: For distance being a line directed end-wise to the eye, it projects only one point in the fund of the eye, which point remains invariably the same, whether the distance be longer or shorter. (*NTV* §2)

he is presenting a summary of the common view of Descartes and others, and his use of *immediately . . . seen* is whatever they meant by that expression. So unlike D. M. Armstrong, who devoted a great deal of space to detailing what *Berkeley* meant by the words *seeing immediately*,[5] we set the discussion in its historical context, give a rough-and-ready account of what *seeing immediately* meant in that context, and attend carefully to see whether Berkeley later developed a more precise definition of the term. This approach is similar to that of Berkeley's early readers and prevents us from begging the questions mentioned above.

Some might consider this approach naïve. Indeed, they might suggest that I am begging the same questions in a different way: they might suggest that *I* am assuming that Berkeley *did not* have a consistent position throughout his philosophical career.

The only way you can tell *whether* Berkeley held the same views throughout his career is by carefully reading the works and making comparisons. This means sometimes you need to compare different editions of the same work. Further, different works are addressed to different audiences, and with differences in audience come differences in argumentative sophistication and presuppositions. Again, the only way you can make judgments about the sophistication of an argument with respect to an audience is by carefully reading the texts.

There are two Berkeleian works that require special comments: his Notebooks and his letters.

Many Berkeley scholars treat his 1707–08 Notebooks—which A. A. Luce called the *Philosophical Commentaries*—as if it were a work like any other published work. I do not believe that is reasonable. The Notebooks were Berkeley's private journals; their intended audience was George Berkeley. They were not published during Berkeley's lifetime: Alexander Campbell Fraser discovered the manuscript in the British Museum in the 1870s. In the Notebooks you find sketches of arguments, bold claims made without argument, memoranda, and some discussions that are found nowhere else. And the positions advanced are not all consistent with one another or with the positions in the published works. Some of the entries are topically marked: they are useful for tracing the *development* of Berkeley's early views, as we shall do when looking at his moral philosophy. But since they reflect Berkeley's *private* thoughts, and since there is no clear way to determine which reflect his considered views apart from consulting his published works, I usually ignore them.

People who regularly read scholarly work on Descartes or Leibniz might be surprised that there will be few references to Berkeley's correspondence. Berkeley's letters are of great biographical value: they are a principal source for knowledge of Berkeley's life. But other than his letters to Samuel Johnson, few contain comments germane to his philosophical work. So they can be safely ignored.

Let us now turn to Berkeley's works on vision.

Further Reading

David Berman (2005). *Berkeley and Irish Philosophy*, Continuum Studies in British Philosophy. London: Continuum.

Edwin S. Gaustad (1979). *George Berkeley in America*. New Haven: Yale University Press.

A. A. Luce (1949). *The Life of George Berkeley, Bishop of Cloyne*. London: Thomas Nelson and Sons.

2
Vision

Berkeley's *An Essay towards a New Theory of Vision* presents both a criticism of an earlier theory of vision and a development of an alternative theory. It is his first account of how things are known through the senses: it is a psychology of vision. It is also a preliminary study that leads to the immaterialism of the *Principles of Human Knowledge* and the *Three Dialogues between Hylas and Philonous*.

In his discussions of vision, Berkeley gives accounts of seeing distance, seeing magnitude, the inversion of visual images on the retina, and he defends the heterogeneity thesis, the claim that the kinds of things perceived by sight are distinct from the kinds of things perceived by touch. One approach to the texts assumes that Berkeley provides explicit arguments for each of his major points and criticizes him if he fails to do so. For example, in Section 2 of the *New Theory of Vision*, Berkeley writes, "It is, I think, agreed by all, that distance, of it self and immediately, cannot be seen." This is sometimes taken to imply that the visual field is two-dimensional (flat). George Pitcher presents a reconstruction of the argument Berkeley allegedly provides for their claim—a reconstruction that pays little attention to the historical context in which Berkeley wrote—and concludes that Berkeley's argument is weak.[1] This ahistorical approach to argument reconstruction is, perhaps, a characteristic of "critical examinations" of Berkeley's work: they *begin* with the assumption that Berkeley is wrong. For example, Pitcher lauds recent psychological research allegedly showing that Berkeley was mistaken.[2]

Margaret Atherton's approach, on the other hand, is sympathetic and historical.[3] She provides a careful discussion of the geometrical model of visual perception in the works of René Descartes and Nicholas Malebranche—the theory Berkeley criticized—before a textual commentary on the *New Theory of Vision*.[4] She recognizes that Berkeley's approach was primarily epistemological and his theory of vision was psychological.

The distinction between an epistemological and a metaphysical approach to the works on vision is significant. When discussing the heterogeneity thesis, an epistemological approach makes appeals to factual evidence, while a metaphysical approach countenances mere possibilities. The epistemological approach grants that if there is no evidence for the existence of abstract ideas, then there is no evidence for the existence of general properties. Thus there is no evidence that we perceive the same property visually and tactually.[5] If it is factually impossible to add visual and tactile points to form a whole, there is reason to believe they are points of different kinds. If a blind-man-made-to-see is, on first sight, unable to distinguish a visual cube from a visual sphere, even though he'd been able to distinguish tactile cubes and spheres, there is reason to believe that visual and tactile objects are distinct from one another.[6] On the other hand, someone approaching Berkeley's theory of vision from a metaphysical perspective—for example, Marc Hight—might reject Berkeley's visual-tactual-line argument by suggesting that there *could be* an olfactory ability that would allow us to measure the length of a line composed of both visual and tactile points on the basis of smell.[7] Similarly, Hight contends that the blind man experiment would be plausible only if he could never match a visual and a tactile cube.[8]

Considerations of Berkeley's method of inquiry are also important. Colin Turbayne recognized that Berkeley presents his account in the *New Theory of Vision* "in the analytical or inductive style," while in the *Theory of Vision . . . Vindicated* he presents it "in the synthetical or deductive style."[9] While Turbayne discusses the differences between analysis and synthesis elsewhere,[10] little work has been devoted explicitly to the role of the method of analysis in the *New Theory of Vision*. It is to that task we now turn.

The Historical Context: Methods of Inquiry and Theories of Vision

In his *Theory of Vision . . . Vindicated* Berkeley distinguishes between two methods of inquiry: analysis and synthesis (*TVV* §38).

Synthesis is the familiar method of deducing theorems from axioms, postulates, and definitions found in Euclid's *Elements*. Analysis is a method by which you discover those fundamental elements. In synthesis you show *that* a theorem deductively follows from the elements taken as true. In analysis you show *that* a certain set of elements will explain a phenomenon whose description is taken as true.

It is important to remember that words often change meanings. Since the work of Immanuel Kant (1724–1804), the word *analysis* in philosophy is usually understood as conceptual analysis. Conceptual analysis is similar to chemical analysis: both attempt to break down compounds into simpler components. But Kant himself was careful to distinguish this from the analytic method: "The analytical method so far as it is opposed to the synthetical . . . signifies only that we start from what is sought, as if it were given, and ascend to the only conditions under which it is possible."[11] It is a search for explanatory principles, for example, the laws of nature. Some proponents of analysis differ from Kant insofar as they grant that there is more than one possible explanation of an event, but analysis shows which is the best of those explanations.

The analytic method was popular in the seventeenth and eighteenth centuries. Descartes, who traced the method to the ancient geometer Pappus (*CSM* 2:5), claimed that the method of analysis was used throughout the *Meditations* (*CSM* 2:111), and it is not implausible to identify the Cartesian method with the method of analysis.[12] It was discussed by scientists[13] and covered in logic textbooks.[14] What are the characteristics of an adequate analysis? 1. It must explain the phenomenon in question, that is, answer the question why or how it came to be. 2. It must be intelligible. 3. It must be general in the sense that it explained not only the phenomenon under investigation, but other similar phenomena. For example, the principles used to explain the properties of a triangle should explain the properties of all plane figures. 4. The principles discovered must be internally consistent and consistent with our observations. 5. The principles discovered should allow you to successfully make predictions. 6. Of two or more hypotheses, it should provide the simplest explanation, that is, it should be based on the smallest number of fundamentally different kinds of things. 7. Of two or more hypotheses, it should explain the largest number of phenomena, particularly phenomena that cannot be explained by the alternative hypotheses. The method of analysis is similar to what later philosophers called "abduction" or "an argument to the best explanation."[15] But how do these methodological principles apply to Berkeley's discussions of vision?

Philosophers seldom work in an intellectual vacuum. They criticize the positions of other philosophers in an attempt to develop a more consistent or broader answer to a question. This is unquestionably what Berkeley is doing in his discussions of vision.

Prior to Berkeley, discussions of vision were found within discussions of optics. Since the work of Johannes Kepler (1571–1630), writers generally agreed on two points: unlike height and width, depth (distance from the eye or the retina) is not visually perceived directly; a perceiver's knowledge of depth is based on an unconscious geometrical calculation (triangulation). As Atherton has shown, since these writers agreed that the calculation is unconscious, it was not subject to empirical verification.[16] Berkeley was almost certainly aware of such views in Descartes (*CSM* 1:167–70), Nicholas Malebranche,[17] William Molyneux,[18] and Isaac Barrow.[19]

But the geometrical solution to the problem of distance perception was not the only hypothesis offered. After presenting his geometrical hypothesis, Descartes presents an alternative. Alluding to a figure he provides, Descartes writes:

> We have yet another way of perceiving distance, namely by the distinctness or indistinctness of the shape seen, together with the strength or weakness of the light. Thus, if we gaze fixedly towards X, the rays coming from objects 10 and 12 do not converge so exactly upon R or T, at the back of our eye, as they would if these objects were at points V and Y. From this we see that they are farther from us, or nearer to us, than X. Then, the light coming from object 10 to our eye is stronger than it would be if that object were near V, and from this we judge it to be nearer; and the light coming from object 12 is weaker than it would be if it were near Y, and so we judge it to be farther away. Finally, we may already have from another source an image of an object's size, or its position, or the distinctness of its shape and its colours, or merely the strength of the light coming from it; and this may enable us to imagine its distance, if not actually to see it. For example, when we observe from afar some body we are used to seeing close at hand, we judge its distance much better than we would if its size were less well known to us. If we are looking at a mountain lit up by sunlight beyond a forest covered in shadow, it is solely the position of the forest that makes us judge it the nearer. And when we look at two ships out at sea, one smaller than the other but proportionately nearer so that they appear equal in size, we can use the difference in their shapes and colours, and in the light they send to us, to judge which is the more distant. (*CSM* 1:171–72)[20]

Call this the empirical account of distance perception. Notice that this combines two distinguishable issues. On the one hand, we have the "distinctness or indistinctness" of the shape seen. On the other, we have previous knowledge of the distance of things perceived. As we shall see, Berkeley uses these as the basis for his account of vision. His account is about the correlation of ideas.

Berkeley on Seeing Distance (*NTV* §§2–51)

Berkeley's account of visually perceiving distance is both a criticism of the geometrical theory of vision and an expansion and clarification of Descartes's empirical account. In recognizing the common view that distance is not perceived directly (*NTV* §2), he is also acknowledging that distance is known in some way. While earlier writers had treated discussions of vision as part of optics, Berkeley differentiates between optics as the science of light and the psychology of vision: the conditions on which one actually makes visual judgments. As we shall see, he explains the perception of distance and magnitude in terms of the confusion and faintness of ideas, and he uses principles from optics to explain the confusion and faintness.

Berkeley begins by almost parroting Descartes's empirical account of distance perception (*NTV* §3). He then turns to accounts of vision at a short distance (near-vision). Here, in particular, the geometrical account of vision was prominent, since the perception of intermediate objects could play no role.[21] With respect to binocular vision, the geometrical theory claims that the object seen is at the apex of a triangle and the pupils or retinas of the eyes are the endpoints of the base line (*NTV* §§4–5); the more obtuse the angle that is formed at the apex, the closer the object is. In the case of monocular vision, the rays of light approach parallel as the distance increases (*NTV* §§6–7). The geometrical approach focuses on necessary connections among 1. the angles, 2. properties of the rays-as-lines, and 3. the distance from the object. The empirical theory rests upon faintness and confusion (blurriness) of the object seen; the relations between the signs of distance and the distance signified are contingent (*NTV* §5).

Earlier writers claimed that distance is perceived indirectly (mediately). Berkeley details that relation in terms of one idea being a sign for another idea: a pale face can show that someone has a feeling of fear or spoken words can represent thoughts (*NTV* §9; cf.

§20). Signification requires no more than the regular correlation of ideas. But if indirect perception is a correlation of ideas, then both ideas must be independently perceivable (*NTV* §10). This provides the basis for his first criticism of the geometrical theory: "But those lines and angles whereof some men pretend to explain the perception of distance are themselves not at all perceived" (*NTV* §12). Since we have no ideas of the geometrical lines and angles, they provide no basis for a signification relation. Berkeley also takes our lack of awareness of the calculation alleged by the geometrical theory to be further evidence against that theory (*NTV* §19). Add to this that calculations take time, while judgments of distance—even those made by beasts and children—are nearly instantaneous (*NTV* §24), and there are further grounds for questioning the geometrical model.

In tandem with his criticisms of the geometrical theory, Berkeley develops his empirical theory. Recall that Descartes's empirical theory allows us to judge distance on the basis of known spatial relations among seen-objects in conjunction with "the distinctness of [the object's] shape and its colours, or merely the strength of the light coming from it" (*CSM* 1:172; cf. *NTV* §3). Berkeley's account develops and modifies this. It is assumed throughout that distance is in some sense seen (*NTV* §11), although Berkeley does not tell you how distance is known directly until later (see *NTV* §45). He focuses on what is known in experience.

Berkeley's account involves a correlation of the ideas of which we are aware, and his method consists of paying careful attention to the sensations that accompany an act of seeing. As an object moves toward or away from us, the eyes move "by lessening or widening the interval between the pupils" (*NTV* §16). This is accompanied by a kinesthetic sensation "which in this case brings the idea of greater or lesser distance into the mind" (*NTV* §16). Because there is a constantly experienced correlation between sensations in the eyes and ideas of distance, the mind develops a habit that correlates those ideas (*NTV* §17). Further, as the object comes closer to the eye, the idea becomes more confused (blurry, *NTV* §21). Again, the mind develops a habit by which it correlates the degree of confusion with ideas of distance: we see the degree of confusion as a sign of the distance (*NTV* §§22, 26). The signification relation is developed from consistently repeated experience. A habit of expectation is developed, and this habit explains 1. why judgments of distance are nearly instantaneous; 2. why children and animals can judge distance without geometric calculation (cf. *NTV* §24); and 3. why people suffering from nearsightedness or farsightedness can successfully judge distances: the habitual correlation of ideas is developed by each individual and varies with individual experience (cf. *NTV* §37). The allusion to animal judgment is interesting insofar as Descartes and his followers claimed that animals do not think—they're complex machines—but they clearly act as if they judge distances.

Berkeley next examines what proponents of the geometric model recognized as an anomaly or counterexample to their account. This was set forth by Isaac Barrow, Sir Isaac Newton's teacher at Cambridge. Barrow discusses it as a problem that arises with respect to both reflection and refraction (*NTV* §24); we'll focus on refraction.

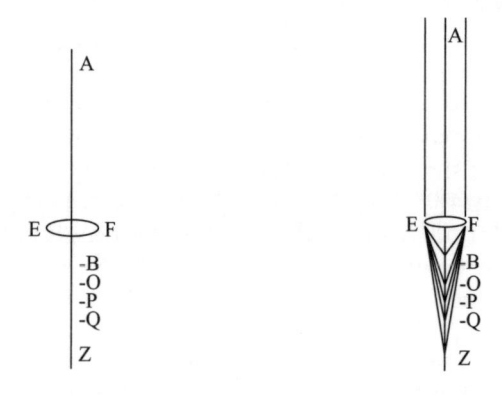

An object *A* is seen through a convex lens, *EF*. At point *B*, *A* appears at its actual location. But moving from point *B* away through points *O*, *P*, *Q*, and *Z*, we appear to be getting *closer* to *A*; at *Z* the image of *A* becomes entirely confused. To understand this problem for the geometric theory, we must remember (*a*) that the lens bends the light rays to form an angle, the apex of which is each successive point on the line, and (*b*) according to the geometric theory, the more acute the angle is, the further is its distance from the eye. In Barrow's case, the apparent distance does not correspond with the account offered by the theory. The angle becomes more acute, and therefore *should* appear more distant, as we proceed from point *B* to point *Z*, but because the perceived object becomes more confused, the object at *A appears* to be coming *closer* as we proceed from point *B* to point *Z*. The Barrow problem shows that the geometric model cannot explain actual appearance of distance.

Optical theory, however, can explain why a certain degree of confusion can occur when the focal point of light is at either a greater or a lesser distance behind the lens of the eye. The image will be clear only if the rays converge on the surface of the retina. If the focal point is either in front of or behind the retina, the image on the retina will be confused, and the same degree of confusion—the same spread of light rays on the retina—can result when the focal point is at a certain distance ahead of or behind the retina (*NTV* §36). This tends to support Berkeley's account of distance perception insofar as it shows that the correlation between confusion and distance is learned.

So Berkeley concludes that calculation in optics can be useful, but it does not explain how we visually perceive distance (*NTV* §38).

But what is the source of the idea of distance? Berkeley introduces what Phillip Cummins called the Molyneux man.[22] In a letter to John Locke, William Molyneux raised a question about a man born blind and made to see. Molyneux's question was whether this man, who had been able to distinguish a cube from a sphere by touch, would immediately be able to distinguish a cube from a sphere upon receiving sight (Locke, *Essay* 2.9.8). Both Locke and Molyneux believed that the blind-man-made-to-see would not be able to visually differentiate the sphere and the cube upon first receiving his sight.

The Molyneux man appears at several points in the *New Theory of Vision* to illustrate and support the conclusions Berkeley draws. Here the issue is whether the Molyneux man could immediately judge distance upon receiving sight. Berkeley's answer is that he could not: the correlation between distance and the ideas of sight is learned (*NTV* §41). Anticipating his discussion of magnitude, Berkeley remarks that the immediate objects of sight are light and color; visible extension and shape are perceivable by means of light and color (*NTV* §43). Visual extension (width in points) varies with distance: if we were to approach the moon, the visually apparent size and shape would change, as do the visually apparent size and shape of any other objects we approach (*NTV* §44). Berkeley draws on Molyneux's original concern with the relation between ideas of sight and touch and identifies the immediate ideas of distance with ideas of touch:

> Having of a long time experienced certain ideas, perceivable by touch, as distance, tangible figure, and solidity, to have been connected with certain ideas of sight, I do upon perceiving these ideas

of sight, forthwith conclude what tangible ideas are, by the wonted ordinary course of Nature like to follow. Looking at an object I perceive a certain visible figure and colour, with some degree of faintness and other circumstances, which from what I have formerly observed, determine me to think, that if I advance forward so many paces or miles, I shall be affected with such and such ideas of touch. (NTV §45)

The ideas of sight signify ideas of touch in much the same way that words signify thoughts (NTV §51). This explains why visual extension can vary with distance, even though the extension of the object itself, which is available only to touch, is constant. Since ideas as such are the immediate objects of perception (NTV §45), since we can immediately perceive distance and extension only by touch, and since mediate perception is perceiving one idea by means of another idea (NTV §9), this habitual relation between ideas of sight and ideas of touch explains how we can mediately perceive distance—an idea of touch—by sight.

Nor is sight the only way by which we can mediately perceive distance. You can also perceive distance by sound. Berkeley illustrates this by discussing a coach:

> Sitting in my study I hear a coach drive along the street; I look through the casement and see it; I walk out and enter into it; thus, common speech would incline one to think, I heard, saw, and touched the same thing, to wit, the coach. It is nevertheless certain, the ideas intromitted by each sense are widely different, and distinct from each other; but having been observed constantly to go together, they are spoken of as one and the same thing. By the variation of the noise I perceive the different distances of the coach, and know that it approaches before I look out. Thus by the ear I perceive distance, just after the same manner as I do by the eye. (NTV §46)

Let us update this example a bit. You are sitting in your house and you hear a car driving down the street. How do you know it's a car? You hear the noises cars normally make. How do you know it's coming toward your house? The sounds change in the ways that they usually do when a car is driving toward your house: some sounds get louder and the perceived pitch of the sound changes. In hearing the car get closer, you're judging distance by sound, just as you typically judge distance by sight: there is a correlation of ideas of sound with ideas of touch.

Berkeley makes an additional point that anticipates his later work. The ideas of the several senses are distinct from one another.

In claiming that a complex object such as a coach is known by the several senses, it is more proper to claim that the complex idea of the coach—and in his later work, the coach itself—is "constructed" from ideas of each the senses that are regularly experienced at the same time (see *DHP* 205). It is because we regularly perceive the ideas of several senses at the same time that the ideas of one sense signify ideas of other senses; we discover natural laws of the correlation of ideas (see *PHK* §§30–33), and we call the multisensory complex by one name.

Perception of Magnitude (*NTV* §§52–87)

Having shown that ideas of touch are the immediate ideas of distance that are mediately perceived by vision, Berkeley is in good stead to provide a similar account of the visual perception of magnitude, that is, extension in height and width. Some optical writers explained seeing magnitude, like seeing distance, on the basis of angles of rays,[23] a position that falls prey to all the criticisms Berkeley raised regarding distance perception. Berkeley's approach is to examine the way tangible magnitude can be perceived by visual signs (*NTV* §54). Identifying tangible magnitude with the "magnitude of the object which exists without the mind" (*NTV* §55; cf. *NTV* §111, but see also *TVV* §§12, 17, 19, 29, and 32), Berkeley examines the visual cues that yield a judgment of the tangible magnitude of an object: the magnitude of the visual object, the confusion or distinctness that is a mark of distance, and the faintness or vigorousness of the visual object (*NTV* §56).

Before looking at Berkeley's account of the visual perception of tactile magnitude, a few words should be said about measuring the magnitude of a visual object. In Section 59 of the *New Theory of Vision* Berkeley distinguishes between minimum visibles and minimum tangibles. Minimum visibles are the minimum points of color that you can see; like mathematical points, they are indivisible (*NTV* §80). David Hume said that to *see* a minimum visible, you can put a spot of ink on the wall and walk backwards: just before it disappears, it's a minimum visible.[24] The visual display of a computer is analogous to Berkeley's visual world: it is composed of pixels, discrete points of color. While Berkeley held that the number of minimum visibles perceived is constant (*NTV* §82), as is the number of pixels on a computer screen, and the size of a minimum visible is consistent across species of animals (*NTV* §80), there is no one-to-one correlation between minimum visibles and minimum tangibles, since the visual size of an object can vary, even though the tangible size of an object remains constant. For example, as I now look at the house next door, I can frame it between my thumb and index finger; but if I move closer to the house, I will no longer be able to do so. Minimum visibles give Berkeley a basis for talking about the magnitude of a visual image (see *NTV* §61).

So what does Berkeley take to be visual cues of tangible magnitude? He answers in terms of "the disposition of the eye, also on the figure, number, and situation of objects and other circumstances that have been observed to attend great or small tangible magnitudes" (*NTV* §57). Fundamentally, it is the faintness of an image in conjunction with its degree of confusion (distance) that is the basis for the judgment of magnitude (*NTV* §§58, 63, 72–73). Remember, Berkeley detailed the notion of faintness in terms of optical theory; namely, faintness concerns the number of rays that pass from an object to the eye (*NTV* §35). In addition, concerns with the direction in which we are looking play some role. Things that will hurt us usually come from in front of us, behind us, or from either side. We are seldom hurt by things falling from above. Berkeley says this fact affects our visual perception of things, particularly our perception of magnitude (*NTV* §§59, 73). His test case for his discussion of judgments of magnitude is the moon illusion.

Consider a harvest moon. The moon at the horizon looks large and yellow. Over the course of the night the moon rises to its apex (the meridian) and appears to shrink and grow brighter. But, based upon our tactile sensations of other objects, we assume that the moon remains the same size throughout its nightly journey. The apparent change in size is an illusion. What will explain it? The apparent changes in magnitude are correlated with different degrees of visual faintness (*NTV* §70). Further, optical theory will explain why the moon perceived at the horizon appears fainter than it does overhead: "the particles which compose our atmosphere intercept the rays of light proceeding from any object to the eye; and by how much the greater is the portion of atmosphere, interjacent between the object and the eye, by so much the more are the rays intercepted; and by consequence the appearance of the object rendered more faint, every object appearing more vigorous or more faint, in proportion as it sendeth more or fewer rays into the eye" (*NTV* §68). Nor is it simply faintness. It is faintness in conjunction with the circumstances in which we usually perceive great tactual magnitude (*NTV* §72). For example, if we have seen a town at the horizon, a town whose magnitude we know from tactile experience is great, and if the appearance of this town was visually faint, we learn to associate visual faintness with great tactual magnitude. It is a contingent relationship; the correlation of faintness with magnitude is simply a fact learned from experience, like the correlation between words and thoughts (*NTV* §64). But it is a fact that explains any visual judgment of magnitude, including the moon illusion. Since Berkeley's account of visually perceiving magnitude explains the moon illusion, it tends to strengthen the evidence for his account. It even explains why the Molyneux man could no more judge magnitude visually than he could judge distance when he was first made to see (*NTV* §79).

Situation and Numerical Heterogeneity (*NTV* §§88–120)

In his *Optics*, Descartes bases his account of visual perception on an analogy to a blind man with two crossed sticks. While analogies between the sticks and light rays might be useful to a defender of a geometrical account of vision, it is particularly apropos insofar as it reflects the fact that the visual image on the retina is inverted even though the object is seen as upright. It is the inversion puzzle that Berkeley identifies with "situation."

Berkeley appeals to experience: anyone not trained in optics has no inclination to suggest that an inverted image is involved in seeing (*NTV* §90). Berkeley appeals to his thought experiment, the Molyneux man who was blind from birth but made to see. Such a one would be able to distinguish between the upper and lower parts of an object by touch, but if made to see "would not at first sight think, that any thing he saw was high or low, erect or inverted" (*NTV* §92). The ideas of sight would be entirely new, and prior to experience, there would be no reason to tie them to ideas of touch. As with perceiving distance and magnitude, the visual array allows you mediately to perceive the tangible up and down, left and right, after learning the correlation between visual and tangible position.

Interesting theories often have unpredicted implications. Berkeley's is no exception. His accounts of distance perception, perception of magnitude, and now the perception of up and down are cases of mediate perception, perceiving tangible ideas through ideas of sight. Already in Section 42 Berkeley suggested that the ideas of sight and touch are distinct. Here he raises the point again: "the ideas which constitute the tangible earth and man, are intirely different from those which constitute the visible earth and man" (*NTV* §102). This is known as the **heterogeneity thesis**, a thesis to which Berkeley returns later in the work. Since everyone agreed that distance is visually perceived mediately, we might believe the conclusion would not be surprising; indeed, the notion of signification requires that there be some difference between the sign and the thing signified. But by identifying the relation as signification, Berkeley presents a challenge to one of the central doctrines of modern philosophy.

Virtually all the moderns held that we sensibly perceive material objects. They also agreed that not all perceived properties are inherent properties of material objects. Descartes limited constitutive properties of material objects to extension, since only extension—the domain of geometry—could be clearly and distinctly perceived. So, for Descartes, colors, sounds, aromas, and temperature are not properties of material objects *as such*. John Locke claimed that the constitutive properties of material objects are limited to solidity, extension, figure, and mobility (Locke, *Essay*, 2.8.9; cf. 2.8.17). He called these the primary qualities of objects; they are all properties perceived both by sight and touch. The secondary qualities of objects—that is, colors, odors, sounds, and temperature—are no more than the perceived effects of actions of bodies (of the primary qualities) on the organs of sense. This led some philosophers to characterize the secondary qualities as nothing but ideas in the mind, although, strictly speaking, Locke held that secondary qualities are combinations of primary qualities that *cause* the ideas (cf. Locke, *Essay* 2.8.8). Locke claimed that the ideas of primary qualities resemble their causes but the ideas of secondary qualities do not (Locke, *Essay* 2.8.15). But if Berkeley's heterogeneity thesis is true—if the objects of sight and touch are distinct—the primary/secondary qualities distinction has to be false: there are no necessary connections between ideas of visual and tangible extension, for example.

A few words should be said about necessary connections. Allusions to necessary connections were popular in eighteenth-century British philosophy, but many scholars are sympathetic with David Hume's remark, "There are no ideas, which occur in metaphysics, more obscure and uncertain, than those of *power, force, energy* or *necessary connection*."[25] Necessary connections are alleged connections between objects. It is usually not difficult to compile a list of which connections a given philosopher took to be necessary; in Berkeley's case the necessary connections are resemblance between ideas, causation, and perception as a connection between mind and ideas. Nor was there disagreement regarding the way in which one would show that there is *not* a necessary connection between two things. Most of the early moderns accepted a conceivability criterion of possibility: if you can (clearly and distinctly) conceive of a state of affairs, then that state of affairs is possible.[26] So, if you can clearly and distinctly conceive two things x and y apart from one another, this is sufficient to show that there is no necessary connection between x and y. The puzzle is finding positive evidence for the existence of necessary connections and a precise account of what they are. Berkeley's concerns here are negative.

"That which I see is only variety of light and colours. That which I feel is hard or soft, hot or cold, rough or smooth. What similitude, what connexion have those ideas with these?" (*NTV* §103). We might say we see *that* a piece of iron is hot—it's red or white—but that is no more than a correlation between seeing red and feeling heat. We may say we see *that* the surface of the table is rough, but the immediate object of vision is the variation of colors we see when seeing a table: we see *that* it is rough by seeing darker lines or points that correspond with the tactile ideas of a rough surface. This is exactly like seeing distance or magnitude by sight. It is a contingent fact that there are these correlations among ideas: we can imagine that the world could be different so there are no necessary connections among those ideas (*NTV* §§104, 63, 64). Hence there is no necessary connection between the visible and tangible head and foot of the person the Molyneux man perceives upon receiving sight. Even ideas of number are visibly and tangibly diverse: in a photograph visible differences (visible edges, changes of color) do not correspond with tangible differences. So, the Molyneux man could not distinguish the visible head from the two visible feet upon obtaining sight (*NTV* §§107–8). Since numbers are composed of units, the fact that what counts as a unit varies with the context in which the word *one* is used shows that there are no necessary connections between the visual and tangible ideas of numbers of objects (*NTV* §109). Since visible and tangible objects are distinct, there is properly no distance between the visible and tangible objects (*NTV* §112).

Following this preliminary discussion of the heterogeneity thesis, Berkeley returns to the question of the inverted retinal image: how can you explain why the image that is inverted on the retina appears upright? The short answer is that the question confuses the visible and tangible earths: as we normally see a person and in the corresponding retinal image, the feet of the person are closest to the visual earth, and the tangible earth is not seen (*NTV* §113). The longer answer is a challenge to the claim that an image is painted on the retina:

> It hath been shewn there is no resemblance between the ideas of sight, and things tangible. It hath likewise been demonstrated, that the proper objects of sight do not exist without the mind. Whence it clearly follows, that the pictures painted on the bottom of the eye, are not the pictures of external objects. (*NTV* §117)

There are no necessary connections between the objects of sight and touch. The objects of touch are *officially* taken to be objects that exist outside the mind (*NTV* §§55, 111). The proponents of the primary/secondary qualities distinction grant that the objects of sight (as light and colors) properly exist only within the mind. So there can be no visual images on the retina which are properly external.

Heterogeneity and the Universal Language of Vision (*NTV* §§121–158)

Up to this point, Berkeley's concern with heterogeneity was properly with the distinctness of the ideas of sight and touch: they are two different kinds of ideas. Even if ideas of sight and touch are distinct, it is still possible that they *represent* one *kind* of thing, in much the same way that the English word *dog* and the German word *Hund* represent the same kind of animal. Berkeley's question then becomes "whether extension, figure, and motion perceived by sight, are not specifically distinct [different in kind] from extension, figure, and motion perceived by touch?" (*NTV* §121). If the proponents of the primary/secondary qualities distinction are correct, then the primary qualities are perceived by both sight and touch: even if the ideas of sight are distinct from the ideas of touch, both kinds of ideas *represent* qualities of material objects that are distinct from ideas: namely, extension, solidity, motion, and number *as such*. If there are qualities of objects that can be known by more than one sense, *how* are they known?

Berkeley begins his assault by examining the alleged abstract idea of extension. Abstract ideas are supposed to provide knowledge of the material world "intirely stript of all other sensible qualities and circumstances that might determine it to any particular existence" (*NTV* §122). But can extension be known in that way?

Berkeley first says that *he* could not "perceive, imagine, or any wise frame in my mind such an abstract idea as is here spoken of" (*NTV* §123). This I-can't-do-it argument provides some (but only some) evidence that the idea cannot be formed. Next, he turns to geometry, which is said to be a haven of abstraction. "But geometry contemplates figures: Now, figure is the termination of magnitude, but we have shewn that extension in abstract hath no finite determinate magnitude, whence it clearly follows that it can have no figure, and consequently is not the object of geometry" (*NTV* §124). If all determinate sensible qualities are stripped away in examining the figure itself, there can be no determinate figure, and therefore nothing to be examined by geometry. But the moderns considered geometry the paradigm of a successful deductive system. So the conclusion has to be rejected as absurd, and the basis of the absurdity is in the tenets of abstraction. Finally, Berkeley turns to Locke, whom he considered the best of the abstractionists (*N* 567). He focuses on Locke's description of an abstract idea of a triangle: "neither equilateral, equicrural, nor scalenum; but all and none of these at once. In effect it is somewhat imperfect that cannot exist; an idea, wherein some parts of several different and inconsistent ideas are put together" (Locke, *Essay* 4.7.9; quoted at *NTV* §125). Appealing to Locke's own claim that inconsistencies cannot be conceived, that is, that one cannot form an idea of an inconsistent state of affairs (Locke, *Essay* 3.10.33), Berkeley concludes that even the best of the abstractionists cannot, on his own principles, form an abstract idea of extension (*NTV* §125).

If there is no clear theory of abstraction, then the alternative grounds for claiming that there is a single property represented by both ideas of touch and sight is weakened. Here the Molyneux man comes into his own. First, ideas of both sight and touch might affect us in the same way. But if the blind-man-made-to-see cannot recognize by sight what he knew by touch, this undercuts any grounds for claiming that there is anything common or similar in ideas of sight and touch (*NTV* §128). Second, ideas of sight conform to ideas of light and color. No ideas of touch are ideas of light or color. So ideas of sight and touch either have nothing in common or they are abstract ideas. The latter possibility was rejected. Thus the ideas have nothing in common (*NTV* §§129–30). Finally, "it is, I think, an axiom universally received, that quantities of the same kind may be added together, and make one intire sum" (*NTV* §131). But this is limited to adding lines to lines or solids to solids: we cannot add lines to solids. Similarly, we cannot form a single idea composed partially of color points and partially of tactile points. If we were able to do so, the Molyneux man would have no problem visually identifying objects when he first saw them, but even Locke, the champion of multiply sensed primary qualities, held that the Molyneux man could not do so (*NTV* §§137–38).

So Berkeley concludes that the *ideas* of sight and touch are heterogeneous (different in kind), as are the properties known by each of the distinct senses.

But both visual and tangible extension are called *extension*. In explaining why this is so, Berkeley introduces what is sometimes called his "divine language."

Throughout the *New Theory of Vision* Berkeley proposed analogies between vision and language. Visual ideas represent tangible ideas just as words represent thoughts. When we hear a word in a familiar language, we immediately form the relevant idea; after a bit of experience, when we are aware of a visual idea we think of the corresponding tangible idea. The correspondence between words and thoughts is arbitrary insofar as it is based solely on conventions. For example, in English the combination of letters *hell* represents an alleged place; in German these same letters in sequence, *hell*, translate to the English adjective *light* or *bright*. Similarly, since there are no necessary connections between ideas of sight and touch, ideas of sight could signify other ideas of touch than they signify. In the cases of both natural (spoken or written) language and vision, we learn what a sign signifies by a constant correlation of different kinds of ideas. The language of vision differs from natural languages, however, insofar as it is universal and learned at an extremely early age. The associations we develop between visual signs and their tactile significations are so tight that we do not notice the difference between those two kinds of ideas without careful attention: the *New Theory of Vision* provides a disentanglement of these distinct kinds of ideas. It is because we tend not to notice the difference between ideas of sight and touch that a word such as *square* is applied to both.

Berkeley concludes the work by declaring vision the language of Nature (first and second editions) or the Author of Nature (later editions). He writes:

> Upon the whole, I think we may fairly conclude, that the proper objects of vision constitute an universal language of the Author of nature, whereby we are instructed how to regulate our actions, in order to attain those things that are necessary to the preservation and well-being of our bodies, as also to avoid whatever may be hurtful and destructive of them. It is by their information that we are principally guided in all the transactions and concerns of life. (*NTV* §147)

Vision is like a language insofar as there are "laws of meaning," that is, constant correlations between ideas of sight and touch that are analogous to the relationship between a word and its meaning. Those laws are contingent. Insofar as they are construed as analogous to meaning relationships, they must be the result of some intentional act. The "Author of Nature" is the being that sets up the relationship between visual and tangible ideas. These visual ideas allow us to predict what tangible ideas we will experience and thereby avoid injuries (*NTV* §148).

A Look Back; A Look Ahead

In this chapter we have examined Berkeley's *Essay towards a New Theory of Vision*. It presents criticisms of geometrical theories of distance perception and perception of magnitude and develops an alternative theory based on the correlation of ideas. Given that Descartes proposed both a geometrical and an empirical account of distance perception, it is not unreasonable to suggest that one of Berkeley's objectives was to discount the geometrical theory as a means of supporting an empirical theory before developing the empirical theory far beyond the modest bounds Descartes proposed.

We have seen how Berkeley used the method of analysis as a means both to criticize the geometrical account of vision and to develop his own empirical account. The method of analysis was widely used by seventeenth- and eighteenth-century scientists, and it is reasonable to read Berkeley's discussion of vision as a scientific enterprise. As a scientific enterprise it is fundamentally epistemological, so criticisms based on metaphysical possibilities carry little or no weight against it. Further, insofar as Berkeley is using the method of analysis his *assumption* that, for example, distance is not seen directly by vision, is *reasonable* insofar as it was common to the discussions of the time, and it is *justified* insofar as the explanation resulting from the analysis can explain how distance is visually perceived indirectly. Thus criticisms that pay no attention to the method, such as Pitcher's, seem to be misplaced.

Some elements of Berkeley's argument remain puzzling. For example, he rejected the geometrical theory of distance perception, in part, because we do not perceive the lines and angles necessary for the geometrical calculations (*NTV* §12). Those lines and angles presumably would be understood in terms of light rays. Then he appeals to the rays of optical theory to explain why his account is correct. Is this legitimate? Doesn't Berkeley assume what he's rejected?

He does not; insofar as Berkeley is engaged in the analytic method, the discovery of an explanation by itself provides *some* evidence that the theory upon which it is based is correct. Further, as we read more Berkeley, we shall discover that one of his common rhetorical moves was to use elements of a theory he was criticizing against those proposing the theory. The opticians can hardly be critical of Berkeley's account of the perception of magnitude if it can be explained, in part, on the basis of their own theory. Similarly, in Section 125 Berkeley showed that Locke could not claim to form an abstract idea of extension given his own account of what is conceivable.

There are themes sounded in the *New Theory of Vision* that arise again in his later works, and, in at least one case, a change. Like most of the moderns, Berkeley sets his discussion in terms of "ideas." How are ideas to be understood? Forty years ago, most scholars believed that Berkeleian ideas are mental images.[27] Any interpretation of the nature of ideas will skew the interpretation of what Berkeley says. In the *New Theory of Vision*, Berkeley does not define *idea* until Section 45: "I take the word idea for any immediate object of sense, or understanding, in which large signification it is commonly used by the moderns." An idea is an immediate object of knowledge (understanding), that is, something that is or can be known by direct experience.[28] This does not necessarily mean it is an image. Nor does it mean he uses the word *idea* in the same way in his later works: it is important to look for any explicit statements Berkeley makes regarding his use of key terms.

In the *New Theory of Vision* Berkeley wrote as if ideas of touch provide access to objects existing outside the mind (*NTV* §§55, 111). In his later works, including the *Theory of Vision . . . Vindicated*, this assumption is rejected: all ideas are on a par, ideas exist only in a mind. But the concern with correlations of ideas remains; indeed, it is expanded.

Other topics also recur. In the Introduction to the *Principles of Human Knowledge*, Berkeley examines abstraction, modifying and generalizing some of the arguments presented in the *New Theory of Vision*. Similarly, discussions of the primary/secondary qualities distinction play a prominent role in Berkeley's criticisms of material substance.

Let us turn next to Berkeley's discussions of abstraction.

Further Reading

D. M. Armstrong (1960). *Berkeley's Theory of Vision: A Critical Examination of Berkeley's Essay towards a New Theory of Vision*. Parkville: Melbourne University Press.

Margaret Atherton (1990). *Berkeley's Revolution in Vision*, Ithaca: Cornell University Press.

Marc A. Hight (2008). *Idea and Ontology: An Essay in Early Modern Metaphysics of Ideas*. University Park: The Pennsylvania State University Press, pp. 218–45.

3
Abstraction

In the Introduction to the *Principles of Human Knowledge,* Berkeley bemoans the fact that philosophers regularly disagree on issues and identifies "abstract ideas" as the cause of this disagreement (Intro. §§1–6). The discussion connects abstract ideas with language, as John Locke had done in his *Essay concerning Human Understanding* (3.3.6ff). Locke's views are unquestionably *one* of the targets of Berkeley's critique. At one time most scholars assumed that Locke's account of abstraction was the *only* object of Berkeley's critique.[1] These same scholars tended to assume that all Berkeleian ideas are mental images. While the view that Berkeley's criticisms are directed solely against Locke is not as prevalent as it once was,[2] the scope of these criticisms remains an important issue.

Berkeley's discussion of abstraction is often tied to the problem of universals, the metaphysical question of general properties. The metaphysical realist answers the question "Do two red things have anything in common?" affirmatively: she claims that both share the universal form of redness. The universal is literally one thing that is related to or exemplified in distinct objects. Those who deny the existence of universals are usually classified as conceptualists or nominalists. Conceptualists hold that the only commonality between two real things is that we form a common concept that applies to both. Nominalists hold that all existents are individual and determinate; objects literally have nothing in common, or, as it is sometimes said, they only share names. Some scholars place Locke and Berkeley in the conceptualist camp.[3] Others declare Berkeley a nominalist.[4]

Among the issues that concern us, then, are the scope of Berkeley's criticisms and the relation of his critique of abstraction to discussions of universals.

We begin by discussing the historical background to Berkeley's discussion, showing that two kinds of activities were commonly called *abstraction*. Next, we examine Berkeley's three principal arguments against abstraction, two of which are found with slight variations in other works. Finally, we briefly examine Berkeley's remarks on selective attention and language.

Historical Context

In one sense it is not surprising that scholars believed Berkeley's criticisms of abstraction were focused solely on Locke. Berkeley's description of the process of abstraction (Intro. §§8–9) borrows heavily from Locke's *Essay* and, as in the *Essay*, abstraction is examined in the context of a discussion of language. Further, Berkeley's criticisms are directed primarily against Locke's account of the meaning of general terms. Since Berkeley considered Locke the best of the abstractionists (*N* 567), the focus is understandable. In another sense, scholarly focus on Locke is puzzling, since Berkeley wrote as if his criticisms are intended to be general and even alludes to the Scholastics, "those great masters of abstraction" (Intro. §17; cf. *Works* 2:131 regarding Aristotle). Further, there are two models of abstraction: the separation model, according to which the properties of a complex idea are taken apart in abstraction, and the selective-attention model, according to which the mind attends to a property of a complex idea without separating the idea from the complex. Berkeley's criticism focuses on the separation model; he himself claims to form general ideas by selective attention (Intro. §§16–17). And some critics of Berkeley argue that Locke himself accepted a selective attention model, and therefore that Berkeley's criticisms do not apply to Locke.[5]

Historically, abstraction does not stand alone. Since it concerns our knowledge of general properties, it is usually tied to the metaphysical problem of universals. Understanding the problem of universals and Berkeley's possible involvement with it requires us to draw some distinctions.

Plato (428–347 B.C.E.) was the first philosopher who was clearly concerned with the problem of universals. His Forms are universals. A thing is a thing of a certain kind insofar as it "participates" in the relevant Form, and it is a better thing of that kind if it participates to a greater degree. Tables are tables because they participate in the Form of Tableness; good actions are good insofar as they participate in the Form of the Good. Platonic Forms are said to exist outside of space and time. They are sometimes called *universalia ante rem*.

Aristotle (384–322 B.C.E.), Plato's pupil, found the relation of participation puzzling and argued that Forms are literally found in ordinary individual objects. Aristotle claimed that Socrates and Plato are both humans—they both contain the Form of Humanity—but the same Form is found in different bits of matter. Aristotelian Forms are sometimes called *universalia in re*. This differentiation between Form-as-universal and matter-as-individuator is also found in the work of St. Thomas Aquinas (1225–1274 C.E.) and many Scholastic philosophers of the medieval period. Philosophers who claim that there are universals in either of these senses are called *metaphysical realists*.

Either there are universals or there are not. Insofar as the problem of universals is a metaphysical problem—it is concerned with what there is—those who deny the existence of universals are *nominalists*. It is unclear that conceptualism is a *metaphysical* position; it seems to be an epistemological position, that is, it is concerned with how we know things as things of a certain kind. Both Locke and Berkeley might be deemed conceptualists insofar as both claim there is some idea involved in the naming of kinds, although, as we shall see, their accounts differ. Both can be deemed nominalists insofar as they contend that everything that exists is individual and determinate, or, as they say, "particular" (*Essay* 3.3.1; *DHP* 192). So, deeming them conceptualists *rather than* nominalists, or vice versa, confuses metaphysical and epistemological issues. While no metaphysical realists are conceptualists, insofar as they claim to know the nature of a thing as a distinct kind of entity (a universal), nominalists who claim words apply directly to objects without a mental intermediary are not conceptualists. And, as we shall see, even the metaphysical realists must provide an account of how universals are known. Some of them appealed to abstraction.

But before returning to the texts, we should ask why anyone would find nominalism appealing.

William of Ockham (1287–1347 C.E.) was the most famous medieval nominalist. Ockham was famous for advocating the **principle of parsimony**, also known as Ockham's Razor: if there are two explanations of a phenomenon, the simpler of the two—the one that assumes the fewest distinct kinds of objects—is more probably true. Ockham argued that similarities can be explained without claiming that there are universals. The principle of parsimony was accepted by many modern philosophers. It was one of the grounds by which they decided which of several theories is more probably true.

"What is there?" is a metaphysical question. "How do we know what there is?" is an *epistemological* question: it is concerned with what we know and how we can know it. Questions of abstraction, as such, are fundamentally epistemological.

If you asked Plato how the Forms are known, he would respond "by recollection." His official claim was that we see the Forms themselves between lives, and learning their natures in this life is an elaborate form of remembering;[6] in practice, recollection is a search for a consistent definition or description of a kind of thing. Since Platonic Forms are not "in" ordinary objects, this is properly an example of neither separation nor selective attention. Conceiving Aristotelian Forms, however, is a case of the conceptual separation of the Form from the matter (conceiving the intentional form), and Aquinas seems to have understood abstraction in the same way.[7] But you do not need to be a realist to be a proponent of a separation theory of abstraction. Locke also uses the language of separation in discussing the meaning of general words:

> Words become general, by being made the signs of general *Ideas*; and *Ideas* become general, by separating from them the circumstances of Time, and Place, and any other *Ideas*, that may determine them to this or that particular Existence. By this way of abstraction they are made capable of representing more Individuals than one; each of which having in it a conformity to that abstract *Idea*, is (as we call it) of that sort. (Locke, *Essay* 3.3.6)

This is the type of abstraction Berkeley describes in his Introduction to the *Principles*, Sections 8–9 (cf. Locke, *Essay* 3.3.9–10). Here the general idea is formed by removing characteristics from particular (determinate) ideas that distinguish them from other ideas of the same kind: place, time, and perhaps color, size, and shape. And the abstract idea of a kind can change with experience (Locke, *Essay* 3.2.3). It is such a constructed abstract idea that provides the meaning of a general term. Where R is a resemblance relation, O is an object, AI is an abstract idea, M is a meaning relation, and W is a word, Locke's account of the meaning of a general word can be represented as follows:

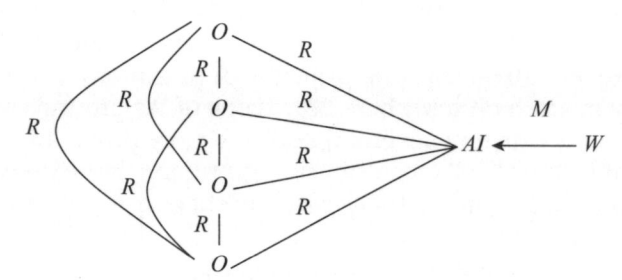

Meaning on the Separation Model

Each of the lines marked R represents a resemblance relation, and, of course, there are indefinitely many other objects that stand in resemblance relations to one another and to the abstract idea. It is the abstract idea that provides the meaning for the general word.

Like the separation model, selective attention is compatible with both realism and nominalism. What Descartes called "true and immutable natures" are common to an indefinite number of objects (CSM 2:44). They might be understood as universals. But when he talks about the meanings of general words (how universals arise), you find something different from Locke's separation model. Descartes wrote:

> These universals arise solely from the fact that we make use of one and the same idea for thinking of all individual items which resemble each other: we apply one and the same term to all the things which are represented by the idea in question, and this is the universal term. When we see two stones, for example, and direct our attention not to their nature but merely to the fact that there are two of them, we form the idea of the number which we call "two"; and when we later see two birds or two trees, and consider not their nature but merely the fact that there are two of them, we go back to the same idea as before. This, then, is the universal idea; and we always designate the number in question by the same universal term "two." In the same way, when we see a figure made up of three lines, we form an idea of it which we call the idea of a triangle; and we later make use of it as a universal idea, so as to represent to our mind all the other figures made up of three lines. Moreover, when we notice that some triangles have one right angle, and others do not, we form the universal idea of a right-angled triangle; since this idea is related to the preceding idea as a special case, it is termed a *species*. And the rectangularity is the universal *differentia* which distinguishes all right-angled triangles from other triangles. And the fact that the square on the hypotenuse

Abstraction 47

is equal to the sum of the squares on the other two sides is a *property* belonging to all and only right-angled triangles. Finally, if we suppose that some right-angled triangles are in motion while others are not, this will be a universal *accident* of such triangles. Hence five universals are commonly listed: *genus, species, differentia, property* and *accident*. (CSM 1:212–13)

On Descartes's model, an abstract idea is a particular idea that functions as a universal; you selectively attend to one aspect of a determinate idea. On his model of meaning, you take one idea to be a paradigm (perfect example) of a thing of a certain kind, and you use it to pick out other ideas of the same kind. His model might be represented as follows:

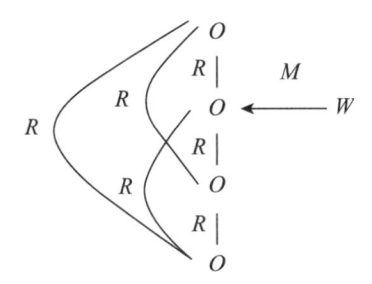

```
              O
           R |
        R    O  ←——— W    M
    R       R |
        R    O
           R |
              O
```

Cartesian Selective Attention

There are several points to notice. First, the two models diagrammed are models of the meaning of general terms. Locke explicitly calls it abstraction; Descartes does not, although he clearly held that the mind can abstract (*CSM* 1:40, 44), even if at some points he suggests that the resulting conception is inadequate (cf. *CSM* 2:83, 86, 143). If you treat these as alternative models of abstraction, you have a situation that is similar to that in the *New Theory of Vision*, where Berkeley supported one model of vision in part by criticizing the other. George Pappas has shown that you find *both* the separation and the selective attention models of abstraction in Locke;[8] indeed, in order to separate a property from an idea, you must first be able to attend to that property.

The separation and selective attention models can be described in three ways: they are accounts of abstraction; they are accounts of the meaning of general terms; they are accounts of how general properties are known. As we shall see in turning to the Introduction to the *Principles*, Berkeley understands selective attention in the last two ways; he assumes abstraction follows the separation model.

The Principal Arguments

In the Introduction to the *Principles*, Berkeley begins by laying out the points of agreement among the abstractionists. He writes:

> It is agreed on all hands, that the qualities or modes of things do never really exist each of them apart by it self, and separated from all others, but are mixed, as it were, and blended together, several in the same object. But we are told, the mind being able to consider each quality singly, or abstracted from those other qualities with which it is united, does by that means frame to it self abstract ideas. For example, there is perceived by sight an object extended, coloured, and moved: this mixed or compound idea the mind resolving into its simple, constituent parts, and viewing each by it self, exclusive of the rest, does frame the abstract ideas of extension, colour, and motion. Not that it is possible for colour or motion to exist without extension: but only that the mind can frame to it self by *abstraction* the idea of colour exclusive of extension, and of motion exclusive of both colour and extension. (Intro. §7)

Berkeley claims that there are two principles that are accepted by all the abstractionists. The first may be called the **principle of abstraction**: it is possible for the mind to frame an idea of a property, quality, or mode in separation from that of which it is a property, quality, or mode. The second principle is that properties, qualities, or modes do not exist apart from objects or substances that have them. Prior to Berkeley, it was commonly held that ordinary objects, human bodies, and minds are substances, that is, things that can exist independently of other things (cf. *CSM* 1:210) and remain the same through time. Substances *have* properties or qualities or modes. A mode or property is a modification of a substance, and no mode can exist apart from a substance. By themselves, these two principles are consistent: both principles can be true at the same time. But the abstractionists assume other principles, and these raise problems of consistency.

After summarizing the Lockean separation model (Intro. §§8–9), Berkeley begins his criticisms. In Section 10 you find this:

> Whether others have this wonderful faculty of *abstracting their ideas*, they best can tell: for my self I find indeed I have a faculty of imagining, or representing to my self the ideas of those particular things I have perceived and of variously compounding and dividing them. I can imagine a man with two heads or the upper parts of a man joined

to the body of a horse. I can consider the hand, the eye, the nose, each by it self abstracted or separated from the rest of the body. But then whatever hand or eye I imagine, it must have some particular shape and colour. Likewise the idea of man that I frame to my self, must be either of a white, or a black, or a tawny, a straight, or a crooked, a tall, or a low, or a middle-sized man. I cannot by any effort of thought conceive the abstract idea above described. And it is equally impossible for me to form the abstract idea of motion distinct from the body moving, and which is neither swift nor slow, curvilinear nor rectilinear; and the like may be said of all other abstract general ideas whatsoever. To be plain, I own my self able to abstract in one sense, as when I consider some particular parts or qualities separated from others, with which though they are united in some object, yet, it is possible they may really exist without them. But I deny that I can abstract one from another, or conceive separately, those qualities which it is impossible should exist so separated; or that I can frame a general notion by abstracting from particulars in the manner aforesaid. Which two last are the proper acceptations of *abstraction*. And there are grounds to think most men will acknowledge themselves to be in my case. The generality of men which are simple and illiterate never pretend to *abstract notions*. It is said they are difficult and not to be attained without pains and study. We may therefore reasonably conclude that, if such there be, they are confined only to the learned.

There are two arguments here. One is a variation on the I-can't-do-it argument found in the *New Theory of Vision* (*NTV* §123) and *Alciphron*. Everyone uses general terms. If the Lockean account is correct, then general terms are signs of abstract general ideas (Locke, *Essay* 3.3.6). If general terms represent abstract general ideas, then you should be able to form an abstract idea composed solely of general properties. Berkeley says he cannot do so, which he takes as evidence that no one else can either, a point that is made explicit in the parallel passage in *Alciphron* (*Works* 3:333). It has a further implication that Berkeley notes in Section 11. Since the ability to form abstract ideas was taken as a fundamental characteristic for distinguishing humans from the lower animals (Locke, *Essay* 2.11.10–11), most of those things we consider human cannot be—which is absurd!

But there is a second argument in Section 10 that relates back to the sketch of abstraction in Section 7. Abstractionists hold that it is possible to conceive of properties apart from objects and that it is impossible for properties to exist apart from objects. Many abstractionists also accepted a conceivability criterion of possibility (*CCP*):

if you can conceive of x, then it is possible that x exists as you conceive of it (*CSM* 2:50, 54; Locke, *Essay* 2.27.1). Since *CCP* entails its contrapositive that if x is impossible, then x is inconceivable (something of which an idea cannot be formed), adding *CCP* to the two principles that are "agreed on all hands" yields an inconsistent triad: not all three principles can be true. Berkeley makes that point by saying, "But I deny that I can abstract one from another, or conceive separately, those qualities which it is impossible should exist so separated." Is he tacitly claiming that the abstractionists are committed to an inconsistent triad? It seems so. In a draft of the Introduction he put it this way, "It is, I think, a receiv'd axiom that an impossibility cannot be conceiv'd,"[9] and he made explicit allusions to the contrapositive of *CCP* in the early editions of *Alciphron* (*Works* 3:334). Inconsistent theories are unacceptable. He is effectively saying to the abstractionists that if they want to retain their commitment to abstraction, they have to either reject the mode-substance relation or *CCP*. Since rejecting either the mode-substance relation or *CCP* would have more pronounced effects on their metaphysics than rejecting the doctrine of abstraction, Berkeley seems to take this as a reason to reject the doctrine of abstract ideas.

If the separation model of abstraction is correct, then there are two fundamentally different kinds of ideas: the typical determinate ideas of experience; and the indeterminate abstract ideas: for example, an idea of color in general that is not an idea of any shade of color. Locke introduced abstract ideas to provide meanings for general terms (Locke, *Essay* 3.3.6). So if the meaning of general terms could be explained without positing abstract ideas as a distinct kind of thing, that theory would be more parsimonious and therefore, in accordance with principles most of the abstractionists themselves accepted, more probably true. Sketching such a parsimonious theory of meaning is Berkeley's task in Sections 11 and 12. After noting Locke's view, that "Words become general, by being made the signs of general *Ideas*" (Locke, *Essay* 3.3.6; Intro. §11), Berkeley proposes an alternative: "But it seems that a word becomes general by being made the sign, not of an abstract general idea but, of several particular ideas, any one of which it indifferently suggests to the mind" (Intro. §11). What does this mean? *By itself*, it seems to mean that there is no idea that stands between a word—a sound or mark, itself an idea—and the objects a mind means by it. The ideas immediately meant are determinate, not abstract. The meaning is arbitrary: it is any idea or ideas of which your mind thinks when you hear a word. Meaning is *extensional*: words pick out objects directly. On Locke's view, meaning is *intensional*: words pick out objects in virtue of characteristics that all things of a certain kind share; the abstract idea provides the criterion for the application of the name of a kind of thing. Where *I* is an idea and *W* a word, Berkeley's model would seem to be like this:

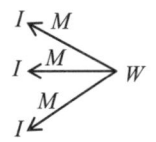

$$I \xleftarrow{M} \quad I \xleftarrow{M} \quad W \quad I \xleftarrow{M}$$

But this is not Berkeley's final word, for he grants that there are general ideas, denying only that there are *abstract* general ideas (Intro. §12).

> Now if we will annex a meaning to our words, and speak only of what we can conceive, I believe we shall acknowledge, that an idea, which considered in it self is particular, becomes general, by being made to represent or stand for all other particular ideas of the same sort. . . . And as that particular line becomes general, by being made a sign, so the name *line* which taken absolutely is particular, by being a sign is made general. And as the former owes its generality, not to its being the sign of an abstract or general line, but of all particular right lines that may possibly exist, so the latter must be thought to derive its generality from the same cause, namely, the various particular lines which it indifferently denotes. (Intro. §12)

There are several points to notice. First, a determinate idea can function as a general idea when it represents all ideas of a certain sort. Sorting is based on resemblance. Thus a general idea of a triangle, for example, is a determinate idea of a triangle that is taken to represent all triangles. It is a case of selective attention: you attend to the triangularity of an idea rather than its color or specific size (cf. Intro. §16). But as readers of the *New Theory of Vision* would claim, it can't be quite that easy. Resemblance alone can account only for a sorting of things known by one sense, but conventional sorting is more complicated and involves the mediate perception of ideas of one sense by ideas of a different sense. So a visual idea of a triangle could represent not only all visual triangles, but all tactile triangles as well, even though they are of properly different sorts (they are not members of a single resemblance class). And Berkeley's remarks on the meanings of words are at least as radical, for here as in

Section 11 he suggests that general terms such as *triangle* or *line* denote all triangles or lines, without the mediation of any general idea. So you do not have the Cartesian model, where one determinate idea goes proxy for all ideas of a sort and the general term primarily denotes that idea. In Berkeley you have a set of resemblance classes—visual, tactual, and so on—each member of which the term denotes. Denoting (signification) is fundamentally a mental act: it is the picking out of individual objects by the use of a term, and the objects actually picked out vary among speakers of a language. The objects in your resemblance classes provide the basis for applying a term to additional objects, as do the objects in my resemblance classes. The objects in resemblance classes will change over time as someone's experience increases.

So Berkeley's account of the meaning of sortal terms is more parsimonious than the abstractionist's: there are no abstract ideas. Nonetheless, the Berkeleian resemblance classes—where the classes are understood as nothing over and above their members—can fulfill the same functions as an abstract idea. Just as the Lockean abstract idea that provides the basis for the meaning of a sortal term—what Locke calls the *nominal essence* (Locke, *Essay* 3.6.26)—can change with increased experience (Locke, *Essay* 3.2.3), the number of resemblance classes into which a thing of a sort is placed can increase with experience. On the Lockean scheme a connotative definition consists of the enumeration of the properties in the abstract idea; on the Berkeleian scheme a connotative definition consists of an enumeration of the resemblance classes that are peculiar to a sort. Both require that one be able to selectively attend to an object; the Berkeleian scheme requires no additional entities that result from that ability. There is no need to introduce abstract ideas as a distinct kind of idea: Berkeley's account is more parsimonious.

Section 13, what Berkeley describes as the "killing blow" in Notebooks entry 687, is based on Locke's account of the abstract idea of a triangle at *Essay* 4.7.9. There Locke writes: "For example, Does it not require some pains and skill to form the *general Idea* of a *Triangle* . . ., for it must be neither Oblique, nor Rectangle, neither Equilateral, Equicrural, nor Scalenon; but all and none of these at once. In effect, it is something imperfect, that cannot exist; an *Idea* wherein some parts of several different and inconsistent *Ideas* are put together." Recall that in *New Theory of Vision* Section 125, Berkeley discussed this passage by quoting Locke against himself: Locke's account is inconsistent with his claim that inconsistencies cannot be conceived. Here Berkeley does not explicitly do that, although he adds emphasis to *all and none* and *inconsistent*. He calls upon his reader to "inform himself whether he has such an idea or no," that is, "the general idea of a triangle, which is, *neither oblique, nor rectangle, equilateral, equicrural, nor scalenon, but all and none of these at once?*" While his explicit focus is on introspection, it is not unreasonable to suggest that Berkeley is making implicit appeals to principles. Berkeley's contemporaries granted that inconsistent states of affairs are impossible. They also assumed a conceivability criterion of possibility, which entails that whatever is impossible is inconceivable.

There is a pattern found in these sections. Berkeley first argues that, as a matter of fact, we cannot form an abstract idea in the manner described (Intro. §10). Then he argues that abstract ideas are not needed for the purposes of communication (Intro. §§11–12). Finally, he argues that the doctrine of abstract ideas rests upon inconsistencies. As we shall see later, this argument pattern emerges again in his criticism of a doctrine of material substance.

Language

By the end of Section 13, Berkeley has raised his principal objections to the separation model of abstraction.[10] He raises a few additional criticisms before identifying the source of the belief in abstraction: language. Constructing abstract ideas is said to be difficult (Locke, *Essay* 3.3.7) and, if Locke's allusions to the inconsistencies contained in abstract ideas are read strictly, impossible. Yet, Berkeley notes, young children "prate together, of their sugar-plumbs and rattles and the rest of their little trinkets" (Intro. §14). He argues that any determinate idea of a geometric figure is sufficient for use in a geometric demonstration regarding a figure of that kind, since the demonstration focuses only on the general properties of that kind of thing, and for this, selective attention is sufficient (Intro. §§15–16). For purposes of knowledge and communication a general definition, that is, an enumeration of the several classes in which objects picked out by a general term are found, is sufficient (Intro. §18).

So, one false assumption that led to the doctrine of abstract ideas was the view that general terms require general ideas (cf. Locke, *Essay* 3.3.6). But Berkeley contends that the error is deeper.

Not only need general terms not denote abstract ideas, they need not denote *any* ideas. In Section 20 Berkeley introduces one of the first cases of **meaning as use**, an account of meaning for which Ludwig Wittgenstein became famous nearly 250 years later.[11] Words are used in "the raising of some passion, the exciting to, or deterring from an action, the putting the mind in some particular disposition; to which the [communicating of ideas] is in many cases barely subservient, and sometimes entirely omitted" (Intro. §20). Favorable emotions are evoked by promises of good things. Fear and dread are evoked by threats of evil. Appeals to noted authorities sometimes convince us that a statement is true. "For example, when a Schoolman tells me *Aristotle hath said it*, all I conceive he means by it, is to dispose me to embrace his opinion with the deference and submission which custom has annexed to that name" (Intro. §20).

Berkeley concludes his discussion with an appeal commonly made by the empiricists: to avoid controversies, examine the bare ideas themselves, don't appeal to language (Intro. §21).[12] This focus on ideas will clear away verbal disputes, that is, disputes that rest solely on the meanings of words. It will free us from the confusions that are hidden by allegedly abstract ideas. In focusing on determinate ideas divested of words, "The objects I consider, I clearly and adequately know," and I cannot be deceived (Intro. §22).

A Look Back; A Look Ahead

In the Introduction to his *Principles of Human Knowledge*, Berkeley presented criticisms of the doctrine of abstraction. He argued that *he* could not form the relevant kind of ideas, that they were not needed to provide the meaning of general terms, and that considerations of the several principles accepted by the abstractionists themselves yields inconsistencies. Abstract ideas, he claimed, are the source of philosophical disagreement, and to avoid perplexities you should examine the determinate ideas themselves.

Does Berkeley's discussion assume an account of the *nature* of ideas? For example, did Berkeley assume that all ideas are mental images?[13] No, he does not. Prior to Section 22, he makes no claims regarding the nature of ideas, nor should he, assuming that he is presenting a general criticism of abstraction. Locke couched his discussion in terms of abstract ideas; the Scholastics couched their discussions in terms of intentional forms. Even if Descartes talked of intentional forms as "little pictures" (*CSM* 1:165), this does not show that a pictorial account reflects the view of all the Scholastics. In Section 22, when Berkeley is considering bare, determinate ideas devoid of language, he says that these "I clearly and adequately know," a remark that is reminiscent of his description of ideas as "the immediate object of sense, or understanding" in the *New Theory of Vision*, Section 45; this anticipates his account of ideas in Part I, Section 1.

Is Berkeley's criticism focused solely on Locke? No, it is not. We have seen that the abstractionists ranged over a number of traditions. Insofar as Berkeley left his notion of *idea* undefined throughout his criticisms, there is no reason to limit his concerns to a single tradition or philosopher. Indeed, his allusion to the Scholastics (Intro. §17) suggests that he intended his critique to extend beyond Locke. Finally, there are allusions to accounts of abstraction that are not found in Locke. For example, in Section 10 he alludes to three "acceptations of *abstraction*." Locke makes no such divisions, but the distinction is found in Antoine Arnauld and Pierre Nicole's *Logic or the Art of Thinking*,[14] one of the most popular logic textbooks of the era. This shows that Berkeley was familiar with and critical of non-Lockean accounts of abstraction. It is reasonable, then, to take his attack to be on the abstractionists across traditions.

But what does he do with his criticisms of abstraction? As we turn to the body of the *Principles*, we shall see that he appeals to abstraction to explain the errors of the philosophers.

Further Reading

E. J. Craig (1968). "Berkeley's Attack on Abstract Ideas," *Philosophical Review* 77: 425–37.

George Pappas (2000). *Berkeley's Thought*. Ithaca: Cornell University Press, pp. 23–79.

George Pitcher (1977). *Berkeley, The Arguments of the Philosophers*. London: Routledge and Kegan Paul, pp. 60–90.

4

The Case for Idealism and Immaterialism in the Principles

Berkeley was an *idealist*: that is, he held that all existents are minds, or things dependent upon minds for their existence. He was also an *immaterialist*: that is, he held that matter does not exist. These are *metaphysical* or *ontological* theses—I shall use the words *metaphysics* and *ontology* synonymously—that is, they pertain to questions of being or existence. On these points nearly all Berkeley scholars agree, although not all scholars give both theses equal emphasis, and some do not seem to distinguish between the two. The first work in which Berkeley defended these theses was his *Principles of Human Knowledge* (1710). Most commentators ignore the fact that the nominal topic of the *Principles* is knowledge; rather, they focus on the conceptual connections among the *kinds* of thing that are found in Berkeley's system, that is, they treat the work as a metaphysical or ontological work. And many scholars find his arguments anything but satisfactory. For example, after lauding the originality and design of Berkeley's philosophy with glowing analogies to great music, art, and architecture, Robert Muehlmann laments that "Berkeley's system presents us with unique puzzles, particularly at its foundation."[1] These foundations are in the first seven sections of Part I. If the foundations are insecure, the edifice he builds upon them must crumble.

Berkeley begins Part I of the *Principles* with the words, "It is evident to any one who takes a survey of the objects of human knowledge, that they are either ideas actually imprinted on the senses, or else such as are perceived by attending to the passions and operations of the mind, or lastly ideas formed by help of

The Case for Idealism and Immaterialism in the Principles 57

memory and imagination, either compounding, dividing, or barely representing those originally perceived in the aforesaid ways" (*PHK* §1). Ideas and minds are the two basic kinds of existents in Berkeley's metaphysics. But as Georges Dicker notes, Berkeley gives no argument for the existence of ideas in the *Principles*.[2] If there is no reason to believe that there are ideas, then there is no reason to accept the theory he builds upon his theory of ideas, and, at best, his subsequent arguments could be persuasive only to those who already accepted the "way of ideas."[3]

In Section 2 Berkeley introduces the notion of minds as things that perceive ideas. It was widely granted that ideas are necessarily mind-dependent.[4] So, *if* there are ideas, then there are minds. But if the existence of ideas is not established, the question of the existence of minds remains open.

In Section 3 Berkeley introduces the *esse* is *percipi* principle: the being of sensible objects is to be perceived. But as George Pitcher notes, "Given this conception of an idea of sense, what principle (α) says is that in every case of sense perception, the perceiver has before his mind—i.e., is aware of—something that is mind-dependent, something that exists only in his own mind. This is very far from being a self-evidently true proposition."[5] Further, Berkeley's "argument" for *esse* is *percipi* consists of examples of how we use the word *exist* when applying that word to sensible things. As Georges Dicker notes, even if it is evident that no idea can exist unperceived, it hardly follows—as Berkeley takes it to follow in Section 4—"that houses, mountains, rivers, and in a word all sensible objects" cannot exist unperceived. Thus Berkeley's arguments in Sections 3 and 4 fail.[6]

In Section 5 Berkeley appeals to abstract ideas. As an *argument* for *esse* is *percipi*,[7] many scholars find Berkeley wanting. Dicker argues that the argument is circular, and therefore unacceptable. It begins, he says, with the premise that a sensible thing cannot exist without being perceived, understanding this to mean that it cannot be thought without being perceived. Given that it cannot be thought without being perceived, the argument concludes that sensible things cannot exist without being perceived—which was the initial premise.[8]

Berkeley's conclusion in Section 6 that "all those bodies which compose the mighty frame of the world, have not any subsistence without a mind" and his conclusion in Section 7 that "there is not any other substance than *spirit*, or that which perceives" (the thesis of idealism) rest upon his earlier arguments. If *any* of the objections to Berkeley's arguments in the first five sections of the *Principles* is cogent, the conclusions in Sections 6 and 7 are unwarranted, and if they are unwarranted, Berkeley's system collapses. For these reasons, scholars might claim that the foundations for Berkeley's philosophy are weak.

I believe there is another way to read Berkeley.

Most scholars assume that Berkeley's arguments are metaphysical. Some suggest that Berkeley developed his metaphysics in order to support a commonsense epistemology.[9] I hope to show that he used his epistemology to ground his metaphysics. That might explain the nominal emphasis on knowledge in the *Principles*. Such an approach was not unprecedented in the modern period: Descartes does the same in his *Meditations*. I hope to show that such an approach provides a consistent reconstruction of the first thirty-three sections of Part I of the *Principles*.

We shall look closely at the texts. We shall assume that Berkeley is a "good philosopher" in the sense that he presents arguments for his major conclusions. Later conclusions are often based, in part, upon earlier conclusions, and no major elements of his philosophical system are presented without argument. Of course, one cannot argue for *all* one's points. We shall acknowledge that some very basic elements of his philosophy, for example, his notion of an idea, are adopted without comment from his predecessors. I hope to show that the first seven sections present a plausible argument for a conceptually lean idealism: ordinary objects are *at least* mind-dependent ideas and, although mental substances are the only substances, questions of the *nature* of mental substance—whether or not it is immaterial—remain open at that point. Next I examine the case for immaterialism in Sections 8–24. Finally, I examine Sections 25–33, where Berkeley develops his case for the claim that real objects are only organized collections of ideas.

The Case for Idealism (Sections 1–7)

Berkeley begins Section 1: "It is evident to any one who takes a survey of the objects of human knowledge, that they are either ideas actually imprinted on the senses, or else such as are perceived by attending to the passions and operations of the mind, or lastly ideas formed by help of memory and imagination, either compounding, dividing, or barely representing those originally perceived in the aforesaid ways" (*PHK* §1). What Berkeley *seems* to claim is that all things known (objects of knowledge) are either ideas of sense, ideas of reflection (ideas of the operations of the mind), or ideas of memory or the imagination. This threefold distinction is found in Locke's *Essay concerning Human Understanding* (Locke, *Essay* 2.1.3–6; 1.2.15), and Locke's influence upon Berkeley is uncontroversial. Berkeley seems to use the expressions *idea* and *object of knowledge* synonymously in Section 2, and he later suggests that the words *perceive* and *know* are synonyms (*PHK* §§2, 6, 26; *DHP* 202, 206), a claim that has Lockean roots (Locke, *Essay* 2.1.9) and is also consistent with the broad use of *perceive* in Descartes's discussions of clear and distinct perception. And we have already seen that Berkeley took an idea to be the immediate object of thought or perception (*NTV* §45, Intro. §22; cf. *NTV* §§43 and 65; *N* 427a).

Berkeley does not give an argument for the existence of ideas; rather, he is using the word *idea* in a way that was common at the time. In doing so he is placing himself in a broad tradition that includes Descartes and Locke. Insofar as he is building on the work of his predecessors—and all philosophers after Thales (the first philosopher) do so—such conceptual borrowing is reasonable—indeed, expected.

But many commentators will find my account implausible. Berkeley was quite clear, they will say, that there are no ideas of reflection. In the second edition of his *Principles* Berkeley claimed that one has ideas of neither minds nor the actions of minds (cf. *PHK* §§27, 89, 136, 139, 142; *DHP* 233). So there can be no ideas of reflection. You can only have *notions* of minds and their states, not ideas of them.[10] Such is the objection.

We shall discuss notions in Chapter 6. Berkeley's alleged rejection of ideas of reflection is puzzling. At several places in the *Principles* he alludes to the difference between ideas of sense and those of reflection (or "reflexion," *PHK* §§13, 25, 35, 68, 74; cf. *PHK* §89, *DHP* p. 233). Further, Berkeley, like his contemporaries, seems to have held that an idea is the *effect* of an act of mind (*PHK* §27), which would explain how ideas could represent actions of the mind even if they do not resemble them (cf. *NTV* §23). Finally, whether or not there are ideas of reflection is irrelevant to Berkeley's arguments for idealism and his arguments against the existence of material substance. So, even if the most natural reading of the sentence were wrong, it would not affect the arguments in the opening sections of the *Principles*.[11]

But the distinction between the first and second editions of the *Principles* is important, for it guides us in understanding Berkeley's remark that "the objects of human knowledge . . . are . . . ideas." This seems to say that *all* objects of human knowledge are ideas, which is consistent with his explicit use of *objects of human knowledge* in the 1710 edition of the *Principles* and implies that minds are not objects of knowledge (cf. N 829). But in 1734 Berkeley added the following to Section 89: "To me it seems that ideas, spirits and relations are all in their respective kinds, the object of human knowledge and subject of discourse: and that the term *idea* would be improperly extended to signify every thing we know or have any notion of." This indicates that ideas are *not* the only objects of knowledge. So, at least in the second edition of the *Principles*, the opening sentence must be understood as *all ideas are objects of human knowledge*, an account we have already found in the *New Theory of Vision* (*NTV* §45) and the Introduction to the *Principles* (Intro. §22).

Our epistemic focus is consistent with what Berkeley discusses in the remainder of the section. First he writes about the five senses and the kinds of ideas that are known by each: by sight you have ideas of light and color, by touch ideas of hard and soft, and so forth. Even ordinary objects *as known* are nothing but collections of ideas that are given a name. Berkeley notes that "as several of these [ideas] are observed to accompany each other, they come to be marked by one name, and so to be reputed as one thing. Thus, for example, a certain colour, taste, smell, figure and consistence having been observed to go together, are accounted one distinct thing, signified by the name *apple*. Other collections of ideas constitute a stone, a tree, a book, and the like sensible things; which, as they are pleasing or disagreeable, excite the passions of love, hatred, joy, grief, and so forth" (*PHK* §1). If Berkeley is concerned only with objects *as they are known*, he is in good intellectual company, for Locke held the same regarding different kinds of substances (Locke, *Essay* 2.23.3ff). An alternative reading of this passage is ontological: Berkeley identified the collections of ideas with trees, books, and so on.[12] Such a reading might be tempting because Berkeley *eventually* identifies ordinary objects with collections of ideas (*PHK* §§30–33), but *at this point* he has given no argument for such an identification. Thus, if we assume that careful philosophers present no significant conclusions without argument, the ontological reading is unwarranted.

In turning to Section 2, Berkeley introduces a contrast between ideas as things known and that which knows them. He wrote:

But besides all that endless variety of ideas or objects of knowledge, there is likewise something which knows or perceives them, and exercises divers operations, as willing, imagining, remembering about them. This perceiving, active being is what I call *mind, spirit, soul* or *my self*. By which words I do not denote any one of my ideas, but a thing entirely distinct from them, wherein they exist, or, which is the same thing, whereby they are perceived; for the existence of an idea consists in being perceived. (*PHK* §2)

If we are concerned with things that are known, there also must be something that knows them. Notice that Berkeley seems to use the words *perceives* and *knows* synonymously (cf. *PHK* §6; see also *N* 74, cf. *N* 174 and 666; *DHP* 202, 204 [knows], 199 [comprehends] (Hylas), and 212, 215, 234 [knows], 240 [understands], 231, 250 [comprehends] (Philonous); *TVV* §26; *Alciphron*, Dialogue 4, §8). John W. Yolton goes so far as to say that Berkeley "was quite clear about his analysis of 'present to' and 'exist in': they mean 'perceived', 'known', or 'comprehended' (i.e. understood)."[13] While for the past century most philosophers have limited the use of the word *perceive* to sense perception and knowledge by the senses, in the early eighteenth century there was a broader understanding of *perceive*. Descartes, for example, was concerned with clear and distinct perception. The ideas Descartes claimed we can clearly and distinctly perceive are ideas of the essences of things, and, as such, they are not limited to ideas of sensation (cf. CSM 2:20–21; see also Locke *Essay* 2.9.2). It should not surprise us then if Berkeley used the words *perceive* and *know* as synonyms.

But notice that Berkeley does not describe the mind or self as merely that which knows; it is also that which "exercises divers operations, as willing, imagining, remembering about them" (*PHK* §2). Is that justified? There must be something that explains the naming of compound ideas, to which Berkeley alluded in Section 1. Naming is a kind of willing. But why can he include other operations of the mind?

Berkeley is working within a fairly established tradition, one that takes the mind to be that which knows and wills, as well as that which remembers and imagines. Nor is that problematic. Remembering is a type of knowing. Imagining is a type of willing: we will to put ideas together in a certain way, and the ideas assembled are themselves known. Further, philosophers do not work in a conceptual vacuum. Insofar as Berkeley can justify the introduction of the category of mind as a thing that knows and acts (wills), he is relatively free to describe its specific activities under those headings. Insofar as he criticizes a certain account of the world and our knowledge of it, but not—with the exception of abstraction—an account of the *activities* of the mind, it is reasonable to accommodate his description of the mind's activities to those assumed by the philosophers he criticizes. Notice what he does not do and ought not do, given his objectives: he does not give an account of the *nature* of the mind as something that is material (such as the brain) or immaterial (such as a Judeo-Christian soul).

If ideas are fundamentally objects of knowledge (things known, perceived), then the concluding remark of Section 2 is hardly shocking: "the existence of an idea consists in being perceived." This is the English version of Berkeley's aphorism, "*esse* is *percipi*," which he introduces in Section 3. Does it mean what it *seems* to say, namely, that existence and being perceived are the same thing, that *existence* is synonymous with *being perceived*?

No, it does not go so far. First, it pertains only to ideas. Given the remarks in Section 2, one would expect the corresponding claim for mind to be "the existence of a mind consists in perceiving and acting" (cf. N 429–429a). Second, such a reading makes little sense.

Existence is the principal concern of metaphysics. As the *philosophical* account of reality, it claims that its categories are more basic than one finds in the sciences.

If Berkeley is basing his metaphysical views on his epistemology, then claims of knowledge function as his **criterion** or standard for determining what there is. Descartes did the same in his *Meditations*: he granted the existence of things only if they could be known. And given Berkeley's initial account of ideas as objects of knowledge, it is reasonable that his criterion for the existence of an idea is that it is known.

Before turning to Section 3, we should say a few words about metaphysics. On some traditional metaphysical schemes, ideas are taken to be **modes** or modifications or states of a *substance*. Descartes held such a view: that a substance is a thing that can exist by itself. Modes are modifications of a substance and, as such, cannot exist without a substance (*CSM* 1:210–12). While we shall see that Berkeley occasionally describes the mind as a substance, it is not clear that he looks at the idea-substance relation in the same way. In *Principles* Section 49 he explicitly writes, "those qualities are in the mind only as they are perceived by it, that is, not by way of *mode* or *attribute*, but only by way of *idea*" (cf. *DHP* 237), and he regularly identifies a mind merely as that which perceives and ideas

The Case for Idealism and Immaterialism in the Principles 63

as those things that are perceived (cf. *DHP* 234 and 236). This *suggests* that Berkeley did not accept a full-blown Cartesian account of substance and modes. There is a temptation to read a fairly determinate account of substance into Berkeley's works,[14] but unless we find that *Berkeley* himself gives us reason to do so, we should resist such a temptation. Why? A determinate concept is straitjacket: it severely limits the ways we can read various passages. If our concept is relatively indeterminate—a mind (mental substance) is that which perceives and wills (acts; *PHK* §§2 and 27)—more possible ways to understand Berkeley's writings remain open. This increases the probability that we can develop a consistent interpretation without having to go back and reexamine our conceptual assumptions.

Returning to the *Principles*, given that Berkeley had already concluded that "the existence of an idea consists in being perceived" (*PHK* §2), Section 3 can be seen as a case study, that is, the application of his general conclusion to the case of ideas of sense. Ideas of the passions, imagination, and other thoughts as such are unproblematic: everyone grants that such ideas cannot exist outside the mind. But ideas of sense seem to be different, since they seem to give you contact with a world outside your mind. But, Berkeley argues, ideas of sense, *as ideas*, do not depart from the general conclusion reached in Section 2. He writes:

> And it seems no less evident that the various sensations or ideas imprinted on the sense, however blended or combined together (that is, whatever objects they compose) cannot exist otherwise than in a mind perceiving them. I think an intuitive knowledge may be obtained of this, by any one that shall attend to what is meant by the term *exist* when applied to sensible things. The table I write on, I say, exists, that is, I see and feel it; and if I were out of my study I should say it existed, meaning thereby that if I was in my study I might perceive it, or that some other spirit actually does perceive it. There was an odour, that is, it was smelled; there was a sound, that is to say, it was heard; a colour or figure, and it was perceived by sight or touch. This is all that I can understand by these and the like expressions. For as to what is said of the absolute existence of unthinking things without any relation to their being perceived, that seems perfectly unintelligible. Their *esse* is *percipi*, nor is it possible they should have any existence, out of the minds or thinking things which perceive them. (*PHK* §3)

Notice that Berkeley appeals to experience: the sole evidence for the existence of an idea of sense is that it is experienced. And this holds

64   *The Case for Idealism and Immaterialism in the* Principles

not only for individual ideas, but also for collections of ideas, that is, sensibly perceived objects—for example, the desk in my study. Further, insofar as an idea of sense is an object of human knowledge, it is necessarily connected with a knower, that is, a mind: this seems to be the point of his appeal to "intuitive knowledge." So, for individual ideas and complex objects of sense *as things known*, their *esse* is *percipi*: to be is to be known or perceived.

If the principle "to be is to be perceived" is limited to ideas as ideas and objects insofar as they are known as collections of ideas, it also makes Section 4 intelligible. On the surface, Section 4 might seem puzzling:

> It is indeed an opinion strangely prevailing amongst men, that houses, mountains, rivers, and in a word all sensible objects have an existence natural or real, distinct from their being perceived by the understanding. But with how great an assurance and acquiescence soever this principle may be entertained in the world; yet whoever shall find in his heart to call it in question, may, if I mistake not, perceive it to involve a manifest contradiction. For what are the forementioned objects but the things we perceive by sense, and what do we perceive besides our own ideas or sensations; and is it not plainly repugnant that any one of these or any combination of them should exist unperceived?

Berkeley identified houses, mountains, and rivers with sensible objects, that is, sensible things as they are immediately known (collections of ideas). Most of his contemporaries held that ideas provide *mediate* or indirect knowledge of objects. They held a version of **representative realism**: ideas represent "real things" in the world outside thought. Such a view might be represented as:

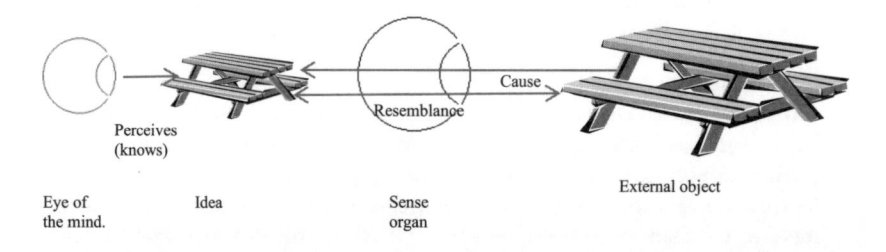

Assuming such a theory, Berkeley's contention that the common view yields a "manifest contradiction" is puzzling. Such a one might read the argument this way:

The Case for Idealism and Immaterialism in the Principles

1. All ordinary objects (mountains, etc.) are objects perceived by sense.
2. All objects perceived by sense are ideas.
3. So all ordinary objects are ideas.
4. No ideas can exist unperceived.
5. So, no ordinary objects can exist unperceived.
6. According to the common view, some ordinary objects can exist unperceived.
7. The common view expressed in 6 is inconsistent with 5.
8. Therefore, the common view is "a manifest contradiction," "plainly repugnant."

On this reading, there is an equivocation on *objects perceived by sense* in going from 1 to 2. On the Lockean and Cartesian accounts, ideas might be the *immediate* objects of sense perception, but ordinary objects are perceived *mediately* (by way of ideas). If there is a shift in the meaning of *objects perceived by sense*, then the surprising conclusion, 3, does not follow from 1 and 2, and if 3 does not follow, then neither 5 nor the "manifest contradiction" in 8 follows. Surely, the critic might add, it defies common sense to suggest that ordinary objects *cannot* exist unperceived. Indeed, this seems to be what is behind Hume's remark that "all his [Berkeley's] arguments, though otherwise intended, are, in reality, merely sceptical."[15]

But Berkeley identified sensible objects with ideas. As we saw when discussing his theory of vision, Berkeleian mediate perception consists of perceiving one idea by way of another (signification). Since he identifies sensible objects with ideas—immediate objects of knowledge—the epistemic focus should be retained in the argument. The argument might be reconstructed as follows:

1'. All ordinary objects (mountains, etc.), as known, are objects known by sense.
2'. All objects known by sense are ideas.
   So, all ordinary objects (mountains, etc.), as known, are ideas.
I. All ideas are objects of human knowledge.
3'. So all ordinary objects, as known, are objects of human knowledge.
4'. No objects of human knowledge can exist unknown.
5'. So, no ordinary objects, as known, can exist unknown.
6'. According to the common view, some ordinary objects, as known, can exist unknown.

7'. The common view expressed in (6') is inconsistent with (5').
8'. Therefore, the common view is "a manifest contradiction," "plainly repugnant."

From 1', 2', and I, 3' follows with necessity (without equivocation). Number 4' is the epistemic version of the *esse* is *percipi* principle, and from 3' and 4', 5' follows with necessity. As epistemic claims neither 3' nor 5' is shocking, but they are sufficient with the commonsensical claim 6' to generate the "manifest contradiction" in 8'. Notice also that this reconstruction of Berkeley's argument does *not* entail that ordinary objects themselves are identical with collections of ideas; it claims such an identity *only as they are known*.

If *esse* is *percipi* is intuitive, and if all ordinary objects exist only as they are known, then why is there the widespread belief that ordinary objects exist unperceived? In Section 5 Berkeley explains how this confusion arises from abstract ideas. He writes:

> [I] If we thoroughly examine this tenet, it will, perhaps, be found at bottom to depend on the doctrine of abstract ideas. For can there be a nicer strain of abstraction than to distinguish the existence of sensible objects from their being perceived, so as to conceive them existing unperceived? Light and colours, heat and cold, extension and figures, in a word the things we see and feel, what are they but so many sensations, notions, ideas or impressions on the sense; and is it possible to separate, even in thought, any of these from perception? For my part I might as easily divide a thing from it self. [II] I may indeed divide in my thoughts or conceive apart from each other those things which, perhaps, I never perceived by sense so divided. Thus I imagine the trunk of a human body without the limbs, or conceive the smell of a rose without thinking on the rose it self. So far I will not deny I can abstract, if that may properly be called abstraction, which extends only to the conceiving separately such objects, as it is possible may really exist or be actually perceived asunder. But my conceiving or imagining power does not extend beyond the possibility of real existence or perception. [III] Hence as it is impossible for me to see or feel anything without an actual sensation of that thing, so is it impossible for me to conceive in my thoughts any sensible thing or object distinct from the sensation or perception of it. (PHK §5)

I have divided the passage into three parts. II is a summary of the position advanced in Introduction, Section 10. Recall that accepting a conditional conceivability criterion of possibility (*CCP*) commits us to accepting the contrapositive of that principle; namely, if x is

The Case for Idealism and Immaterialism in the Principles 67

impossible, then x is inconceivable (*Contra-CCP*). In Introduction, Section 10, *Contra-CCP* together with the principle that it is impossible for a mode or quality to exist apart from a substance (Intro. §7) entails that it is impossible to conceive of a mode or quality apart from a substance, that is, to abstract. As in Introduction Section 10, Berkeley allows that one can conceive integral parts of objects distinct from the objects of which they are parts. He applies *Contra-CCP* to the objects in *his* system: "But my conceiving or imagining power does not extend beyond the possibility of real existence or perception," that is, if x is impossible, then x cannot be conceived (we cannot form an idea of x). An idea is an object of human knowledge. So, the application of *Contra-CCP* to the present case can be restated as follows: If x cannot be known, then x cannot be an object of human knowledge, that is, if x cannot be known, then x cannot be known. This is the conclusion in **Part III**, which may be restated as follows:

> If it is impossible to see or feel anything without the relevant kind of object of human knowledge, then it is impossible to form the relevant kind of idea (object of human knowledge).
>
> It is impossible to see or feel anything without the relevant kind of object of human knowledge.
>
> So, it is impossible to form the relevant kind of idea (object of human knowledge).

Since the objects of human knowledge are ideas of sensation, ideas of reflection, and ideas of memory or imagination composed of ideas of either of the previous kinds (*PHK* §1; cf. Locke, *Essay* 2.2.2–3), the call to see or feel something without the relevant kind of idea is an impossible state of affairs. Since Berkeley parses *abstraction* in terms of conceiving of impossible states of affairs, it is reasonable for him to suggest in I that the doctrine of abstract ideas explains the confusion of the philosophers, for at bottom the philosophers' position requires that sensible objects exist unknown, that they be at once known and unknown.

Section 6 is a summary of Berkeley's conclusions, a summary that seems to include the claim that ordinary objects are at least collections of ideas. Berkeley writes:

> Some truths there are so near and obvious to the mind, that a man need only open his eyes to see them. Such I take this important one to be, to wit, that all the choir of heaven and furniture of the earth,

in a word all those bodies which compose the mighty frame of the world, have not any subsistence without a mind, that their being is to be perceived or known; that consequently so long as they are not actually perceived by me, or do not exist in my mind or that of any other created spirit, they must either have no existence at all, or else subsist in the mind of some eternal spirit: it being perfectly unintelligible and involving all the absurdity of abstraction, to attribute to any single part of them an existence independent of a spirit. To be convinced of which, the reader need only reflect and try to separate in his own thoughts the being of a sensible thing from its being perceived. (§6)

Several points should be noticed. First, here Berkeley *explicitly* introduces the equation of perceiving and knowing, "their being is to be perceived or known." Second, while Berkeley's remarks in §3 on the existence of the table in his study when *he* is not perceiving it might be taken to suggest that there is an eternal spirit that knows all ideas we do not know—though recall that all he said there was that if I am not perceiving the table in my study it is possible "that some other spirit actually does perceive it," a position that is consistent with the table being seen by a finite spirit—here he *suggests* that there might be ideas that are perceived only by an eternal spirit. But, notice, he *does not* posit the existence of such a spirit; he merely suggests that it is the alternative to claiming that objects that are not perceived by a finite mind have no existence. Third, the language *seems* ontological: he suggests that ideas might *subsist* in the mind of an eternal spirit. If we take the wording seriously—rather than as merely the claim that if God knows all sensible objects, God knows them in a way that is different from the way in which humans know them (cf. *DHP* 240–41)—the wording shows the relationship between Berkeley's epistemology and his ontology. If our reconstruction of Berkeley's arguments to this point is sound, Berkeley is primarily an epistemologist. He is concerned with what is known and the conditions for knowing. If he is also building an ontology, then there is an isomorphic relationship between the elements in his epistemology and those in his ontology. So ideas have two aspects. As epistemic elements (objects of human knowledge), ideas require that there be a knower that is distinct from them. Call this knower *mind*, *soul*, or *spirit*. The knower as an epistemic posit, that is, something the existence of which is necessary in order to give an adequate account of the knowing situation. As an epistemic posit, the mind, as such, has no characteristics beyond "that which knows." Knowing is a necessary connection between the idea as

The Case for Idealism and Immaterialism in the Principles   69

object of human knowledge and the mind or spirit as knower.[16] Ideas as ontological elements, that is, fundamental components of the world, must reflect the same kind of dependence relation to a mind. Call this relation "perceiving." When speaking ontologically, we tend to use words such as *exist* and *subsist*.

Notice that he suggests that "all the choir of heaven and furniture of the earth, in a word all those bodies which compose the mighty frame of the world, have not any subsistence without a mind, that their being is to be perceived or known." This suggests that ordinary objects are *at least* composed of ideas. This is a radical departure from the representative realism of Descartes and Locke, who held that ordinary objects are distinct from our ideas of them. Does this commit Berkeley to the claim that ordinary objects are *only* composed of ideas? No; Berkeley has made no explicit commitments to the nature of ordinary objects *beyond* the claim that they are composed of ideas. As we shall see, this is an issue he addresses beginning in Section 8.

With the end of Section 6, the argument for *esse is percipi* is effectively finished. In Section 7 Berkeley concludes that there are only spiritual substances and begins his transition to the argument for immaterialism. He writes:

> From what has been said, it follows, there is not any other substance than *spirit*, or that which perceives. But for the fuller proof of this point, let it be considered, the sensible qualities are colour, figure, motion, smell, taste, and such like, that is, the ideas perceived by sense. Now for an idea to exist in an unperceiving thing, is a manifest contradiction; for to have an idea is all one as to perceive: that therefore wherein colour, figure, and the like qualities exist, must perceive them; hence it is clear there can be no unthinking substance or *substratum* of those ideas. (*PHK* §7)

Assuming an epistemic reading of the first six sections of the *Principles*, the conclusion follows that there is no substance other than spirit, that is, a knower. All that is required to account for the knowing situation is an object known and a knower together with the knowing (perceiving) relation between the two. Ordinary objects are composed of *at least* ideas, and ideas depend for their existence on minds. So, there could be no ordinary objects if there were no minds. The only substances are mental substances. Thus everything that exists either is a mind or depends for its existence upon a mind. Berkeley was an idealist.

Does this commit Berkeley to the existence of an *immaterial* substance? No. Berkeley has provided no analysis of the nature of spirit. Idealism comes in many flavors. Kant claimed that Descartes was an idealist.[17] Insofar as God is a mind, and, as an infinite Cartesian substance, everything depends upon God for its existence, Descartes was an idealist even though he distinguished between and was committed to the existence of mental and physical finite substances.

Thus a commitment to idealism, as such, does not show that matter does not exist. To show that ordinary objects are *at least* ideas does not show that they have no other properties. To show that the only kind of substance that exists is mental does not also show that it is not composed of matter. Defending immaterialism is Berkeley's next task.

The Attack on Matter (Sections 8–24)

If you were going to show that something does not exist, how would you go about it? Some things are easy, you reply: I can show that there are no round squares by showing that the notion of roundness is inconsistent with the notion of squareness. But showing that there is not an existent imperceptible elephant in the corner of my office might be a little harder. What would count as evidence? How do you establish a negative claim? Can you do so? Would it be enough to say, "I can develop a coherent account of the world without claiming that there are imperceptible elephants, so, there is no reason for me to believe such things exist"?

I shall argue that Berkeley launches his attack against *theories* of matter. Criticisms of theories proceed on several fronts. If a theory is plausible, it must be coherent, that is, 1. you must be able to understand the meanings of the terms of which it is composed; 2. it must be internally consistent: the concepts of which it is composed must not yield contradictions; and 3. it must explain what it is intended to explain. So, if Berkeley could show that a theory is composed of meaningless terms he would strike a blow against the theory. Showing that a theory entails inconsistencies would be a serious blow against it: it would show that the theory, *as stated*, is false; it would at least shift the burden of proof to its proponents, who might be able to "patch" it in such a way that it became consistent. If he can show that a theory fails to explain, or that the explanations cannot work in the ways the proponents claimed, there is another blow against the theory. If, in addition to any of these, it is possible to provide an alternative explanation of the phenomenon that is simpler—that assumes fewer fundamentally different kinds of things than the proposed theory—there are good reasons to reject the theory.

Two theories of material substance were current during the early eighteenth century. One was a traditional substratum theory of substance, a theory that can trace its roots at least to Aristotle. According to that theory, a substance is something that has properties: it is said to support or lie under observable properties or accidents. The other theory is drawn from the "new science" of the seventeenth century. Many scientists adopted an atomic theory of matter, a theory that traced its roots to Democritus. As the atomic theory was developed by John Locke and Robert Boyle, it was deemed the "corpuscular hypothesis." Corpuscles, the basic physical components of material objects, have only certain properties, which were deemed the primary qualities. These primary qualities are the properties of matter as such. On Locke's lists they are extension, solidity, figure, and mobility (Locke, *Essay* 2.8.9), to which he sometimes adds bulk, texture, and number (Locke, *Essay* 2.8.10 and 17). As the fundamental components of matter, they cause humans to perceive other properties, the secondary qualities: colors, heat and cold, flavors, sounds, and aromas (Locke, *Essay* 2.8.10). Secondary qualities can be said to be "in" a material object only insofar as the object contains the peculiar arrangement of corpuscles that cause a mind to form an idea of a particular color, sound, or other secondary quality (Locke, *Essay* 2.8.8 and 10). Locke claimed that a quality *as such* is a power in an object to produce a certain idea (Locke, *Essay* 2.8.8), meaning that secondary qualities as powers exist in objects. But secondary qualities *as powers* can be reduced to (explained in terms of) the operations of corpuscles composed solely of the primary qualities. Since ideas of the primary qualities are said to resemble the properties in the objects themselves, while ideas of secondary qualities do not (Locke, *Essay* 2.8.15), it was commonly claimed that secondary qualities exist only in the mind.[18]

Berkeley develops arguments against both accounts of matter. He first attacks the primary/secondary qualities distinction. He begins that discussion with an argument supporting his **likeness principle**, the principle that nothing can be like an idea except an idea. This is presented in Section 8 (cf. *DHP* 206):

But say you, though the ideas themselves do not exist without the mind, yet there may be things like them whereof they are copies or resemblances, which things exist without the mind, in an unthinking substance. I answer, an idea can be like nothing but an idea; a colour or figure can be like nothing but another colour or figure. If we look but ever so little into our thoughts, we shall find it impossible for us to conceive a likeness except only between our ideas. Again, I ask whether those supposed originals or external things, of which our ideas are the pictures or representations, be themselves perceivable or no? If they are, then they are ideas, and we have gained our point; but if you say they are not, I appeal to any one whether it be sense, to assert a colour is like something which is invisible; hard or soft, like something which is intangible; and so of the rest.

How does the argument go? It might be reconstructed like this:

1. Experience suggests that it is impossible for us to conceive a likeness between any things other than ideas.
2. So it is impossible for there to be a likeness between anything other than ideas.

But the conclusion does not follow from the premise. The premise is a simple statement of fact. The conclusion claims that it is impossible for an idea to resemble anything but an idea. Experience can show that something is *possible*: a claim of possibility is weaker than a claim of actuality, so if something is actually experienced it is possible to experience it. The conceivability criterion of possibility (CCP)—if I can conceive of p, or clearly and distinctly conceive of p, or conceive of p as a whole in terms of all of its parts and their interrelations, then p is logically possible (consistent)—might be reasonable. But it does not follow from CCP that if, as a matter of fact, I cannot conceive of p then p is impossible. Berkeley seems to be making exactly that move in his discussion of the likeness principle. Does that mean it should be rejected?

Our discussion of CCP understood it in a modest way; we claimed it is merely a conditional statement. Some scholars[19] hold that Berkeley accepted a more powerful version of the principle: p is conceivable if and only if p is possible, that is, if p is conceivable, then p is possible, and if p is possible, then p is conceivable. This principle entails an **inconceivability criterion of impossibility** (*ICI*): if p is inconceivable, then p is impossible. It is to such a principle that Berkeley seems to appeal in Section 8.

The Case for Idealism and Immaterialism in the Principles 73

But what does *ICI* mean? Is it plausible?

There are two points to keep in mind. First, *inconceivable* means "it is not possible to conceive." Second, we're concerned with a criterion by which to judge impossibility. So, while it might be reasonable to say that if p is logically inconceivable, then p is logically impossible, it's not the kind of inconceivability that can function as a criterion. What Berkeley must mean by *inconceivable* might be called "factual inconceivability": I try but I find I cannot form the relevant idea. But, just as we needed to clarify what Berkeley probably meant by *inconceivable*, we must also clarify what he meant by *impossible*. There are several modes (types) of impossibility. The strongest mode of impossibility is **logical impossibility**. Logically impossible states of affairs are represented by logical contradictions, statements of the form "p and not p." Such statements are formally false: the form or structure of the statement precludes the possibility of its truth. **Conceptual impossibility** is weaker. Here the part of the content of the subject term of a statement is denied by the predicate. Here there is a contradiction, but it is based on the content, for example, "some bachelors are married." **Epistemic impossibility** is weaker still. It is merely the claim that it is impossible to know. And this seems like a plausible candidate for *ICI*: If I cannot, in fact, form an idea of p, then it is impossible to know that p exists (ICI_E). Since Berkeley posits the existence of objects if and only if they can be known, the fact that an object cannot be conceived entails that there is no basis for positing its existence. If there is no basis for positing its existence, there is no basis for claiming resemblance (likeness). Thus there are no epistemic grounds for claiming a resemblance between an idea and any non-idea.

If you think about it a bit, this is quite reasonable. Consider an analogous case. Does the woman in Leonardo da Vinci's *Mona Lisa* resemble the subject he painted (cf. *DHP* 203–4)? How could you answer that question? It is not merely that art historians disagree regarding who the subject was—assuming it was not a compilation from several subjects—even if there were incontrovertible proof that it was Leonardo's Irish cousin Lisa O'Malley, there is no way a comparison could be made. The portrait was painted more than five hundred years ago. The subject has been dead for more than four hundred years. Bodies deteriorate. There is nothing left to compare. It's an unanswerable question. But the presumed material objects are as unavailable as Lisa O'Malley's body: they are posits outside the domain of ideas. There is no ground for claiming resemblance. An idea only can be known to be like another idea. In a world that is constructed on the basis of what is known, therefore, it is impossible for an idea to be like something that is not an idea.

In Section 9 Berkeley begins his attack on the primary / secondary qualities distinction itself. He writes:

> Some there are who make a distinction betwixt *primary* and *secondary* qualities: by the former, they mean extension, figure, motion, rest, solidity or impenetrability and number: by the latter they denote all other sensible qualities, as colours, sounds, tastes, and so forth. The ideas we have of these they acknowledge not to be the resemblances of any thing existing without the mind or unperceived; but they will have our ideas of the primary qualities to be patterns or images of things which exist without the mind, in an unthinking substance which they call *matter*. By matter therefore we are to understand an inert, senseless substance, in which extension, figure, and motion, do actually subsist. But it is evident from what we have already shewn, that extension, figure and motion are only ideas existing in the mind, and that an idea can be like nothing but another idea, and that consequently neither they nor their archetypes can exist in an unperceiving substance. Hence it is plain, that the very notion of what is called *matter* or *corporeal substance*, involves a contradiction in it. (PHK §9)

Berkeley's model of the primary/secondary qualities distinction is Lockean. While acknowledging that the primary qualities are the alleged constitutive properties of matter, Berkeley also associates the distinction with the traditional theory of substance: matter is the inert substance in which the primary qualities subsist, a point that is not made in Locke's discussion of primary and secondary qualities but which is consistent with his overall philosophical position. Berkeley claims that such a position is inconsistent. Why? Insofar as we can claim that the primary qualities exist, they must be ideas, that is, objects of knowledge. As we learned in the Introduction to the *Principles*, things are divided into kinds on the basis of resemblance. So, if there were extensions, figures, motions, and solidities that were not ideas, they would have to resemble ideas. The likeness principle blocks that move in two ways. The first is epistemic: by limiting the applicability of the resemblance relation, it undercuts any ground for representative realism. So even if there were extensions in a world outside the domain of ideas, they could not be known. Hence, there is no ground for claiming they exist. The second is categorial: it assumes that two things can be things of the same kind without resemblance. The doctrine of primary qualities

The Case for Idealism and Immaterialism in the Principles

thus takes extension, for example, to be both inherently knowable and inherently unknowable. If only ideas can resemble ideas, ideas cannot resemble "external objects." So, there would need to be a basis for claiming that sensible extension and nonsensible extension are the same kind of things, a basis that is not founded on resemblance. This is inconsistent with Locke's account of how the world is divided into kinds (*Essay* 3.3). Hence, the doctrine of primary qualities is inconsistent; it is built on contradictory principles.

What elements of the primary / secondary qualities distinction has Berkeley attacked? He used his likeness principle to argue that Locke's claimed resemblance between ideas of primary qualities and the qualities in material objects (*Essay* 2.8.15) is incoherent. Some might argue that the resemblance thesis is secondary to the causal thesis. After all, Locke's notion of *quality* is defined in terms of the power to cause or produce an idea of a certain sort (*Essay* 2.2.8). Nothing Berkeley has said is inconsistent with the causal thesis *unless* there must be a resemblance between a cause and its effect. But Locke's *denial* of a resemblance between the ideas of secondary qualities and their causes entails that the likeness principle alone leaves the causal thesis intact. But, as we shall see, one way to read part of Section 10 is as an attack on the causal thesis.

Section 10 reads:

> They who assert that figure, motion, and the rest of the primary or original qualities do exist without the mind, in unthinking substances, do at the same time acknowledge that colours, sounds, heat, cold, and such like secondary qualities, do not, which they tell us are sensations existing in the mind alone, that depend on and are occasioned by the different size, texture and motion of the minute particles of matter. This they take for an undoubted truth, which they can demonstrate beyond all exception. Now if it be certain, that those original qualities are inseparably united with the other sensible qualities, and not, even in thought, capable of being abstracted from them, it plainly follows that they exist only in the mind. But I desire any one to reflect and try, whether he can by any abstraction of thought, conceive the extension and motion of a body, without all other sensible qualities. For my own part, I see evidently that it is not in my power to frame an idea of a body extended and moved, but I must withal give it some colour or other sensible quality which is acknowledged to exist only in the mind. In short, extension, figure, and motion, abstracted from all other qualities, are inconceivable. Where therefore the other sensible qualities are, there must these be also, to wit, in the mind and no where else. (*PHK* §10)

After acknowledging that the resemblance thesis does not apply to (ideas of) secondary qualities with respect to their putative originals in matter, Berkeley argues that since secondary qualities exist only in the mind, primary qualities also exist only in the mind. The argument may be put this way:

1. If primary qualities are inseparably united with secondary qualities, and if secondary exist only in the mind, then primary qualities exist only in the mind.
2. Primary qualities are inseparably united with secondary qualities.
3. Secondary qualities exist only in the mind.
4. So primary qualities exist only in the mind.

The argument is valid. The interesting point is the argument for 2, where Berkeley appeals to ICI_E. Berkeley's evidence for 2 consists of a challenge to conceive of extension apart from the secondary qualities together with an "I tried, but I can't do it" claim. "In short, extension, figure, and motion, abstracted from all other qualities, are inconceivable. Where therefore the other sensible qualities are, there must these be also, to wit, in the mind and no where else." If he appeals to ICI_E, Berkeley can claim that insofar as he cannot conceive of extension, figure, and motion apart from the secondary qualities, it follows that he cannot know that they are distinct from and independent of the secondary qualities. Insofar as his ontology follows his epistemology, there is no ground for claiming that primary qualities exist apart from secondary qualities. So, primary qualities cannot exist apart from secondary qualities. If the secondary qualities exist only as perceived, that is, in the mind, then the primary qualities must also so exist.

Here one might object, "So what? The primary / secondary qualities distinction is primarily a causal hypothesis. Why would it make *any* difference if I cannot conceive of the cause apart from its effect? Why can't I posit an object composed solely of the primary qualities as an unknown something that causes the ideas I perceive?" To answer this objection we must look at the conceptual constraints on considerations of efficient causality.

It was commonly claimed that the cause of an entity must be something numerically distinct from its effect. This is found in the late scholastic philosopher Francesco Suarez's discussion of efficient causality,[20] and it was the basis for Arnauld's objection to Descartes's claim that God can be self-caused (CSM 2:147). If the primary qualities, as known, are inseparable (indistinguishable insofar as they are known to exist) from some secondary qualities, there is no basis for claiming that a combination of the primary qualities is the cause of a secondary quality: to make such a claim is inconsistent with the distinctness condition.[21]

While Berkeley had already suggested that the primary / secondary qualities distinction is a philosophical error that can be explained by a commitment to the doctrine of abstract ideas— "In short, extension, figure, and motion, abstracted from all other qualities, are inconceivable" (*PHK* §10)—his discussion in Section 11 makes this connection explicit. He writes:

> Again, *great* and *small*, *swift* and *slow*, are allowed to exist no where without the mind, being entirely relative, and changing as the frame or position of the organs of sense varies. The extension therefore which exists without the mind, is neither great nor small, the motion neither swift nor slow, that is, they are nothing at all. But say you, they are extension in general, and motion in general: thus we see how much the tenet of extended, moveable substances existing without the mind, depends on that strange doctrine of *abstract ideas*. And here I cannot but remark, how nearly the vague and indeterminate description of matter or corporeal substance, which the modern philosophers are run into by their own principles, resembles that antiquated and so much ridiculed notion of *materia prima*, to be met with in Aristotle and his followers. Without extension solidity cannot be conceived; since therefore it has been shewn that extension exists not in an unthinking substance, the same must also be true of solidity. (*PHK* §11)

All known cases of size and movement are determinate, yet we make comparative claims regarding size and motion. Our basis for claiming that one object is larger than another or that one movement is faster than another is experience. Comparative concepts are strictly mental. So either those concepts do not apply to putative material objects, in which case material objects are extended but have no relative size and move but at no relative speed (which is absurd), or only extension in general and movement in general are applicable to material objects, in which case the notions of extension and motion are unintelligible. If the notions of extension and movement as applied to putative material objects are unintelligible, then the doctrine of matter assumed by the primary / secondary qualities distinction is no better than the Aristotelian doctrine of prime matter, which is matter in general that is not the matter of any particular thing. In either case, the attempt to ascribe extension to matter as such is unintelligible. But, since even Locke allowed that the notion of solidity could be construed only as impenetrability or resistance, since only extended substances can be known to be impenetrable, and since Berkeley already argued that extension can exist only in the mind, solidity also can exist only in the mind.

Sections 12 and 13 are extensions of the conclusions reached in Section 11. While Section 11 focuses on vague concepts such as *swift* and *slow*, Berkeley focuses on explicit measurements in Section 12. Determinate measurements are always made relative to some conventional scale. One thing can be at once one yard, three feet, or thirty-six inches long, depending upon your chosen standard of measurement. And measurement is always made by comparing one sensibly perceived object with another. Given the conclusions in Section 11 as well as the likeness principle, it is incoherent to apply standards of measurement to imperceptible objects. Thus it is implausible to suggest that number is a property as of matter as such. And in Section 13 Berkeley argues that the root problem is with the notion of unity (oneness). If units are relative to a system of measurement, then, contrary to Locke (*Essay* 2.16.1), it makes no sense to suggest that we have a determinate simple idea of unity. The idea of unity can be derived only by a putative act of abstraction, which explains the philosophical error in claiming that number is a primary quality.

Berkeley concludes his criticisms of the primary / secondary qualities distinction by contending that the arguments used to show that secondary qualities are dependent upon the mind can be turned against the contention that primary qualities have an existence outside the mind. Here is an example: it is proved that sweetness is not really in the sapid thing, because, the thing remaining unaltered, the sweet flavor is changed into bitter by a change in the perceiver, for example, a fever. Similarly, Berkeley suggests, it is reasonable to claim that motion does not exist outside the mind, since if the succession of ideas in the mind become swifter, the motion will appear slower even if there is no alteration in an external object (*PHK* §14).

In Section 15 Berkeley summarizes his conclusions. Alluding to the arguments in Section 14, he writes:

> it must be confessed this method of arguing doth not so much prove that there is no extension or colour in an outward object, as that we do not know by sense which is the true extension or colour of the

object. But the arguments foregoing plainly shew it to be impossible that any colour or extension at all, or other sensible quality whatsoever, should exist in an unthinking subject without the mind, or in truth, that there should be any such thing as an outward object. (*PHK* §15)

What is going on? Doesn't Berkeley grant in the first sentence that all we *really* know is that we don't know what the extension or color of a putative external material object is, while claiming in the second sentence that he has proven that external material objects do not exist? Can he have it both ways? He can, if our interpretive hypothesis is correct. If Berkeley posits the existence of only what can be known directly and of those things whose existence is entailed by what can be known directly, then the fact that we cannot know anything about material objects on the basis of what is known directly implies that there is no ground for positing the existence of such objects. If anything admitted to his ontology must have epistemic warrant, the absence of such warrant is a sufficient condition for denying the existence of the putative object. So, since his arguments show that the primary / secondary qualities distinction provides no epistemic warrant for claiming the existence of "an outward object," he is warranted in denying the existence of material substance *as it is construed* on the basis of the primary / secondary qualities distinction.

Having completed his discussion of the primary / secondary qualities distinction, Berkeley turns to the older notion of substance. Even among those philosophers who were committed to the new science, the older notion of substance persisted. Thus, Descartes held that a substance is a thing that can exist by itself as the subject of attribution and modification (CSM 1:210–11); Locke held that a substance as such is a substratum that underlies properties (Locke, *Essay* 2.23.1–3). We shall see that Berkeley criticizes the notion of *material* substance, and that his arguments have close parallels to his criticisms of abstraction in Introduction, Sections 10–13: he argues 1. that one cannot form the relevant idea of a material substance, 2. that the doctrine of material substratum plays no explanatory role with respect to our knowledge of the world, and 3. that the situation required to show that a material substance is even *possible* is internally inconsistent. I argue that it differs from the structure in Introduction Sections 10–13 only insofar as Berkeley's epistemic theory of ideas is integral to establishing 3.

The Case for Idealism and Immaterialism in the Principles

Berkeley begins by describing the substratum theory of material substance and arguing that one cannot form an idea of substance. He writes:

> It is said extension is a mode or accident of matter, and that matter is the *substratum* that supports it. Now I desire that you would explain what is meant by matter's *supporting* extension: say you, I have no idea of matter, and therefore cannot explain it. I answer, though you have no positive, yet if you have any meaning at all, you must at least have a relative idea of matter; though you know not what it is, yet you must be supposed to know what relation it bears to accidents, and what is meant by its supporting them. It is evident *support* cannot here be taken in its usual or literal sense, as when we say that pillars support a building: in what sense therefore must it be taken? (*PHK* §16)

Berkeley is asking whether we have an idea of substance. His discussion focuses on Locke's discussion of the idea of substance in general. At *Essay* 2.23.2, Locke wrote, "The *Idea* then we have, to which we give the general name Substance, being nothing, but the supposed, but unknown support of those Qualities we find existing, which we imagine cannot subsist, *sine re substante*, without something to support them, we call that Support *Substantia*; which, according to the true import of the Word, is in plain *English, standing under* or *upholding*." This Locke describes as "An obscure and relative *Idea* of Substance in general" (Locke, *Essay* 2.23.3). We do not know what substance itself is other than it is that which supports. As Locke remarked at another place, "we have no *Idea* of what it is, but only a confused and obscure one of what it does," (*Essay* 2.13.19).

If you claim the existence of substance, there should be some evidence for it. One type of evidence is an idea. But it was generally conceded that we have no *positive* idea of substance itself, that is, we have no ideas of the constitutive properties of substance. The best we can do is what Locke called a "relative idea." What is that? In his *Reply to Edward, Bishop of Worcester*, Locke suggests that it is the singling out of an object on the basis of its relation to something that is known directly. He wrote:

> To explain myself, and clear my meaning in this matter: all the ideas of all the sensible qualities of a cherry come into my mind by sensation; the ideas of perceiving, thinking, reasoning, knowing, &c. come into my mind by reflection: the ideas of these qualities and actions, or powers, are perceived by the mind to be by themselves

inconsistent with existence; or, as your lordship well expresses it, "we find that we can have no true conception of any modes or accidents, but we must conceive a substratum or subject, wherein they are;" i.e. that they cannot exist or subsist of themselves. Hence the mind perceives their necessary connexion with inherence or being supported; which being a relative idea superadded to the red colour in a cherry, or to thinking in a man, the mind frames the correlative idea of a support. For I never denied, that the mind could frame to itself ideas of relation, but have showed the quite contrary in my chapters about relation. But because a relation cannot be founded in nothing, or be the relation of nothing, and the thing here related as a supporter or support is not represented to the mind by any clear and distinct idea; therefore the obscure, indistinct, vague idea of thing or something, is all that is left to be the positive idea, which has the relation of a support or substratum to modes or accidents; and that general indetermined idea of something, is, by the abstraction of the mind, derived also from the simple ideas of sensation and reflection: and thus the mind, from the positive, simple ideas got by sensation or reflection, comes to the general relative idea of substance; which, without the positive simple ideas, it would never have.[22]

Insofar as the mind perceives a relation between a positive idea and something else, even if it has no positive idea of that to which that positive idea is related, one is able to single out that "something." But the mind must perceive the relation if one can plausibly claim to single out the related object. Berkeley's initial criticism is that we have no determinate notion of support, or, insofar as we do, it cannot be the notion of support operative in the relative idea of substance (cf. *DHP* 199). Hence, we cannot single out the relevant kind of object.[23]

In Section 17 Berkeley extends his criticism by relating it to his earlier conclusions. He writes:

If we inquire into what the most accurate philosophers declare themselves to mean by *material substance*; we shall find them acknowledge, they have no other meaning annexed to those sounds, but the idea of being in general, together with the relative notion of its supporting accidents. The general idea of being appeareth to me the most abstract and incomprehensible of all other; and as for its supporting accidents, this, as we have just now observed, cannot be understood in the common sense of those words; it must therefore be taken in some other sense, but what that is they do not explain. So that when I consider the two parts or branches which make the signification of the words *material substance*, I am convinced there is no distinct meaning annexed to them. But why should we trouble ourselves any farther, in discussing this material *substratum* or support of figure and motion, and other sensible qualities? Does it not suppose they have an existence without the mind? And is not this a direct repugnancy, and altogether inconceivable? (*PHK* §17)

Once again Berkeley stresses that the notion of *support* is problematic, but he adds two elements. First, if we *were* able to single out a material substance, this would be deemed *being in general*—"that general indetermined idea of something" as Locke called it in his letter to Stillingfleet—that supports accidents. But the notion of "being in general" is abstract in the extreme. If Berkeley's critique of abstract ideas is sound, such a general notion is unintelligible. Second, this unintelligibility is compounded by the presumption that material substances have an existence that is independent of a mind. Thus, the notion of material substance contains a "direct repugnancy" and is therefore inconceivable.

What is the general conclusion from Sections 16 and 17? Section 16 argues that we cannot, in fact, form an idea—not even a relative idea—of material substance. Section 17 argues that the notion of material substance is inconsistent, and therefore it is impossible to form an idea of material substance. At bottom, Berkeley's claim is that we have no idea of material substance, so there is no reason to believe it exists.

But not all things that exist are things of which we have ideas. In Section 2 Berkeley granted that there must be minds-as-knowers insofar as there are objects of human knowledge (ideas). Minds are known by reason, not by immediate perception. In Sections 18–20 Berkeley asks whether the demands of reason require the existence of material substance. Sense experience provides us only with immediate knowledge of ideas, a point even the proponents of material substance acknowledge. Does reason demand the existence of material substance? No. As Berkeley writes:

> It remains therefore that if we have any knowledge at all of external things, it must be by reason, inferring their existence from what is immediately perceived by sense. But what reason can induce us to believe the existence of bodies without the mind, from what we perceive, since the very patrons of matter themselves do not pretend, there is any necessary connexion betwixt them and our ideas? I say it is granted on all hands (and what happens in dreams, phrensies, and the like, puts it beyond dispute) that it is possible we might be affected with all the ideas we have now, though no bodies existed

The Case for Idealism and Immaterialism in the Principles 83

without, resembling them. Hence it is evident the supposition of external bodies is not necessary for the producing our ideas: since it is granted they are produced sometimes, and might possibly be produced always in the same order we see them in at present, without their concurrence. (*PHK* §18)

Appeals to reason are of two sorts, although in Berkeley's philosophy they would seem to be two sides of a single coin. First, reason can demand the existence of an entity if there is a necessary connection between an object of one sort and that of another. The connection between an object of human knowledge and a knower in Section 2 is such a necessary connection: one cannot exist without the other. Second, there might be a causal connection, which, prior to Hume, was often deemed a species of necessary connection.[24] Berkeley cites the "materialists" themselves as an authority for claiming that there is no necessary connection between what is perceived and material substance (cf. Locke, *Essay* 4.3.28). While we might believe Berkeley is concerned with necessary connections of the first sort, it is clear that he is concerned with at least causal connections. In the case of dreams and hallucinations, there is no presumed necessary connection between the occurrence of the idea and a resembling object that causes it. Granting that it is *possible* that some idea is not caused by a material object is sufficient to show that there is no necessary connection between all ideas and material substances. So, given the constraints on causal explanation assumed by Berkeley and his contemporaries, namely, that causal relations involve necessary connections, this is sufficient to show that the *presumption* of material substance cannot explain the occurrence of ideas. So *reason* provides no ground for claiming that there are material objects. In Section 19, Berkeley concludes that since the doctrine of material substance is of no explanatory value, his ontology would be more parsimonious if material substance were excluded from it. Since the ontologically simpler theory is more probably true, this is a reason to exclude material substance. It has the additional advantage of dissolving the problem of mind-body interaction. "In short, if there were external bodies, it is impossible we should ever come to know it; and if there were not, we might have the very same reasons to think there were that we have now" (*PHK* §20). This is not to deny that ideas must be caused; it requires that the cause be mental.

We should notice what Berkeley has done to this point. First, he asked whether we have an idea of material substance, to which his answer was a resounding "No!" Second, he asked whether—assuming that the existence of material substance is at least *possible*—it could play an explanatory role in our conceptual scheme. Again his answer is "No." Notice that we have seen a similar pattern of argumentation in Introduction Sections 10–12. First he argued that we cannot form abstract ideas. Then he argued that we do not need them to explain linguistic meaning. This was followed by the "killing blow" in Introduction, Section 13, the argument that Locke's abstract idea of a triangle is inconsistent and therefore impossible and therefore inconceivable. Berkeley makes a similar move in Sections 22 and 23. His so-called Master Argument shows that the condition necessary to show that a material substance is merely possible is internally inconsistent.

In Section 22 he writes:

> I am afraid I have given cause to think me needlessly prolix in handling this subject. For to what purpose is it to dilate on that which may be demonstrated with the utmost evidence in a line or two, to any one that is capable of the least reflexion? It is but looking into your own thoughts, and so trying whether you can conceive it possible for a sound, or figure, or motion, or colour, to exist without the mind, or unperceived. This easy trial may make you see, that what you contend for, is a downright contradiction. Insomuch that I am content to put the whole upon this issue; if you can but conceive it possible for one extended moveable substance, or in general, for any one idea or any thing like an idea, to exist otherwise than in a mind perceiving it, I shall readily give up the cause: And as for all that *compages* of external bodies which you contend for, I shall grant you its existence, though you cannot either give me any reason why you believe it exists, or assign any use to it when it is supposed to exist. I say, the bare possibility of your opinion's being true, shall pass for an argument that it is so. (*PHK* §22)

This is nothing if not bold. Dropping the assumption that the existence of material substance is at least possible, Berkeley claims that if it can be shown that the existence of material objects—or even unperceived qualities of material substance—is possible, he will grant that unperceived objects exist. He assumes a conditional conceivability criterion of possibility (*CCP*). If one can conceive of a quality distinct from being perceived, then Berkeley will allow that they so exist. And if there are grounds for claiming the existence of *one* object that exists unperceived, there is no reason why one should place *any* restrictions on the number of mind-independent objects:

The Case for Idealism and Immaterialism in the Principles 85

if you are developing an ontology, you are concerned with the number of distinct **categories** or fundamentally different *kinds* of objects in one's world, not with the number of objects of a given kind.

So how can Berkeley make this bold claim? Won't it do to simply conceive of a color patch? This will not suffice. Berkeley addresses this issue in Section 23. There he argues that, given *CCP*, it is impossible to show that you can so much as conceive of something existing apart from a mind, since anything you conceive is related to at least one mind, namely, yours. Thus there can be no evidence that the existence of a material object is so much as possible.

But doesn't this blur a distinction? As Kenneth Winkler put it, "It is true that we conceive of the object, but it need not be unconceived in order for us to represent it as unconceived."[25]

On the epistemic interpretation, we need not blush at Berkeley's argument. Nor need we take the discussion in Section 23 to be the heart of the argument. The argument is presented in two sentences in Section 22: "It is but looking into your own thoughts, and so trying whether you can conceive it possible for a sound, or figure, or motion, or colour, to exist without the mind, or unperceived. This easy trial may make you see, that what you contend for, is a downright contradiction." How should that be understood? What is involved in conceiving of a sound, or figure, or motion, or color? You form an idea of a sound, or an idea of a thing that has a certain figure and color. And what is an idea? An idea is an object of human knowledge. To perceive is to know. So, Berkeley's challenge is to conceive of an object of human knowledge that exists unknown. Having argued already in Section 4, that there is a "manifest contradiction," that it is "plainly repugnant" for an object of human knowledge to exist unknown, Berkeley's Master Argument is little more than a reiteration of that argument, although it is a reiteration of that argument for a different purpose. In Section 4, Berkeley was concerned with immediate objects of knowledge. Here, as he indicates in Section 23, he is concerned with material substance: "A little attention will discover to any one the truth and evidence of what is here said, and make it unnecessary to insist on any other proofs against the existence of material substance."

So what have we seen in the progression from Section 16 through Section 23? There have been three points: 1. we cannot form the relevant idea of a material substance, so there's no positive evidence for the existence of material substance; 2. the doctrine of material substratum plays no explanatory role with regard to our knowledge of the world, so there's no indirect evidence for the existence of material substance; and 3. the situation required to show that a material substance is even *possible* is internally inconsistent. And this is how Berkeley summarizes his discussion in Section 24:

> It is very obvious, upon the least inquiry into our own thoughts, to know whether it be possible for us to understand what is meant, by *the absolute existence of sensible objects in themselves, or without the mind*. To me it is evident those words mark out either a direct contradiction [1. and *PHK* §4], or else nothing at all [1. and 2.].

We should notice that Berkeley's conclusion is broader than the issues discussed in Sections 16–23; it is a summary of the conclusions reached to this point in the *Principles*.

Onward to Ordinary Objects (Sections 25–33)

So far Berkeley has argued that ordinary objects are *at least* composed of mind-dependent ideas (*PHK* §§1–7), and, since there are no grounds for claiming the existence of material substance (*PHK* §§9–24), ordinary objects are composed *only* of ideas and minds are immaterial. But of what kind of ideas are ordinary objects composed? How are those ideas of which ordinary objects composed distinguished from others? And what more can be known about minds?

Berkeley answers some of those questions in Sections 25–33. Our focus will be on the argumentative moves Berkeley makes in distinguishing ordinary objects ("real things," *PHK* §33) from other ideas.

Beginning with Section 25, Berkeley explores the implications of his earlier conclusions. Recall that, while he argued that there are no material substances, he has *not* introduced any positive characterization of mental substance beyond the claim that it is that which knows, remembers, imagines, and wills (*PHK* §2). Beginning in Section 25, Berkeley develops a positive argument for the immateriality of mental substance.

Section 25 presents Berkeley's passivity thesis. The passivity thesis was proposed by his predecessors as a ground for claiming the existence of material objects (see CSM 2:54; Locke, *Essay* 4.11.5). Berkeley uses the passivity thesis to prove the existence and provide a characterization of mental substance. He writes:

The Case for Idealism and Immaterialism in the Principles

> All our ideas, sensations, or the things which we perceive, by whatsoever names they may be distinguished, are visibly inactive, there is nothing of power or agency included in them. So that one idea or object of thought cannot produce, or make any alteration in another. To be satisfied of the truth of this, there is nothing else requisite but a bare observation of our ideas. For since they and every part of them exist only in the mind, it follows that there is nothing in them but what is perceived. But whoever shall attend to his ideas, whether of sense or reflexion, will not perceive in them any power or activity; there is therefore no such thing contained in them. A little attention will discover to us that the very being of an idea implies passiveness and inertness in it, insomuch that it is impossible for an idea to do any thing, or, strictly speaking, to be the cause of any thing: neither can it be the resemblance or pattern of any active being, as is evident from Sect. 8. Whence it plainly follows that extension, figure and motion, cannot be the cause of our sensations. To say therefore, that these are the effects of powers resulting from the configuration, number, motion, and size of corpuscles, must certainly be false. (*PHK* §25)

Berkeley claims that ideas are inactive (passive), that is, they have no causal powers. He claims that we can recognize the passivity of ideas simply by attending to them. If ideas are the immediate objects of human knowledge and exist only as they are known, they must be epistemically transparent: they can have all and only those qualities that can be known by attending to them. Phillip Cummins calls this the "Manifest Qualities Thesis."[26] So, if ideas "are visibly inactive," they cannot properly act on one another. Since the primary qualities of extension, figure, and motion are ideas, they cannot be causally efficacious.

On its face, this might seem a bit strange. Locke listed the idea of power as one derivable from both sense and reflection (*Essay* 2.7.1). Powers can be understood only in terms of their effects (cf. *Essay* 2.8.25, 2.21.72, 2.22.11). You see flame coming into contact with gold. Then you see the gold in liquid form. Do you see the cause or power? As Hume later claimed, "No, of course not!" One thing happens, then another thing happens. Being limited to the realm of sense perception, we see *that* certain events regularly follow one another; we do *not* perceive the causal relationship. So it is not unreasonable to claim that we do not sensibly perceive that there are causal relations among (powers in) objects.

Still, there is something strange about the passage. Look at your ideas. Do you see any causal relations among them? Compare this with the following: "Look at this picture. Do you see a gwalf in it?" I suspect you would answer, "What's a gwalf?" You have to be in a position to know what you are looking for if you are to "see" its absence. Already in Section 2 Berkeley suggested that the mind is active. In his terminology, he would allow that we have a *notion* of power on the basis of our own mental activities: we know *that* the mind acts, even though we cannot form an idea of how it acts. So, if we have a notion of power on the basis of the actions of our mind, we should be in a position to see whether there are active powers—as opposed to merely the effects of those powers—among our ideas.

But even if powers are not perceivable among ideas, the fact that there are observed changes is undeniable. If these changes cannot arise from the ideas themselves, then there must be some other cause of them. As Berkeley writes:

> We perceive a continual succession of ideas, some are anew excited, others are changed or totally disappear. There is therefore some cause of these ideas whereon they depend, and which produces and changes them. That this cause cannot be any quality or idea or combination of ideas, is clear from the preceding section. It must therefore be a substance; but it has been shewn that there is no corporeal or material substance: it remains therefore that the cause of ideas is an incorporeal active substance or spirit. (PHK §26)

There is a succession of ideas. There must be a cause of this succession: Berkeley, like nearly all of his predecessors, held that every event or existent must have a cause. This cause of ideas cannot itself be an idea, since ideas are passive. So it must be a substance. It cannot be a material substance, since his earlier arguments concluded that there is no coherent notion of matter. So it must be an immaterial substance or spirit.

Berkeley continues by describing this immaterial substance:

> A spirit is one simple, undivided, active being: as it perceives ideas, it is called the *understanding*, and as it produces or otherwise operates about them, it is called the *will*. Hence there can be no idea formed of a soul or spirit: for all ideas whatever, being passive and inert, *vide* Sect. 25, they cannot represent unto us, by way of image or likeness, that which acts. A little attention will make it plain to any one, that to have an idea which shall be like that active principle of motion and change of ideas, is absolutely impossible. Such is the nature of spirit or that which acts, that it cannot be of it self perceived, but only by the effects which it produceth. If any man shall doubt of the truth

of what is here delivered, let him but reflect and try if he can frame the idea of any power or active being; and whether he hath ideas of two principal powers, marked by the names *will* and *understanding*, distinct from each other as well as from a third idea of substance or being in general, with a relative notion of its supporting or being the subject of the aforesaid powers, which is signified by the name soul or spirit. This is what some hold; but so far as I can see, the words *will, soul, spirit*, do not stand for different ideas, or in truth, for any idea at all, but for something which is very different from ideas, and which being an agent cannot be like unto, or represented by, any idea whatsoever. Though it must be owned at the same time, that we have some notion of soul, spirit, and the operations of the mind, such as willing, loving, hating, in as much as we know or understand the meaning of those words. (*PHK* §27)

Berkeley describes spirit as "one simple, undivided, active being." There are two reasons why Berkeley might claim that it is *one* simple being: because it was the view of common sense and the common philosophical view that the self is one thing throughout its existence;[27] or because he held that there was no distinction between the will and understanding as active elements of the mind (*N* 848, 871). Simplicity again involves an implicit appeal to philosophical tradition, as well, perhaps, as the contention that *extension* is inherently complex, and spirit as immaterial is unextended. So, it is one thing that acts. The distinction between understanding and will represents two aspects of one thing. Since spirit is active, we cannot have an idea of it; as Berkeley notes in the last sentence of the section—a sentence added to the 1734 edition of the *Principles*—we can only have a *notion* of it. Notice that Berkeley suggests that a spirit can be known only by its effects.

In Section 28 Berkeley continues his discussion of mind. He writes:

I find I can excite ideas in my mind at pleasure, and vary and shift the scene as oft as I think fit. It is no more than willing, and straightway this or that idea arises in my fancy: and by the same power it is obliterated, and makes way for another. This making and unmaking of ideas doth very properly denominate the mind active. Thus much is certain, and grounded on experience: but when we talk of unthinking agents, or of exciting ideas exclusive of volition, we only amuse our selves with words. (*PHK* §28)

This is little more than an appeal to experience to show that we are conscious of the activities of the mind. We can cause ideas (form ideas of the imagination), which is nothing more than an act of the will. So, minds are active. We are not aware of the activity of any alleged material entity. Thus the presumption that matter is a cause is no more than playing with words.

But not all the ideas of which I am aware are ideas I am aware of causing. This provides the ground for claiming that there is another mind. As Berkeley writes:

> But whatever power I may have over my own thoughts, I find the ideas actually perceived by sense have not a like dependence on my will. When in broad day-light I open my eyes, it is not in my power to choose whether I shall see or no, or to determine what particular objects shall present themselves to my view; and so likewise as to the hearing and other senses, the ideas imprinted on them are not creatures of my will. There is therefore some other will or spirit that produces them. (*PHK* §29)

This is the argument from passivity. There are ideas that I do not produce. Every existent must have a cause. If there is an idea that I do not produce, then there must be something outside of me that is the cause of that idea. The mind is passive in sense perception: when I sensibly perceive something, my mind is not the cause of the idea. To put it differently, if you open your eyes, you *see* things: you have no say regarding *that* you see or *what* you see. Indeed, you are aware of "a continual succession of ideas" (*PHK* §26) and, whether this is construed as perceiving objects (compilations of ideas) or simply as a succession of ideas, there must be a causal explanation for it. Given Berkeley's arguments in Sections 8–24, the cause cannot be a material substance (contrary to earlier proponents of the passivity argument, see CSM 2:54; Locke, *Essay* 4.11.5). So there has to be at least an other spirit that is the cause of those ideas.

Given that Berkeley later alludes to the Author of Nature as this cause (*PHK* §33), should we assume that Section 29 provides an argument for *exactly one* cause of all those ideas? Is this, as many scholars have claimed, an argument for the existence of God?[28] The short answer is "No." Given that we are aware of a "continual succession of ideas" (*PHK* §26) and, although we cause some of the ideas of which we are aware (*PHK* §28), we do not cause all of them (*PHK* §29), it follows that there must be some other cause. Given that only mental substances are causes (*PHK* §§25–26), it follows that there must be some other mental substance that is the cause of those ideas we do not cause. Just as Berkeley's predecessors held

The Case for Idealism and Immaterialism in the Principles 91

that there are many material substances that cause some of our ideas, it is consistent with the argument in Section 29 to claim that there are many immaterial substances that cause some of our ideas. And even when Berkeley suggests that there is *one* cause (*PHK* §30), which he identifies with the Author of Nature (*PHK* §33), this being is described as merely a "more powerful spirit" (*PHK* §33), rather than an omnipotent spirit (God). If Berkeley was a careful philosopher, proportioning his conclusions to the premises he has established and choosing his words carefully, then the most he has proven is that there is at least one mind distinct from his own. On the other hand, as we shall see in Chapter 6, Section 29 is a stage along the way to proving the existence of the Judeo-Christian God.

But what does Berkeley do with the conclusions he has drawn up to this point? Recall that in Section 1, Berkeley claimed that ideas of sensation, reflection, memory, and the imagination are alike objects of human knowledge. On the surface, such a view is peculiar, since it *suggests* that all our ideas are equally "real." In Sections 30–34 Berkeley introduces a number of distinctions that set aside this apparent peculiarity. He distinguishes between ideas of the sense and imagination, and he distinguishes between "real things" and imaginary things. These distinctions are drawn *entirely* on the side of ideas.

In Section 30, Berkeley introduces two distinctions between ideas of sensation and ideas of the imagination. He writes:

> The ideas of sense are more strong, lively, and distinct than those of the imagination; they have likewise a steadiness, order, and coherence, and are not excited at random, as those which are the effects of human wills often are, but in a regular train or series, the admirable connexion whereof sufficiently testifies the wisdom and benevolence of its Author. Now the set rules or established methods, wherein the mind we depend on excites in us the ideas of sense, are called the Laws of Nature: and these we learn by experience, which teaches us that such and such ideas are attended with such and such other ideas, in the ordinary course of things. (*PHK* §30)

There are two differences between ideas of sensation and ideas of the imagination. First, ideas of sense are "more strong, lively, and distinct than those of the imagination." This is a phenomenal criterion. In contradistinction to this, Berkeley introduces a second criterion, namely, ideas of sensation "have likewise a steadiness, order, and coherence, and are not excited at random, as those which are the effects of human wills often are." These regularities Berkeley calls "Laws of Nature." The concern with natural laws is important in understanding Berkeley's philosophy. Natural laws are *strictly* relations of succession and co-existence among ideas. In Section 31 he remarks, "This [presence of natural laws regarding ideas] gives us a sort of foresight which enables us to regulate our actions for the benefit of life" (cf. *PHK* §62). In Section 32 he comments that "this consistent, uniform working which so evidently displays the goodness and wisdom of that governing spirit whose will constitutes the Laws of Nature, is so far from leading our thoughts to him, that it rather sends us wandering after second causes." The constancy of our perceptions naturally leads us to the absurd position—given the conclusions in Section 25—that ideas cause one another. This allusion to natural laws among ideas leads to one of Berkeley's two meanings of *real things*, and is a virtual restatement of the divine language thesis in the *Essay towards a New Theory of Vision*, in the *Theory of Vision . . . Vindicated*, and in *Alciphron*.

In Section 33, Berkeley identifies "real things" with ideas of sensation and collections of such. He writes:

> The ideas imprinted on the senses by the Author of Nature are called *real things*: and those excited in the imagination being less regular, vivid and constant, are more properly termed *ideas*, or *images of things*, which they copy and represent. But then our sensations, be they never so vivid and distinct, are nevertheless *ideas*, that is, they exist in the mind, or are perceived by it, as truly as the ideas of its own framing. The ideas of sense are allowed to have more reality in them, that is, to be more strong, orderly, and coherent than the creatures of the mind; but this is no argument that they exist without the mind. They are also less dependent on the spirit, or thinking substance which perceives them, in that they are excited by the will of another and more powerful spirit: yet still they are *ideas*, and certainly no idea, whether faint or strong, can exist otherwise than in a mind perceiving it. (*PHK* §33)

The identification of ideas of sensation with real things is also emphasized in the *Three Dialogues between Hylas and Philonous* (*DHP* 215, 229, 235, 244, 260, 262; cf. 258, N 823). But the emphasis on laws of nature and the recognition of laws of nature on the basis of experience (*PHK* §32) suggest that "real things" are not identical with individual ideas of sensation. 1. Any idea of sensation is, as such, a real thing. 2. Those collections of successive ideas of sensation that we actually perceive in perceiving what we deem a single object, for example, a tree or a table, are real things. 3. But we also claim to know that certain complex objects exist. Here we are concerned with not only those ideas we actually perceive by sense, but those that we would perceive by sense were we in the appropriate situations—the table in my office when I am not present, or the rings of a tree that is not cut down. We noted that the discussion of the apple in Section 1 was reminiscent of Locke's concern with nominal essences. Insofar as it left open the possibility that the collection of ideas *we take to be* constitutive of a thing of a kind can expand with increased experience—can expand when we discover additional laws of nature—it is an *epistemic construct*. It is what we take to be the ideas constituting an object or an object of a certain kind. Properly speaking, this construct includes ideas of the memory and imagination, as well as ideas of sensation, although it is rooted in ideas of sensation that provide the basis for ideas of the memory and the imagination. These epistemically real things are almost always incomplete: there are almost always additional kinds of ideas that, once they are associated on the basis of experience with other ideas of sensation we have, can be and are added to that collection of ideas we deem constitutive of a thing of a kind. These *epistemically real things* are mind-dependent. But senses 1 and 2 of *real things* also exist only as objects of human knowledge, that is, as perceived or, insofar as they are always known by the Author of Nature, knowable by human minds. So, insofar as 1 is the fundamental sense of *real things*, there is not the epistemic or ontological gulf between the mind and reality that one finds in the representationalism of Locke or Descartes. Insofar as 3 is a construct, it provides room for error and incomplete knowledge while explaining the commonsense belief that those things we sensibly perceive are real. Thus, Berkeley's remarks in Section 34 are entirely reasonable:

> By the principles premised, we are not deprived of any one thing in Nature. Whatever we see, feel, hear, or any wise conceive or understand, remains as secure as ever, and is as real as ever. There is a *rerum natura*, and the distinction between realities and chimeras retains its full force. This is evident from Sect. 29, 30, and 33, where we have shewn what is meant by real things in opposition to chimeras, or ideas of our own framing; but then they both equally exist in the mind, and in that sense are alike *ideas*. (*PHK* §34)

A Look Back; A Look Ahead

In this chapter we have examined Berkeley's principal arguments for idealism and immaterialism in the *Principles*. Berkeley identifies ideas with objects of knowledge (*PHK* §1). Insofar as something is known, there must also be something that knows (*PHK* §2). By Section 7, Berkeley had concluded that ordinary objects are *at least* collections of ideas, and the only substances that exist are mental substances. But it is consistent with these conclusions that minds are material objects, and that matter is an additional component of ordinary objects. In Sections 8–24 Berkeley argues that there is no evidence for the existence of matter, either construed in terms of primary qualities or as a substratum. In Sections 25–33 he begins his account of the nature of the mind as an immaterial substance, and gives criteria for distinguishing between collections of ideas that are, and those that are not, real things.

Does our account sidestep the problems posed by Berkeley's critics? Let us review the alleged problems. Does Berkeley prove the existence of ideas in Section 1? No. Without proving the existence of ideas, any *inference* concerning the existence of minds in Section 2 is unwarranted. If the conclusions in Section 2 are unwarranted, then Berkeley has no grounds for claiming that "the existence of an idea consists in being perceived" (*PHK* §2). Section 3 cannot be a mere case study of a conclusion already justified in Section 2. Thus if Berkeley is to show that the *esse* of sensible objects is *percipi*, Section 3 must provide an independent argument for that principle. But Dicker is certainly right in claiming that what he calls "the argument from the meaning of *exist*" will not establish *esse* is *percipi*.[29] While we have seen that there is a reconstruction of the argument in Section 4 that will yield the "manifest contraction" Berkeley finds, our argument is plausible only if the conclusions in the earlier sections are founded. Similarly, treating the discussion of abstraction in Section 5 as an error rather than as an argument for *esse* is *percipi* might be plausible, but as an explanation it provides no evidence for *esse* is *percipi*. It would seem, then, that the conclusion in Section 6 that "all those bodies which compose the mighty frame of the world, have not any subsistence without a mind" and the conclusion in Section 7 that "there is not any other substance than *spirit*, or that which perceives" are unwarranted, and if they are unwarranted, the subsequent conclusions he built on those foundations crumble.

So, what are we to do? Should we paraphrase Hamlet and say, "Alas, poor Berkeley! I knew him, Horatio: a fellow of infinite jest, of most excellent fancy,"[30] for surely his idealism and immaterialism cannot be taken seriously?

No! Nor need we suggest that if Berkeley borrowed his notions of ideas and mind from Descartes and Locke, he only wanted to convert their followers to his views.[31]

Compare the argumentative structure of the opening thirty-three sections of *Principles*, Part I with that in the *New Theory of Vision*. The *New Theory of Vision* followed the method of analysis. It started with a *supposition* that distance is not perceived immediately. It provided an explanation according to which the supposition would be true. Following the method of analysis, the initial supposition is deemed true only if the theory proposed successfully explains it. As Descartes said of his own use of analytic method, "I take my reasonings to be so closely interconnected that just as the last are proved by the first, which are their causes, so the first are proved by the last, which are their effects" (CSM 1:150). We have seen that Berkeley begins Part I of the *Principles* with the *supposition* that there are ideas (things known) and minds (knowers). Given this, he spins an account of the world that is just like the world we all assume exists—there are ordinary physical objects and minds (things that know them)—except it does not contain "material substance." An epistemic basis for metaphysical conclusions is exactly what you would expect from a practitioner of the method of analysis, and if the overall account has epistemic warrant, given the *assumption* that there are ideas, that assumption is justified. So, unlike Harry Bracken, who once remarked, "Once one starts to unravel the strands in the argument of those thirty-three sections and to identify them, it seems as though there is no way to weave them back together,"[32] I believe that once one sees how the strands fit together, one beholds an elegant tapestry.

In the *Three Dialogues between Hylas and Philonous*, Berkeley presents another defense of idealism and immaterialism. Some of his arguments parallel those in the *Principles*, but his general approach focuses on common sense and the avoidance of skepticism. So, let us turn to the *Three Dialogues*.

Further Reading

Georges Dicker (2011). *Berkeley's Idealism: A Critical Examination*. New York: Oxford University Press.

Marc A. Hight (2008). *Idea and Ontology: An Essay in Early Modern Metaphysics of Ideas*. University Park: The Pennsylvania State University Press, pp. 138–76.

George S. Pappas (2000). *Berkeley's Thought*. Ithaca: Cornell University Press, pp. 103–208.

George Pitcher (1977). *Berkeley*, Arguments of the Philosophers. London: Routledge & Kegan Paul, pp. 91–179.

5
Three Dialogues between Hylas and Philonous

In 1713 Berkeley recast his arguments in dialogue form. In the *Three Dialogues*, Berkeley's spokesman, Philonous (Greek for "friend of mind"), raises objections to the theories of material substance posed by Hylas (from the Greek word for "matter") and defends immaterialism from the objections Hylas raises.

Most scholars mine arguments from the *Principles* and the *Three Dialogues* as if they were a single work. They might note the parallels among the arguments or claim that the statement of the argument in one work clarifies the statement of an argument in the other. Sometimes, we are told, the *Three Dialogues* provide arguments for assumptions made in the *Principles*.[1] Some scholars take selected arguments from the *Three Dialogues* as the basis for Berkeley's entire case for idealism and immaterialism.[2] Few scholars focus exclusively on the *Three Dialogues*.[3]

But even a cursory examination of the *Principles* and the *Three Dialogues* shows a difference in focus. While the *Principles* develops a positive case for idealism and immaterialism, the *Three Dialogues* assumes Berkeley's views are already articulated and defends them. While the principal argument for idealism and immaterialism in the *Principles* makes no allusions to common sense and the defeat of skepticism, they are the focus throughout the *Three Dialogues*. While the *Principles* provides distinguishable arguments for idealism and immaterialism, the *Three Dialogues* focuses on immaterialism (cf. *DHP* 172). If you treat the *Three Dialogues* as no more than a mine for individual arguments, you will fail to see the overall structure of Berkeley's argument in that work.

In this chapter I argue that, as in the *Principles*, the Berkeley of the *Three Dialogues* constructs his metaphysics on epistemological foundations. But rather than the linear, analytic approach we found in the *Principles*, Berkeley's spokesman, Philonous, argues that immaterialism entails fewer skeptical consequences than the alternative posed by the doctrine of material substance; that it entails no skeptical consequences that are not also entailed by the doctrine of material substance; and that immaterialism possesses other theoretical virtues not enjoyed by the doctrine of material substance.

We shall follow the skeptical arguments Philonous raises against accounts of material substance that Hylas champions in Dialogue I. Most of these are classical skeptical arguments. They appear to be drawn from Sextus Empiricus's *Outlines of Pyrrhonism*. I have found no positive evidence that Berkeley read the *Outlines*, but the skeptical arguments were part of the intellectual coin of the time. In Dialogue II, Philonous presents arguments for immaterialism based upon theoretical simplicity. In Dialogue III Hylas turns the tables on Philonous and argues that no fewer skeptical consequences accrue to immaterialism than to materialism—arguments to which Philonous replies.

To understand these arguments, we begin by examining the skeptical tradition.

Background

Skepticism is the philosophical view that knowledge is severely limited. The skeptic argues that there are strict limits to our knowledge of the nature and existence of things and that the evidence for the truth of a proposition is always balanced by the evidence for the falsehood of the same proposition.[4] According to the ancient skeptics, we can trust appearances, but inferences that go beyond appearances are unwarranted.[5] There is a sense in which skepticism was a minor tradition among the ancients: it did not have the impact on the development of positive philosophies that was enjoyed by Plato's or Aristotle's works. Nonetheless, Pyrrho of Elis (360–270 B.C.E), who is often deemed the founder of the skeptical tradition, was like Aristotle one of Alexander the Great's tutors, and two generations after Plato's death his Academy took a decidedly skeptical turn. Richard Popkin has argued that the rediscovery of the *Outlines of Pyrrhonism* fueled the questioning of authority that characterized the Renaissance and early modern period.[6] Pierre

Bayle's *Historical and Critical Dictionary* (1697 and 1702), was a monumental work whose skeptical arguments became the hallmark of skepticism in the modern period. Some of Bayle's arguments influenced Berkeley.

The fact that skeptical arguments were well known in the modern period does not imply that they were popular. Epistemology is the principal focus of the modern period; skepticism is the foil against which epistemologies were tested. René Descartes's *Meditations on First Philosophy* are often read as founding a positive philosophy by pushing skeptical arguments to their most extreme and absurd conclusions. The closing remarks of Berkeley's Third Dialogue—his analogy between skepticism and a fountain (*DHP* 263)—suggests that Berkeley saw his work in much the same way. Even Berkeley's *Principles* were cast as a defense against skepticism (see subtitle and Intro. §1), even though his discussion of the skeptical implications of the doctrine of material substance only begins in Section 86.

Dialogue One

One morning Hylas visits Philonous. Hylas had suffered a sleepless night, having been plagued by the common views of "those men who have in all ages, through an affectation of being distinguished from the vulgar, or some unaccountable turn of thought, pretended either to believe nothing at all, or to believe the most extravagant things in the world" (*DHP* 171; cf. Intro. §1). His visit to Philonous is not happenstance, since Philonous had been represented as a skeptical philosopher insofar as he held "that there is no such thing as *material substance* in the world" (*DHP* 172). Philonous replies, "That there is no such thing as what philosophers call *material substance*, I am seriously persuaded," (*DHP* 172), which draws the reply from Hylas, "What! can any thing be more fantastical, more repugnant to common sense, or a more manifest piece of scepticism, than to believe there is no such thing as *matter*?" (*DHP* 172). Since Hylas and Philonous both take skepticism to be the hobgoblin of philosophical inquiry, they agree to examine their views and "to admit that opinion for true, which upon examination shall appear most agreeable to common sense, and remote from scepticism" (*DHP* 172), where *skepticism* is understood as "distrusting the senses, of denying the real existence of sensible things, or pretending to know nothing of them" (*DHP* 173).

There are several points to notice. First, this is a conceptual contest. For Philonous to carry the day, he must show both that skeptical consequences follow from the doctrine of material substance—what Berkeley calls "materialism"[7]—and that any skeptical consequences that follow from immaterialism also follow from materialism. If something cannot be known on either theory, that "skeptical consequence" counts neither for nor against either theory. Second, Berkeley contrasts skepticism with common sense. Some scholars have devoted considerable effort to detailing what Berkeley meant by *common sense*.[8] We shall take the naïve approach and assume that common sense affirms what skepticism denies. Common sense places faith in the senses, affirms the existence of sensible things, and contends that we have knowledge of sensible things. As we shall see, in the early eighteenth century the term *sensible things* was construed to include ordinary physical objects. At the time, the existence of God as the cause of the natural world was generally taken as a piece of philosophical common sense. With respect to any point on which the materialist and the immaterialist might agree, the advantage would go to either side only if that side could provide a stronger argument for the mutually accepted conclusion.

The First Dialogue focuses on theories of material substance. There are several distinct theories, which Hylas champions. As Philonous raises objections to one theory, Hylas shifts to another. If a theory of material substance is plausible, we must be able to distinguish material substance from everything else. There must be criteria for drawing that distinction, and the criteria must be stated and justified. The criteria for the identification of material substance can take either of two forms. If material substance is immediately known, the issue is whether there are adequate criteria for distinguishing the properties of material objects from other properties that are immediately known. Alternatively, if material substance is not immediately known, then it must be distinguished from other things on the basis of its (alleged) essential properties and those properties must be knowable. Philonous appeals to the classical arguments of the skeptics to show that theories of material substance can meet none of those conditions.

If material entities such as fire are immediately known by the senses, then heat is the property of a material object. As a material property, Hylas takes heat to be "a real absolute being, distinct from, and without any relation to their being perceived" (*DHP* 175), that is, it exists "without the mind" (*DHP* 175). Both Hylas and

Philonous grant that pain and pleasure are *not* properties of material objects (*DHP* 176). When you come too close to the fire, you experience heat as a form of pain. If the heat and pain are distinct, then there must be criteria for distinguishing between them. But, as perceived, we experience "one simple uniform sensation" not "two distinct sensations" (*DHP* 176). At least with respect to great heat, Hylas can provide no criterion for distinguishing heat from pain. If great heat cannot be distinguished from pain, there is no ground for claiming heat can exist apart from pain, which exists only in the mind. Since the burden of proof is on Hylas to show that there are material substances, he faces the skeptical consequences of his position and concedes that "I begin to suspect a very great heat cannot exist but in a mind perceiving it" (*DHP* 177).[9]

But great heat is one thing; warmth is something else. Even if the inability to distinguish pain from great heat or extreme cold gives no reason to believe they exist apart from the mind, Hylas contends the same cannot be said about moderate degrees of temperature. Hylas and Philonous agree that if a theory yields absurd consequences, it must be false (*DHP* 178). Philonous appeals to some of the classical skeptical arguments to refute Hylas:

> PHILONOUS. Suppose now one of your hands hot, and the other cold, and that they are both at once put into the same vessel of water, in an intermediate state; will not the water seem cold to one hand, and warm to the other?
> HYLAS. It will.
> PHILONOUS. Ought we not therefore by your principles to conclude, it is really both cold and warm at the same time, that is, according to your own concession, to believe an absurdity.
> HYLAS. I confess it seems so. (*DHP* 178–179; cf. *OP* I, §101)

Similarly, if you hold that sweetness is an inherent property of a material object, this assumption is reduced to absurdity by an argument from circumstances (*DHP* 181): what appears sweet to a person who is well appears bitter to a person who is ill, so if flavor is inherent in an object, the object must be both sweet and bitter, which is absurd (cf. *OP* I, §92 and §§101–2). The contention that odor is an inherent property of material objects is challenged by an argument from the differences among animals: "Or can you imagine, that filth and ordure affect those brute animals that feed on them out of choice, with the same smells which we perceive in them?" (*DHP* 181; cf. *OP* I, §51). If we follow Hylas and identify sounds with the motions of air, we have to distinguish between sound as perceived by us and sound as it really is (*DHP* 181–82). This results in a philosophical paradox, namely, "*real sounds are never heard*, and the idea of them is obtained from some other sense" (*DHP* 183). This does *not* entail that sound is *not* an inherent property of material objects; it does imply that we might never be in a position to distinguish those movements that constitute sound from other motions. Thus it is not clear that sounds as motions are knowable.

Finally, Hylas and Philonous turn to light and color. What is visible is perceived by sight (*DHP* 183). Color raises the skeptics' familiar problems: for example, that the colors of clouds appear to change with distance (*DHP* 184), which leads Hylas to the distinction between real and apparent color (*DHP* 184) and the suggestion that apparent colors are those that change with one's distance from the object perceived (*DHP* 184).[10] If what is perceived from the smallest perceptual distance—or greatest magnification—is most clearly perceived, then the actual color is more properly determined by a microscope than it is by the naked eye. But a microscope introduces an entirely new world of appearance: what grounds are there for claiming that apparent colors under the microscope constitute real colors? Further skeptical problems are raised by variations in appearance among animals, jaundice, differences correlated with the different humors in a body, and so forth (*DHP* 184–85). All these suggest there is no single criterion by which the actual color of an object can be known. Hence, there are no grounds for claiming that color is a property of a material object. Since skeptical doubts arise regarding each of the immediate objects of sense, there is no reason to believe that material substance can be immediately known.

What is going on? Why should Hylas and Philonous begin with an examination of sensible qualities when trying to unravel a theory of material substance?

Hylas claimed that an external object is "a material substance with sensible qualities inhering in it" (*DHP* 176). This reflects an inherence model of substance, and allusions to inherence are common throughout the discussion. It was not uncommon to maintain that substance itself might not be immediately perceived, but it is known either by one of its attributes or a collection of qualities. Descartes put it this way:

> We cannot initially become aware of a substance merely through its being an existing thing, since this alone does not of itself have any effect on us. We can, however, easily come to know a substance by

one of its attributes, in virtue of the common notion that nothingness possesses no attributes, that is to say, no properties or qualities. Thus, if we perceive the presence of some attribute, we can infer that there must also be present an existing thing or substance to which it may be attributed. (CSM I:210)

Descartes tells us substances are known and distinguished on the basis of their principal attributes: extension and thought (CSM I:210, 2:54). Locke, famously, claimed that a substance is "only a supposition of he knows not what support of such qualities, which are capable of producing simple ideas in us" (Locke, *Essay* 2.23.2), while claiming that we can distinguish kinds of substances on the basis of the several ideas of qualities they produce in us (Locke, *Essay* 2.23.3ff; cf. Locke, *Essay* 2.13.19). On such a model, we could, in principle, distinguish a material substance from an immaterial substance on the basis of its essential properties. But if, as Philonous argues, no property that is not immediately perceived can be distinctly and determinately known, there is no ground for deeming such an alleged property an essential property of material substance. Therefore, it provides no ground for introducing the category of material substance (*DHP* 187).

With the failure of an inherence model of material substance, Hylas shifts to the "modern" view, and suggests that matter is differentiated from mind by the primary qualities: extension, figure, solidity, gravity, motion, and rest (*DHP* 187). The problem is the same: namely, what are deemed the essential properties of material substance either cannot be known or cannot be distinguished from nonessential properties. The procedure is also the same: Philonous raises classical skeptical arguments to bolster his case that material substance is unknowable.

If you assume, as Hylas does (*DHP* 188), that extension and figure are immediately perceived, then apparent extension and actual extension are the same. But what appears small to a human will appear large to a mite and enormous to a creature smaller than a mite (*DHP* 188). If extension is a property existing apart from a mind, it must be determinate. Since humans do not have privileged access to extension, it is impossible to know the determinate extension of an object. Visual extension varies with distance (*DHP* 189; cf. *OP* I, §118), so either extension cannot be known by sight or it is indeterminate, both of which are inconsistent with the assumptions operative by proponents of the primary / secondary qualities distinction. There are similar inconsistencies in apparent figures given distance and perspective (*DHP* 189; cf. *OP* I, §118). Again, insofar as motion requires a notion of time, and insofar as time is measured by the succession of ideas (Locke, *Essay* 2.14.4), what appears fast to one person can appear slow to another (*DHP* 190; cf. *OP* I, §112). Apparent solidity can vary among animals (*DHP* 191). These variations among perceivers imply that one cannot know the determinate extensions, motions, figures, or degrees of solidity that are said to be constitutive properties of material objects.

Philonous goes so far as to argue that the primary qualities are inconceivable apart from some secondary qualities. One of his remarks should be noted, insofar as it tends to support my contention that Berkeley introduced entities into his ontology only insofar as they can be known. After a brief discussion of abstraction, Philonous remarks: "Since therefore it is impossible even for the mind to disunite the ideas of extension and motion from all other sensible qualities, doth it not follow, that where the one exist, there necessarily the other exist likewise?" (*DHP* 194)

Because no primary qualities can be conceived apart from some secondary qualities, Philonous suggests, it is impossible for them to exist apart from those qualities. What does that mean? If we are concerned with *logical* impossibility, why should we take the fact that we cannot conceive of a state of affairs as a ground for claiming that it is impossible? There are many things that we, *as a matter of fact*, cannot conceive simply because we do not have the appropriate background, but that hardly shows that they are logically impossible. On the other hand, if Berkeley was concerned with *epistemic* possibility and impossibility, then the fact that we cannot now form a conception of x entails that we cannot now know x. If we cannot know x, we have no ground for claiming the existence is x. It would seem, then, that a plausible reading of Berkeley's concerns with inconceivability supports an epistemic account of Berkeley's ontological commitments.

Toward the end of the First Dialogue, there is a shift from immediate perception to mediate perception. Hylas claims that material substance "is not itself sensible; its modes and qualities only being perceived by the senses" (*DHP* 197). After Philonous argues that "corporeal substance being the *substratum* of extension, must have another extension by which it is qualified to be a substratum: and so no to infinity" (*DHP* 198), he presents the Master Argument: "If you can conceive it possible for any mixture or combination of qualities, or any sensible object whatever, to exist without the mind, then I will grant it actually to be so" (*DHP* 200). As we noted in the last chapter, this challenge calls for us to conceive of something that is both known and unknown at the same time. It *does not* show that it is impossible for a material substance to exist. It shows only that conceivability cannot show that it is even possible to know the nature of material substance.

Similarly, Berkeley presents a version of the likeness principle. If there are material objects, they have "a fixed and real nature, which remains the same, notwithstanding any change in our senses" (*DHP* 205). But since ideas are

> continually changing upon every alteration in the distance, medium, or instruments of sensation; how can any determinate material objects be properly represented or painted forth by several distinct things, each of which is so different from and unlike the rest? Or if you say it resembles some one only of our ideas, how shall we be able to distinguish the true copy from all the false ones? (*DHP* 206).

In short, even if there were material objects and some aspects of them resembled ideas, there would be no way to know that.

By the end of Dialogue One, Hylas has presented numerous accounts of material substance. In each case, Philonous argued that substance, according to the given conception, cannot be known. There are no criteria for drawing the distinction between material objects and ideas. If there were properties that would allow us to draw the distinction, those properties could not be known. Indeed, insofar as conceivability is the ground for claiming possibility, we cannot even provide grounds for claiming that the existence of material substance is possible.

Dialogue Two

In *Principles*, Part I, Section 18, Berkeley says that if there are material substances, "Either we must know [them] by sense, or by reason." The First Dialogue was concerned primarily with alleged knowledge by sense. The Second is concerned with knowledge by reason. It is concerned, as Hylas says, with "the modern way of explaining things," "the way of accounting for our sensations or ideas" (*DHP* 208). Since Berkeley held that all existents must be caused, if a theory of material substance were necessary to explain the origin of ideas, there would be grounds for introducing it. The fact that such a substance could be known only mediately is not a problem (cf. *DHP* 232). Philonous argues that appeals to theoretical grounds for positing material substance fail. The discussions focus on two issues: the internal consistency of the theories posed, and questions posed by the theoretical virtues, particularly parsimony.[11]

The Dialogue begins with a brief argument showing that if the brain is a sensible object, and therefore composed of ideas (as Hylas concedes), then "you talk of ideas imprinted in an idea, causing that same idea, which is absurd" (*DHP* 209). The absurdity is grounded in a widely accepted position that nothing can be the efficient cause of itself.[12] After this, Philonous turns to a point of agreement with the materialists and argues that his argument is superior to theirs.

Berkeley and the Christian materialists agreed that God exists and that the existence of God is an important fact. Given that ideas exist only when they are perceived and that it is necessary to explain why ordinary objects as composites of ideas can continue to exist when they are unperceived by humans, it follows that they must be perceived by another spirit. If they are perceived and ordered by God, this would explain the phenomenal world. So, Berkeley concludes, *his* account is superior to that of the Christian materialist insofar as it provides a stronger proof of the existence of God. As Philonous says:

> Men commonly believe that all things are known or perceived by God, because they believe the being of a God, whereas I on the other side, immediately and necessarily conclude the being of a God, because all sensible things must be perceived by him. (*DHP* 212; cf. *DHP* 214–15)

Berkeley claims that his theory provides better evidence for the existence of God than is provided by alternative theories, and is therefore superior to them.

Hylas turns to the notion of seeing all things in God, Nicholas Malebranche's theory, suggesting Philonous' theory is very similar (*DHP* 213). Philonous replies that, according to Malebranche, one perceives ideas in the essence of God, but insofar as God is a wholly active being and ideas are purely passive, it is absurd to suggest that ideas can be part of God's essence (*DHP* 213–14). Further, since Malebranche proposed his theory to account for a way in which we can have ideas of material objects, even if it is impossible for spiritual substance to be united—or to causally interact—with material substance. Finally, material substance does not explain how one comes to have ideas. Philonous' theory is simpler:

Beside all which it hath this peculiar to itself; that it [Malebranche's metaphysics] makes that material world serve to no purpose. And if it pass for a good argument against other hypotheses in the sciences, that they suppose Nature or the divine wisdom to make something in vain, or do that by tedious round-about methods, which might have been performed in a much more easy and compendious way, what shall we think of that hypothesis which supposes the whole world made in vain? (*DHP* 214)

The principle of parsimony was accepted by both Berkeley and the materialists. According to that principle, if two theories will explain a phenomenon but one is simpler (posits fewer different kinds of entities), the simpler theory is more probably true. Berkeley's theory is more parsimonious. According to Berkeley, God is the immediate cause of ideas of sense, and real things are composed of those ideas (*DHP* 215; cf. *PHK* §33). He can thus explain the occurrence of ideas without positing material substance.

Hylas' next move is to suggest that matter is distinct in nature from both spirits and ideas, and it is nothing other than that which causes ideas (*DHP* 215). Philonous deems this unintelligible. Either it reduces to the standard notion of matter—the primary qualities—which he and Philonous had already agreed cannot exist apart from thought (*DHP* 216), or, as Hylas suggests, it produces, "that kind of action which belongs to matter, *viz. motion*" (*DHP* 217). But motion is a sensible quality, and therefore an idea, and therefore inactive. Therefore, such a notion is inconsistent.

Hylas tries for a variation on this by describing matter as an instrument subordinate to the supreme being that is used to produce ideas (*DHP* 217). Conceding that an instrument is "applied in doing those things only, which cannot be performed by the mere act of our wills" (*DHP* 218), it is inconsistent with the presumption that God is an all-powerful being to assume that God needs an instrument to act (*DHP* 219). Philonous concludes, therefore, that there is no reason to introduce matter as an instrument.

Both of these are subject to considerations based on parsimony. If Berkeley's theory is true, then God acts directly to form ideas. Hylas' assorted theories all grant that God *could* cause ideas directly. Hence, there is no reason to introduce secondary causes, that is, causal entities below the status of God (cf. *DHP* 258; *N* 433 and 485; *PHK* §32; cf. *S* §§160 and 173). Similarly, suggesting that matter is an independent order of nature that provides the occasion on which God causes ideas in us falls to considerations of parsimony, since that order can be explained on the basis of the wisdom and power of God alone (*DHP* 220). Finally, Hylas' objection that the reality of things cannot be maintained without the postulation of material substance (*DHP* 224), is met with the response that everyone takes the fact that we can see, feel, and wear a glove as sufficient evidence for its existence (*DHP* 224), that is, Berkeley's account of real objects in terms of ordered collections of ideas of sense (*DHP* 215; *DHP* 235; *PHK* §33) is sufficient to account for real objects, and it is an account that leaves the properties of objects in principle knowable.

By the end of Dialogue Two, then, Philonous has shown that material substance can be known neither by sense nor by reason. Dialogue Two shows that immaterialism provides a better explanation of experiential phenomena than materialism.

Dialogue Three

If Berkeley defends immaterialism by arguing that fewer skeptical consequences are entailed by immaterialism than materialism, then his case is far from finished. He must show that skeptical objections to immaterialism can be answered. So in the Third Dialogue, Hylas assumes the role of the skeptic with respect to Philonous' position. Indeed, Hylas begins in a state of skeptical despair and contends that Philonous' position results in the same sorry state as his own. Given the agreed objective in Dialogue One (*DHP* 173–74, *DHP* 259), this is what we should expect. It is incumbent upon Philonous to reply to the skeptical arguments Hylas raises. This is what we find in Dialogue Three.

Upon professing his skepticism, Hylas claims it is impossible to know either the essence or the existence of things. The context suggests the concern is with Locke's contention that real essences of things cannot be known (Locke, *Essay* 2.31.6; cf. the discussion of the medieval notion of *quiddities*, *DHP* 238 and 256), since the focus is on Locke's favorite example, the essence of gold. Hylas laments the fact that we can only know the sensible qualities of objects (*DHP* 228). After identifying the source of Hylas' skepticism with the doctrine of material substance (*DHP* 229), Philonous explains how the Berkeleian identification of real things with collections of sensible qualities sidesteps skepticism regarding both essence and existence (*DHP* 229–30). Berkeley collapses Locke's nominal / real essence distinction.

Locke drew a distinction between real essences and nominal essences. A *nominal* essence is nothing more than an abstract idea that provides a name for a kind of thing; it is a collection of ideas. A *real essence* is the arrangement of corpuscles in a material object that causes ideas (Locke, *Essay* 3.3.15–18). If there are no material objects—if all the ideas are caused immediately by God—then the notion of a Lockean real essence disappears; there is no distinction between a real essence and a nominal essence.

Berkeleian real essences are in principle accessible, even if we never know all the properties constituting an object of a kind. This means that Berkeleian real essences entail no more skeptical consequences than Lockean nominal essences (cf. Locke, *Essay* 4.9.17).

Hylas continues with the parity argument, his argument that the same problems with material substance apply to immaterial substance. There are two points that are relevant to an epistemic approach to Berkeleian ontology. First, Philonous contends that material and immaterial substance are not on a par because immaterial substance is knowable, while material substance is not (*DHP* 233). Then, Philonous notes, "I know what I mean, when I affirm that there is a spiritual substance or support of ideas, that is, that a spirit knows and perceives them" (*DHP* 234). The theme that *the* relation between a mind and an idea is epistemic is recurrent in Dialogue Three. It is the relationship between an idea and the infinite mind: "the real tree existing without his mind is truly known and comprehended by (that is *exists in* [Berkeley's emphasis]) the infinite mind of God" (*DHP* 235). Identifying sensible qualities with ideas, Philonous concludes, "It is therefore evident there can be no substratum of those qualities but spirit, in which they exist, not by way of mode or property, but as a thing perceived in that which perceives it" (*DHP* 237; cf. *PHK* §49). This suggests that the Berkeleian concept of substance is conceptually thin, though less "confused and obscure" than Locke's. Recall Locke's remark, "so that of *Substance*, we have no *Idea* of what it is, but only a confused obscure one of what it does" (Locke, *Essay* 2.13.19). We have a clear notion of what Berkeleian substance does: it knows and causes ideas. It is less clear that the epistemic relation of perception can be mapped onto an ontological counterpart such as inhesion.[13]

Hylas continues to raise objections to Philonous' position. He presents a version of the argument from evil: "in making God the immediate author of all the motions in Nature, you make him the author of ... heinous sins" (*DHP* 236). In reply, Philonous indicates that the potential problem is independent of immaterialism: at worst, immaterialism is on a par with materialism regarding the moral turpitude of God. He then sketches an account of moral turpitude that is based on motives and indicates that it is consistent with immaterialism that finite spirits are causes of some motions (*DHP* 237; cf. *PHK* §147).

Hylas raises standard skeptical objections concerning the bent oar, the round-square tower, and so forth (cf. *OP* I, §118). These pose no problem for Berkeley's position. Real things are identified with ideas of sense that are bundled in such a way that previous and subsequent members of the bundle are predictable (*DHP* 235). God "exhibits them to our view in such a manner, and according to such rules as he himself hath ordained, and are by us termed the *Laws of Nature*" (*DHP* 231; cf. *PHK* §30). Proponents of material substance were also committed to the existence of such descriptive laws of nature. Hence, Philonous can reply that "in the case of the oar, what he immediately perceives by sight is certainly crooked; and so far he is in the right. . . . But his mistake [that the oar will appear bent when removed from the water] lies . . . in the wrong judgment he makes concerning the ideas he apprehends to be connected with those immediately perceived" (*DHP* 238). If real things are limited to appearance, and if what counts as one thing (or kind of thing) is formed of temporally disparate ideas united by laws of nature (cf. *DHP* 243, 245), the skeptical arguments lose their force.

Hylas asks whether Philonous' position commits him to the claims that God suffers pain:

> But you have asserted, that whatever ideas we perceive from without, are in the mind which affects us. The ideas therefore of pain and uneasiness are in God; or in other words, God suffers pain: that is to say, there is an imperfection in the Divine Nature, which you acknowledged was absurd. So you are caught in a plain contradiction. (*DHP* 240)[14]

Philonous replies that since God is omniscient, God knows what pain is. But suffering pain requires being affected in accordance with the laws of nature. Since nothing can cause changes in God, God cannot suffer pain (*DHP* 240–41).

The question of microscopic entities is raised again (*DHP* 245). Recall that Philonous argued that considerations of microscopic appearances suggest that if color is an inherent property in material substance, it is unknowable (*DHP* 184–85). Philonous replies to Hylas' objection in terms of the heterogeneity thesis and the meanings of words. Since every variation in thought forms a new idea, it is impossible to name individual ideas. So

> men combine together several ideas, apprehended by divers senses, or by the same sense at different times, or in different circumstances, but observed however to have some connexion in Nature, either with respect to co-existence or succession; all which they refer to one name, and consider as one thing. Hence it follows that when I examine by my other senses a thing I have seen, it is not in order to understand better the same object which I had perceived by sight, the object of one sense not being perceived by the other senses. And when I look through a microscope, it is not that I may perceive more clearly what I perceived already with my bare eyes, the object perceived by the glass being quite different from the former. But *in both cases my aim is only to know what ideas are connected together; and the more a man knows of the connexion of ideas, the more he is said to know of the nature of things.* (DHP 245, emphasis added)

The remarks on words are reminiscent of Locke on general terms (Locke, *Essay* 3.3.2–5). The remarks on the development of an idea of a kind are reminiscent of Locke on nominal essence (Locke, *Essay* 3.3.18). In both cases, they tend to show that Berkeley's concern is with *knowing* the connections of ideas that are taken to constitute a thing of a certain kind. Thus, they tend to support my thesis that "to be is to be perceived" is understood as "to be is to be known."

Philonous briefly alludes to the justification of the likeness principle on the basis of the variation of ideas of a supposed real thing relative to such things as distance.

> Farther, as our ideas are perpetually varied, without any change in the supposed real things, it necessarily follows they cannot all be true copies of them: or if some are, and others are not, it is impossible to distinguish the former from the latter. And this plunges us yet deeper in uncertainty. (DHP 246)

Insofar as objects are as they are known, the variations in ideas are components of the real thing.

Hylas objects that on Philonous' principles that no two people can see the same thing (*DHP* 247). Philonous' reply is reminiscent of Locke's differentiation of senses of diversity (Locke, *Essay* 2.27) and seems to anticipate Hume's discussion of blurring of senses of *identity*.[15] While Philonous seems to blur the distinction between numerical and specific identity (identity of kind) when complaining about the philosopher's disposition to abstraction, he gives a Berkeleian account of visual perspective: two people see the same qualitatively and temporally complex thing by perceiving distinct ideas that are components of that thing.

While Philonous can meet Hylas' challenge only if he can reply to all skeptical challenges that are peculiar to immaterialism, any problem that is equally challenging to the materialist and the immaterialist does not count against the immaterialist. So when Hylas raises an objection based on the question of whether God executed the decree resulting in creation "from all eternity, or at some certain time began to will what he had not actually willed before, but only designed to will" (*DHP* 254), Philonous notes that the objection applies to *any* account of creation (*DHP* 254). This is sufficient to meet the terms of the initial challenge (cf. *DHP* 173; *DHP* 259).

A Look Back; A Look Ahead

Philonous' success consists in the fact that fewer skeptical consequences follow from immaterialism than materialism: "the same principles which at first view lead to scepticism, pursued to a certain point" collapse on themselves like the column of water in a fountain and "bring men back to common sense" (*DHP* 263). By subjecting the basic epistemic principles of Lockean empiricism to skeptical argumentation, empiricism is shown to be limited to appearance. On those grounds, if existence claims are limited to what is known, the result is Berkeleian immaterialism.

We have also seen that the *Three Dialogues* need not be taken as a supplement to the *Principles*. It provides an independent defense of immaterialism, a defense that shows how immaterialism overcomes the skepticism raised by the doctrine of material substance. While defeating skepticism was one of the objectives of the *Principles* (title page), it was not the primary focus of that work. Given Berkeley's remark in the Preface to the first edition of the *Three Dialogues*, "*I* thought it requisite to treat more clearly and fully of certain [my emphasis] *principles laid down in the First* [part of the *Principles*], *and to place them in a new light. Which is the business of the following* Dialogues" (*Works* 2:168–169), the focus on immaterialism and the refutation of skepticism—rather than all the elements examined in the *Principles*—should not be surprising.

But Berkeley was an idealist: he held that everything that exists is either a mind or depends for its existence upon a mind. So far, we have found little discussion of mind as such in Berkeley's works, and there is a good reason for that absence. His original plan was to write the *Principles* as a book in several parts. The second part was to present an account of mind, God, and morals (B-J 2.6, ¶2; cf. N 508, 807). That part was never completed. This is not to say there are no discussions of mind in the *Principles* and *Three Dialogues*, but those discussions are brief. In the 1734 editions of the *Principles* and the *Three Dialogues*, Berkeley added several passages in which he alluded to our *notions* of mind and relations. It is to these that we shall next turn.

Further Reading

Aaron Garrett (2008). *Berkeley's Three Dialogues: A Reader's Guide*. London: Continuum.

Alan Hausman and David Hausman (1995). "A New Approach to Berkeley's Ideal Reality," in Muehlmann (1995a). *Berkeley's Metaphysics: Structural, Interpretive, and Critical Essays*. University Park: The Pennsylvania State University Press, pp. 47–65.

Tom Stoneham (2002). *Berkeley's World: An Examination of the Three Dialogues*. Oxford: Oxford University Press.

6

Minds
Yours, Mine, and God's

Berkeley originally intended the *Principles* to be a book in several parts. His Notebooks suggest that second part was to cover issues relating to mind (*N* 807, 878) and morality (*N* 508), and the third part was to cover issues relating to the sciences (*N* 583). But it was not to be. Berkeley told his American correspondent Samuel Johnson, "As to the second part of my treatise concerning the principles of human knowledge, the fact is that I had made a considerable progress in it, but the manuscript was lost about fourteen years ago during my travels in Italy; and I never had leisure since to do so disagreeable a thing as writing twice on the same subject" (B-J 2.6). But it is not that Berkeley ignored those issues. We find discussions of moral issues in *Passive Obedience* and *Alciphron*. *De Motu* is a sketch of physics on immaterialist principles. Further considerations of mind, however, are limited to several brief additions to the 1734 editions of the *Principles* and the *Three Dialogues*, additions telling us we have *notions*, but not ideas, of mind (*PHK* §§27, 89, 140, 142; *DHP* 232–34).

In this chapter we examine themes in Berkeley's discussions of mind. We focus on two questions: What is the nature of mind? How are minds known? We end with a discussion of our knowledge of minds other than our own.

Scholars defend one of two accounts of the nature of Berkeleian minds. Most scholars hold that Berkeleian minds are immaterial substances. All scholars agree that in his published works Berkeley wrote as if the distinction between ideas and minds is absolute (*PHK* 2; *DHP* 233). But if you look at Berkeley's Notebooks, you'll find that he at least briefly entertained a **congeries** or **bundle** theory of mind: a mind is nothing but a collection of ideas and acts of will. This is an account David Hume made famous.[1] Robert Muehlmann and Stephen Daniel have argued that Berkeley never abandoned the congeries analysis, even though he disguised that fact in his published works.[2]

Our focus in this book is on Berkeley's published works. While the congeries approach has an epistemic appeal—knowing the mind is nothing but knowing the ideas and acts of will that compose it—if the published works contain a coherent account of how mind as an immaterial substance is known, it is reasonable to deem that Berkeley's account.

The question, "How are minds known?" disguises two distinct questions: If having a notion tells us *what* something is, how is the notion known? Next, are minds known directly or indirectly?

At one time I believed that Berkeley knew his own mind and other minds indirectly on the basis of "relative notions."[3] This was based on a model of relative notions found in the works of Thomas Reid, a model that allows us to single out a thing on the basis of its relationship to things known directly.[4] I held that a relative notion is comparable to a definite description, a phrase beginning with the word *the*. The language of "relative ideas" and "relative notions" was common in the eighteenth century, particularly with respect to the doctrines of substance. Locke claimed we have nothing but "An obscure and relative idea of substance in general" (Locke, *Essay* 2.23.3).[5] We have seen that some of Berkeley's criticisms of Locke's account of our alleged relative idea of material substance is that we have no clear notion of *support*, the relation that is supposed to allow us to pick out the substance itself (*PHK* §16). But my account was inconsistent with Philonous' remarks in Dialogue Three: "I know what I mean by the terms *I* and *myself*; and I know this immediately, or intuitively, though I do not perceive it as I perceive a triangle, a colour, or a sound" (*DHP* 231, all editions), and "My own mind and my own ideas I have an immediate knowledge of" (*DHP* 232, all editions), and, perhaps, "I know or am conscious of my own being" (*DHP* 233, 1734 edition). So my earlier conclusions need to be reexamined.

We begin by examining the relevant passages in the *Principles*: Sections 1–2, 26–27, 89, and 135–42. These passages show that Berkeley holds first that a mind is that which perceives ideas and acts with respect to ideas, and second, that, properly speaking, we neither have nor can have an idea of mind. This discussion will give reason to believe that while Berkeley claimed that ideas, minds, and relations are objects of knowledge (*PHK* §89, 1734 edition), ideas are *only* objects of human knowledge, while minds have other properties. Next, we examine passages in the Third Dialogue in which Berkeley claims we know our own minds immediately (*DHP* 231–33). This will also be the occasion for discussing the remark at *PHK* Section 89 that we know ourselves by an "inward feeling or reflection," his notions of relations, and the "large sense" in which we might be said to have an idea of the mind. We conclude with a brief discussion of our knowledge of other finite minds and God.

The *Principles*

In the 1734 editions of the *Principles* and *Three Dialogues* Berkeley claims that we have notions, but not ideas, of minds and relations (*PHK* §§27, 89, 140, 142; *DHP* 232–33). Presumably notions provide us with some knowledge of the nature of minds and relations, since they were added to the list of objects of human knowledge (*PHK* §89) and Berkeley claims we have a notion of mind and its operations insofar as we know the meanings of the corresponding terms (*PHK* §27, 140; *DHP* 231). Since Berkeley occasionally uses the words *notion* and *definition* synonymously (*DHP* 233; *A* 3.1, p. 113), it is reasonable to suggest that a notion provides knowledge of *what* something is. Thus we begin our examination of notions of mind at the beginning of *Principles*, Part I.

Recall that in Chapter 4 we worried about how to read the opening sentence of *Principles*, Part I: "the objects of human knowledge . . . are . . . ideas." Does this mean that all objects of human knowledge are ideas, or all ideas are objects of human knowledge, or that the terms *objects of human knowledge* and *ideas* are synonymous (coextensive)? We concluded that, given the additions to Section 89 in the 1734 edition stating that minds and relations are also objects of human knowledge, Berkeley must have meant that all ideas are objects of human knowledge. Section 1 set the stage for the distinction between ideas as things known and "*mind, spirit, soul* or *myself*" as "something which knows or perceives [ideas] and exercises diverse operations, as willing, imagining, remembering about them" (*PHK* §2). If a notion tells us *what* something is, Section 2 presents us with a notion of mind, and with only slight variations in the wording, this is Berkeley's "definition" of mind throughout the *Principles* and *Three Dialogues* (*PHK* §§27, 138, 139; *DHP* 231, 233; spirit as perceiver: *PHK* §71, *DHP* 234; spirit as cause: *PHK* §§26, 28, 29, 33, 57, 61, 102, 105, *DHP* 215, 217, 236, 239, 240; see also *N* 429–29a).

Since minds are understood in contradistinction to ideas, since notions tell us *what* something is, and since as we have a *notion* of a mind as that which knows ideas and acts, we also have a *notion* of ideas *as ideas*, as those things that are known. And there is reason to believe that Berkeley's notion of ideas is that they are *only* objects of knowledge. In Section 25 he claims that they are "visibly inactive" and therefore cannot be agents, and "since they and every part of them exist only in the mind, it follows that there is nothing in them but what is perceived." If nothing is epistemically hidden in ideas, they are only as they are known. Hence, they are inactive. So there is good reason to believe that they are *only* objects of knowledge. While minds are also objects of knowledge (*PHK* §89, 1734 edition), being known does not exhaust their function within Berkeley's philosophical system; they also cause ideas. Perceiving is a "necessary relation" between ideas and minds (*DHP* 235–36). Given that an idea is perceived, it follows that there must be a mind perceiving it. Perceiving is an asymmetrical relation: minds know or perceive ideas, but ideas do not know or perceive minds. On the other hand, minds cause ideas (*PHK* §§26 and 28). Like most of his contemporaries, Berkeley held that all ideas and actions have a cause (cf. *PHK* §60). Causality is also an asymmetrical relation. Only minds as mental substances can be causes (*PHK* §26). Given his remark in Section 27 (all editions) that "such is the nature of *spirit* or that which acts, that it cannot be of it self perceived, but only by the effects which it produceth," it follows that given any idea you can *infer* that there is some mind that caused it. This suggests that, in the *Principles*, Berkeley held that it is possible for minds (mental substances) to be known by inference. Given his remark in the Second Dialogue, "That from a cause, effect, operation, sign, or other circumstance, there may reasonably be inferred the existence of a thing not immediately perceived" (*DHP* 223), there is no inconsistency in claiming that *one* way that minds can be known is by inference. Whether you can also know your own mind in another way remains an open question. But *if* the existence of minds—any minds—can be known by inference, it would require that we have notions of the necessary relations (or connections) of perception and causality. Whether that is possible is a question to which we return below.

Since Berkeley couched his discussion of mind in terms of substance, I shall say a few words about the notion of substance before turning to his arguments that there are not and cannot be ideas of mind.

Doctrines of substance can be traced back to Aristotle. In *Metaphysics*, Book V (Δ), Chapter 8, Aristotle presents four definitions of the word *substance* followed by a general summary: "It follows, then, that substance has two senses, *(a)* the ultimate substratum, which is no longer predicated of anything else, and *(b)* that which is a 'this' and separable—and of this nature is the shape or form of each thing."[6] In the modern period, the notion of substance as substratum—that which lies under and functions as the subject of predication (has properties)—became the dominant notion. Locke wrote, "so that if any one will examine himself concerning his notion of pure substance in general, he will find he has no other idea of it at all, but only a supposition of he knows not what support of such qualities, which are capable of producing simple ideas in us" (Locke, *Essay* 2.23.2). By *qualities* Locke means "the power to produce any idea in our mind" (Locke, *Essay* 2.8.8). Famously, Lockean substance is *unknown* in the sense that we are not immediately aware of it; we are only aware of the ideas produced by its powers. This causal function of substance also has roots in Aristotle[7] and is found in Berkeley. Notice that, according to Locke, we know little or nothing of the nature of substance itself: we know it only through its effects. As Locke wrote at one point, "so that of substance, we have no idea of what it is, but only a confused obscure one of what it does" (Locke, *Essay* 2.13.19). We know this substance on the basis of its relation to ideas; ideas are known immediately. We have only "an obscure and relative idea of substance in general" (Locke, *Essay* 2.23.3). Given what we have found in Berkeley to this point, it would seem that Berkeley's notions are similar: we know mind only as that which perceives ideas and causes ideas.

Locke's notion of substance is conceptually thin: it tells us very little about the nature of substance. There are, however, richer notions of substance in the modern period. Descartes held that a substance is a thing that can exist by itself (CSM 1:210; CSM 2:30; cf. CSM 2.9); in the case of a finite substance, it is something that depends only upon God (CSM 1:210). Descartes's metaphysics is a metaphysics of substances and modes (or accidents). Descartes says, "we employ the term *mode* when we are thinking of a substance as being affected or modified" (CSM 2:211). Modes are states of substances; they cannot exist apart from a substance. Hence, ideas as modes of mental substance cannot exist apart from a mental substance (cf. CSM 2:28–29). Does Berkeley subscribe to such a Cartesian model of substance? There is some reason to believe that he does not, since in both the *Principles* and the *Three Dialogues* he denies that sensible qualities as ideas are modes of the mind.

At *Principles*, Section 49, Berkeley writes, "qualities are in the mind only as they are perceived by it, that is, not by way of *mode* or *attribute*, but only by way of *idea*; and it no more follows, that the soul or mind is extended because extension exists in it alone, than it does that it is red or blue, because those colours are on all hands acknowledged to exist in it, and no where else." This point is even clearer in the Third Dialogue:

> That there is no substance wherein ideas can exist beside spirit, is to me evident. And that the objects immediately perceived are ideas, is on all hands agreed. And that sensible qualities are objects immediately perceived, no one can deny. It is therefore evident there can be no *substratum* of those qualities but spirit, *in which they exist, not by way of mode or property, but as a thing perceived in that which perceives it*. (DHP 237, emphasis added)

Notice that in both passages the central point is that sensible qualities are ideas,[8] and, as ideas, Berkeley denies that they are modes of a mental substance. The model of a mode assumed here is one of modification: a thing is a thing of a certain kind in virtue of the qualities that inhere in it. On such a model, it would be reasonable to claim that a triangle is a triangle in virtue of a particular modification of extension, namely, the property of triangularity. Berkeley's point is that only ideas are extended, but insofar as ideas are *not* modes of mind, minds are *not* extended.

Is this significant? Perhaps. Berkeley's denial that ideas are modes avoids the absurd view that a mind is modified according to its ideas—for example, that having a red or square idea entails that the mind is red or square. As far as I know, Berkeley's contemporaries avoided this absurdity and never predicated the determinate properties of ideas-as-modes to the substance that has those ideas.[9] But the denial that ideas are modes raises another issue.

One of the problems Berkeley faced in proposing a theory of mental substance is that he had to specify a relation or relations between a substance and those "things" (traditionally called attributes, modes, or accidents) that are dependent upon it. Already in *Principles* Section 2, Berkeley delineated the meaning of *mind* in terms of the relations of perceiving ideas and acting with respect to them. But perception is a historically odd candidate for a relation between a substance and one of its dependents. Certainly it could not hold with respect to *material* substance. It was incumbent upon Berkeley, then, to examine other candidates for the relation between a substance and its dependents to show that there is no intelligible relation that will provide grounds for claiming the existence of material substance. He criticized Locke's claim that substances *support* accidents, contending that the notion of *support* was unintelligible (*PHK* §16), and his broader discussions of the alleged notions of material substance tend to show that alternative candidates are either missing or unintelligible. For example, in the Second Dialogue Berkeley allows that inferential knowledge of things distinct from ideas is in principle acceptable, but he denies any basis for inferring the existence of material substance (*DHP* 223), and one of the additions to Dialogue Three, the parity argument (*DHP* 232–34), contends that the notion of material substance is inconsistent and therefore unintelligible.[10] Berkeley finds no such problems with the relations of perceiving (knowing) and causing. Hence, they are viable candidates for the relations between substances and ideas.

There might be another reason for Berkeley's denial that ideas-qualities are Cartesian modes, although I have found no explicit textual evidence to support this. Descartes claimed that only finite substances have modes; infinite substance has only attributes (CSM 1:211–12). But Descartes's God is omniscient, that is, God knows all, including the ideas of individual human beings. So, in the case of the Cartesian God, there must be distinct relations between God and God's attributes and between God and what God knows. In the case of Cartesian humans, there must be both the metaphysical relation between a mind-as-substance and an idea-as-mode, and the epistemic relation between the mind-as-knower and the idea-as-known. In treating ideas as objects of knowledge, regardless of the knower, and rejecting a modal construal of ideas, Berkeley assumes a simpler metaphysics than Descartes assumed: the knowing (perceiving) relation is the only relation between a substance and an idea. Since we have seen that Berkeley takes parsimony to be an intellectual virtue, he might also have rejected modes and attributes on grounds of parsimony.

Returning to the *Principles*, a second major theme is that we do not and cannot have ideas of minds. The concern behind this is expressed in Section 89 (all editions):

> *Thing* or *being* is the most general name of all, it comprehends under it two kinds entirely distinct and heterogeneous, and which have nothing common but the name, to wit, *spirits* and *ideas*. The former are *active, indivisible substances*: the latter are *inert, fleeting, dependent beings*, which subsist not by themselves, but are supported by, or exist in minds or spiritual substances.

There is an *assumption* that fundamentally different kinds of things are known in fundamentally different ways—an assumption we first encountered in the *New Theory of Vision*—and in *Principles* Sections 90–134 Berkeley works out the implications of what can be known by ideas. In Sections 135–44 he argues that there are not and cannot be ideas of minds. He lays the explicit groundwork for this argument in Sections 25 and 27, and we shall begin by looking there.

Recall that in Section 25 Berkeley argued that ideas are inactive: they cannot function as causes. Ideas as things known can have no unknown properties. We examine them and discover they have no "power or activity" (causal properties). This sets the stage for the argument in Section 27. Since ideas can resemble nothing but ideas (*PHK* §8), and since minds are active and ideas are passive, ideas cannot resemble minds or actions of minds.

Berkeley returns to this theme in Section 135. Citing Section 27, he wrote:

> But surely it ought not to be looked on as a defect in a human understanding, that it does not perceive the idea of *spirit*, if it is manifestly impossible there should be any such *idea*. And this, if I mistake not, has been demonstrated in *Sect.* 27: to which I shall here add that a spirit has been shown to be the only substance or support, wherein the unthinking beings or ideas can exist: but that this *substance* which supports or perceives ideas should it self be an *idea* or like an *idea*, is evidently absurd. (*PHK* §135)

This sets the stage for further discussions of our knowledge of mind. Given the passive nature of ideas, it is impossible that they represent inherently active beings (*PHK* §27). His earlier discussion showed that the passivity of ideas entails that they cannot fulfill the active functions of substance. Here he focuses on perception. Why does perceiving alone entail that a spirit cannot be an idea or a collection of ideas? Ideas are unthinking beings. Perceiving is a kind of thinking. So, ideas as unthinking beings cannot constitute a mental substance.

But, you might ask, "Isn't Berkeley just playing with words? Sure, if you characterize a mind as *a thing that thinks* and an idea as *an unthinking thing*, it would be inconsistent to claim that minds are ideas. But his original characterization of ideas was *objects of human knowledge* (*PHK* §1), and in the 1734 edition of Section 89 he extended the class of objects of knowledge to include minds. So, even if ideas cannot perceive themselves, why can't there be 'stacks' of ideas, as it were, each idea being supported (perceived) by another?"

I'll grant that Berkeley's argument is not as precise as we might desire, but if it were "ideas all the way down," we'd have an infinite regress: since an idea's existence depends upon being perceived, if there is no unperceived perceiver there could be no ideas "above" it. Further, our *notion* of an idea is exhausted in being perceived: it is *only* an object of knowledge. Our notion of the self is *not* exhausted in being known; it is also a thing that perceives and acts. So, in spite of its truncated nature, Berkeley's point is that a mind cannot *be* an idea. But if an idea can neither be a mind nor represent a mind, no augmentation of the sensible modalities could provide knowledge of mind (*PHK* §136). Since "by the word *spirit* we mean only that which thinks, wills, and perceives" (*PHK* §138), any attempts to delineate other respects in which an idea might represent a mind fail (*PHK* §137).

In Section 139 Berkeley considers the objection that if there is no idea of the mind, then the word *mind* and its synonyms are meaningless. In replying to this objection in the *Third Dialogue*, Berkeley discusses how we know minds, and we'll examine that reply in detail below. Here he simply replies, "I answer, those words do mean or signify a real thing, which is neither an idea nor like an idea, but that which perceives ideas, and wills, and reasons about them. What I am my self, that which I denote by the term I, is the same with what is meant by *soul* or *spiritual substance*." The focus in Section 139 is on the fundamental difference between ideas and spirits, a point he had already raised in Section 2 and stressed in Section 89 (all editions). Words such as *mind* denote things that are fundamentally different from ideas. "It is therefore necessary, in order to prevent equivocation and confounding natures perfectly disagreeing and unlike, that we distinguish between *spirit* and *idea*." He revisits this concern with clarity in his 1734 additions to Section 142. After noting that, strictly speaking, we do not have an idea of minds or spirits, but only a notion of them, he remarks: "What I know, that I have some notion of. I will not say, that the terms *idea* and *notion* may not be used convertibly, if the world will have it so.

Minds

But yet it conduceth to clearness and propriety, that we distinguish things very different by different names." The verbal idea/notion distinction was introduced to mirror the idea/spirit distinction: ideas and spirits are fundamentally different kinds of things and are known in different ways. This is supported by Berkeley's closing remark in the section, "But if in the modern way the word *idea* is extended to spirits, and relations and acts; this is after all an affair of verbal concern," and he explains problems regarding the conceptual distinctions between minds and ideas on the basis of the doctrine of abstract ideas (*PHK* §143).

Before asking how minds are known, we should examine Berkeley's remarks on relations. In his additions to the 1734 edition of the *Principles* Berkeley claimed, "In like manner we know and have a notion of relations between things or ideas, which relations are distinct from the ideas or things related, inasmuch as the latter may be perceived by us without our perceiving the former. To me it seems that ideas, spirits and relations are all in their respective kinds, the object of human knowledge and subject of discourse" (*PHK* §89, 1734 edition), and "It is also to be remarked, that all relations including an act of the mind, we cannot so properly be said to have an idea, but rather a notion of the relations or habitudes between things." (*PHK* §142, 1734 edition). These are Berkeley's only remarks on our notions of relations. They are, at best, suggestive. Assume you have an idea described as, "A cup is to the left of a computer." You can consider the cup by itself; you can consider the computer by itself. If you take either the cup or the computer away, "to the left of" would also disappear. Is the "to the left of" something more than the cup and the computer? Berkeley's sole hint is the cryptic remark, "all relations including an act of the mind, . . ." What does that mean?

If Berkeley had anything like a coherent notion of relations, he probably drew it from John Locke's discussion in the *Essay concerning Human Understanding*. Locke's discussion is the longest and most coherent account of relations that was available to Berkeley. Locke begins his discussion "Of Relations" as follows:

> Besides the *Ideas*, whether simple or complex, that the Mind has of Things, as they are in themselves, there are others it gets from their comparison one with another. The Understanding, in the consideration of any thing, is not confined to that precise Object: It can carry any *Idea* as it were beyond itself, or, at least look beyond it, to see how it stands in conformity to any other. (*Essay* 2.25.1, see also 2.25.5, 2.28.1)

This suggests that relations are acts of comparing. Locke claims that there are several ways in which we naturally compare ideas. This suggests that contemplating ideas naturally causes certain comparisons in much the same way as an arrangement of particles causes you to have an idea of red (see Locke, *Essay* 2.26). So, *if* Berkeley is following Locke, the "to the left of" we considered above is an act of comparing.[11]

But if the same model would allow you to have a notion of perception and causation as relations, then you must be able to compare ideas and minds in much the same way you can compare ideas with ideas. Such comparisons are blocked by the likeness principle: "an idea can be like nothing but an idea" (*PHK* §8). Further, if perception and causation are relations, then they're special relations: they're "necessary relations," they are used to define *mind* as that which perceives ideas and causes ideas, and to define *idea* as that which is perceived. So while a cup is a cup whether or not it is to the left of a computer—"being to the left of" is a contingent relation—an idea would not be an idea if it were not perceived, and a mind would not be a mind if it could neither perceive nor cause ideas. We must be able to have notions of perceiving and causal relations if it is possible to conceive of minds indirectly, that is, on the basis of their relations to ideas, something Berkeley seemed to allow as early as *Principles* Section 2. But in the *Principles* Berkeley never indicates how we can have notions of perceiving and causing as such. Indeed, he says little about how minds are known. That topic is the focus of a passage in the Third Dialogue.

Knowing Minds: Dialogue Three

In the *Principles*, Berkeley's sole clue to how our own minds are known is in the 1734 addition to Section 89: "We comprehend our own existence by inward feeling or reflexion, and that of other spirits by reason." The allusion to an "inward feeling or reflexion" *suggests* that we know ourselves on the basis of "ideas of reflection." Locke claimed that we know the operations of our own minds by ideas of reflection: "In time, the Mind comes to reflect on its own *Operations* about the *Ideas* got by *Sensation*, and thereby stores itself with a new set of *Ideas*, which I call *Ideas* of *Reflection*" (Locke, *Essay* 2.1.24). Eighteenth-century philosophers agreed that all ideas are caused. Ideas of reflection are caused by the actions of our own minds. There was no requirement that effects resemble their causes, as is shown by the presumption that ideas of secondary qualities do not resemble their causes (Locke, *Essay* 2.8.15). Since Berkeley claimed that "such is the nature of *spirit* or that which acts, that it cannot be of it self perceived, but only by the effects which it produceth" (*PHK* §27, all editions), there is no reason Berkeley could not countenance ideas of reflection. And he could do this even if we grant A. A. Luce that "One of [Berkeley's] cardinal contentions, urged over and over again, is that there are no ideas of the mind or its operations,"[12] so long as the *of* is not the *of* of resemblance or identity. Of course, if minds are known only by their effects, then we know our own minds indirectly: I would know my own mind as merely that which causes certain ideas of reflection. There are two problems with such an account. First, as we noted above, if you can know minds indirectly, you must be able to know the relations on which the conception is based (cf. *PHK* §16). As necessary relations, it is not clear that perception and causation can be known independently of their relata. Second, in the Third Dialogue, Philonous claims that we know minds immediately. Perhaps the Third Dialogue will provide us with an alternative understanding of *reflection*, and so we turn to it.

The discussion of mind in the Third Dialogue can be divided into two parts. The first is a long speech that many commentators take as the key to understanding Berkeley's knowledge of mind (*DHP* 231–32).[13] The second part is the parity argument (*DHP* 232–34), four speeches added in the 1734 edition in which Philonous argues that none of the conceptual problems posed by the putative notion of material substance apply to immaterial substance. Philonous' remark, "I know or am conscious of my own being" (*DHP* 233), is consistent with his claims of immediate knowledge of himself in the first passage. His allusions to knowing himself by reflection (*DHP* 233) echo his remark in *Principles* Section 89 (1734 edition), but are little more than passing remarks. If we are to put any meat on the conceptual bone of *reflection* that takes us away from ideas of reflection as mere effects, we can only hope to find that in the first passage in Dialogue Three.

Hylas was concerned with the implications of having no idea of God. Philonous' reply concerns our knowledge of both our own minds and the minds of others, including God. He says:

> [1] As to your first question; I own I have properly no idea, either of God or any other spirit; for these being active, cannot be represented by things perfectly inert, as our ideas are. [2] I do nevertheless know,

that I who am a spirit or thinking substance, exist as certainly, as I know my ideas exist. [3] Farther, I know what I mean by the terms *I* and *myself*; and I know this immediately, or intuitively, though I do not perceive it as I perceive a triangle, a colour, or a sound. [4] The mind, spirit or soul, is that indivisible unextended thing, which thinks, acts, and perceives. [5] I say *indivisible*, because unextended; and *unextended*, because extended, figured, moveable things, are ideas; and that which perceives ideas, which thinks and wills, is plainly it self no idea, nor like an idea. [6] Ideas are things inactive, and perceived: and spirits a sort of beings altogether different from them. [7] I do not therefore say my soul is an idea, or like an idea. [8] However, taking the word *idea* in a large sense, my soul may be said to furnish me with an idea, that is, an image, or likeness of God, though indeed extremely inadequate. [9] For all the notion I have of God, is obtained by reflecting on my own soul heightening its powers, and removing its imperfections. [10] I have therefore, though not an inactive idea, yet in my self some sort of an active thinking image of the Deity. [11] And though I perceive Him not by sense, yet I have a notion of Him, or know Him by reflexion and reasoning. [12] My own mind and my own ideas I have an immediate knowledge of; and by the help of these, do mediately apprehend the possibility of the existence of other spirits and ideas. [13] Farther, from my own being, and from the dependency I find in my self and my ideas, I do by an act of reason, necessarily infer the existence of a God, and of all created things in the mind of God. [14] So much for your first question. [15] For the second: I suppose by this time you can answer it your self. [16] For you neither perceive matter objectively, as you do an inactive being or idea, nor know it, as you do your self by a reflex act: neither do you mediately apprehend it by similitude of the one or the other: nor yet collect it by reasoning from that which you know immediately. [17] All which makes the case of *matter* widely different from that of the *Deity*. (*DHP* 231–32)

I've numbered the sentences to facilitate the discussion.

Some of these themes are very familiar: we do not have ideas of the self or God [1], ideas are inactive and perceived [10], spirits are wholly different from ideas [6], my soul neither is nor is like an idea [7], and I have immediate knowledge of my own ideas [12]. There are other themes that concern knowing other minds and using our own mind as an "image" or model for understanding other minds [8]–[11] (see also *PHK* §140), and arguments for the existence of God [13], themes to which we return below. The interesting claims are that we have immediate knowledge of our own minds [3], [12].

There is no question that the Philonous of Dialogue Three claims immediate knowledge of his own mind; it is a point stated twice,

[3], [12], and his allusion to knowing himself by "reflex act" [16] might be taken as a third. In the course of his first speech in the parity argument, he says, "the being of my self, that is, my own soul, mind or thinking principle, I evidently know by reflexion" (*DHP* 233) and "I do not perceive it as an idea or by means of an idea, but know it by reflexion" (*DHP* 233). *Reflection* is ambiguous. As we noted above, it *could* be understood as an allusion to an idea of reflection, which would mean that mind is known by inference (reasoning). Interestingly, Berkeley's allusion to knowing God by reflection in [11] suggests that he understood the word *reflection* as synonymous with *reasoning*, which is a common suggestion in his works (see Intro. §18; *PHK* §§22, 51, 149; *DHP* 169, 197, 205, 212, 213, 232, 248, 261). But if reflection provides *immediate* knowledge of the mind, it must be comparable to the perceiving relation, which provides immediate knowledge of ideas. His allusion to a reflex act by which one knows oneself in [16] might do so (cf. Locke, *Essay* 2.21.4). If it is comparable to a perceiving relation, the two relations might be represented as follows:

Mind Perceiving Idea   Mind Reflex Act

Will this do? Perhaps. It would allow the mind to be aware of itself, to know itself immediately, to be self-conscious. Isn't that all that's required? No.

Our discussion of the passages in the *Principles* shows that *given* a notion of mind as a thing that perceives and acts, it is possible to have at least indirect knowledge of mind. Reflex acts explain how we can know our own minds directly. But nothing in the *Principles* tells us the source of the notion itself. We must ask, then, whether reflex acts can explain how we can have a *notion* of mind as a thing that perceives and acts.

It is not clear they can do so. To see why, consider the analogy to immediate visual perception. We normally say: I open my eyes and see my coffee cup. On Berkeley's scheme, properly speaking, I open my eyes and perceive an array of minimum visibles, some collection of which I identify as my coffee cup. Seeing a collection of minimum visibles as my coffee cup is an act distinct from the bare perceiving. Should you doubt this, consider an infant. She presumably immediately sees what you see, but she doesn't see these visibles as objects of certain kinds: she has not learned to differentiate the visual display into determinate objects, or she hasn't learned the language that allows her to make that differentiation, or whatever psychological story you would like to tell. If you're immediately aware of your mind by a reflex act, you are in a state that is analogous to the infant: to *describe* your mind as a thing that perceives and acts is to go beyond the immediate awareness.

The problem is only exacerbated if you take seriously Berkeley's remark at the beginning of *Principles* Section 27: "A spirit is one simple, undivided, active being." On *one* understanding of *simple*, this means it is not qualitatively complex. It means you might be aware of simple qualities, or you may point to them, but you can't define them. If Berkeley allowed that there are simple ideas,[14] a red minimum visible would be such. What can you say about it? It's red. And what is it to be red? You cannot verbally define it. You can only ostensively define *red* by physically or verbally pointing to things, for example, the outer rim of a rainbow, a fire truck, or an apple. In the case of a simple mind, you might pick this mind out by its relations to other things, or what it does—it is that which perceives and acts—but that tells you nothing about the thing itself.

Of course, this might not be the sense of *simple* Berkeley had in mind. He *might* have meant no more than that it is unextended, which would parallel his account of natural immortality (*PHK* 141; cf. [5]).

Knowing the perceiving and causal relations by reflex act seems even more difficult. If it is similar to the way we know relations between ideas, it requires that the mind be aware of both itself *and* an idea by a reflex act. Every idea is distinct from but necessarily connected to *some* mind as perceiver and *some* mind as its cause. This seems to require more than having the mind know itself by reflex act. The reflex act is sufficient to provide the extensional meaning of *mind*: it is a case of direct acquaintance. If this is an acquaintance with a mind as a *simple* thing, it cannot involve the connections between a mind and its ideas. Thus it cannot be the basis for a notion of mind as that which perceives and acts.

But the Berkeley of the *Three Dialogues* suggests another way in which the mind is known. In [3] Berkeley says, "I know what I mean by the terms *I* and *myself*, and I know this immediately, or intuitively." Reflex acts allow you to know *that* your mind exists; they do not allow you to know that your mind is a thing that perceives and causes ideas. Perhaps we need to also look at the intuitive side of "immediately, or intuitively."

Several notions of *intuition* were available to Berkeley. What Locke called "intuitive knowledge" is based on a comparison of ideas: "Thus the mind perceives, that *White* is not *Black*, That a *Circle* is not a *Triangle*, That *Three* are more than *Two*, and equal to *One* and *Two*. Such kinds of Truths the Mind perceives at the first sight of the *Ideas* together, by bare *Intuition*, without the intervention of any other *Idea*; and this kind of Knowledge is the clearest and most certain, that human Frailty is capable of" (Locke, *Essay* 4.2.1).[15] If this is limited to a comparison of ideas, it cannot be Berkeley's model of intuition.

The Scholastics and, perhaps, Descartes held that we have intuitive knowledge of the natures of things. Unlike many of his contemporaries, Berkeley was not ill disposed toward the Scholastics (*N* 716). If perceiving and causing ideas are essential properties of mind, an appeal to Scholastic intuition could provide the basis for such a notion. The notion would reflect the real essence of mind. If Berkeley accepted a Scholastic notion of *intuition*, then the nominalism assumed in the Introduction to the *Principles* must be limited, since nominalism eschews real essences. Further, this appeal to intuition is found exactly where we would expect to find appeals to intuition or self-evidence, namely, at the foundations of the theory. Is Berkeley then an implicit Scholastic?

He is not. An appeal to Scholastic intuition solely to justify his notion of mind would be *ad hoc*. *Ad hoc* appeals show that a philosophical theory is weak and unsystematic. Further, if Berkeley allows one essential essence, there is no reason to dismiss others: limited nominalism is implausible. But there seems to be a sense of *intuition* that avoids these untoward consequences.

Philosophical inquiries are based on general assumptions. Metaphysicians assume something exists. Epistemologists assume that something is known, a point granted by even the most extreme skeptics.[16] These assumptions are so basic that we might call them *intuitions*. Intuitions might go beyond the most basic assumptions. For example, if something is known, then there must be a knower. If there are actions, there must be an actor. If things persist through change, there must be something that remains the same. These are assumptions that are granted across philosophical traditions. They are conceptually necessary truths. As *conceptually* necessary truths, they entail no existence claims. Berkeley's notion of a mind as that which perceives ideas and acts might be understood in this way. Conceptually necessary truths might have the status of the supposition or hypothesis that is the basis for an inquiry by the method of analysis.[17] Is there evidence that Berkeley understood *intuition* in this way?

Yes, but it is quite limited. Apart from the passage in the *Three Dialogues*, there are few allusions to intuition. In *Alciphron*, Berkeley alludes to the "bare intuition of ideas" (*A* 7:11, p. 304; cf. *N* 547, 563), which is irrelevant to our present considerations. His claim that we have no immediate intuition of matter (*DHP* 234) is comparable to a concern with intuition by ideas. His allusion to Descartes—"What a jest is it for a philosopher to question the existence of sensible things, till he hath it proved to him from the veracity of God: or to pretend our knowledge in this point falls short of intuition or demonstration?" (*DHP* 231)—is consistent with using *intuition* as an allusion to self-evidence, but it provides no insight into Berkeley's use of the term.

There is a remark, however, in *Principles*, Section 3, that seems to imply the relevant sense of *intuitive*, since an idea as an object of knowledge entails the existence of a knower (*PHK* §§1–2): "I think an intuitive knowledge may be obtained of this [that an idea of sense cannot exist apart from a mind], by any one that shall attend to what is meant by the term *exist*, when applied to sensible things." Further, Berkeley's additions to the 1734 edition of the *Principles* tie the notion of mind to meaning. In Section 27 you find this: "Though it must be owned at the same time, that we have some notion of soul, spirit, and the operations of the mind, such as willing, loving, hating, inasmuch as we know or understand the meaning of those words." In Section 142, there is this: "I have some knowledge or notion of my mind, and its acts about ideas, inasmuch as I know or understand what is meant by those words." In the 1734 edition of the *Three Dialogues* he added: "Farther, I know what I mean, when I affirm that there is a spiritual substance or support of ideas, that is, that a spirit knows and perceives ideas" (*DHP* 234). In the 1752 edition of *Alciphron* he added, "Certainly it must be allowed that we have some notion, that we understand, or know what is meant by, the terms *myself, will, memory, love, hate,* and so forth, although, to speak exactly, these words do not suggest so many distinct ideas" (*A* 7:5, p. 292). The sense of *means* here cannot be purely extensional, insofar as it ties the meaning of *mind* to *idea*. It seems reasonable to suggest, then, that intuition in the Third Dialogue is a source of conceptual necessity, in the sense that it is what all philosophers assume as a basis for inquiry.

Someone might ask, however, "Doesn't this introduce too much? Prior to Berkeley, nearly all philosophers had assumed a notion of material substance. Wouldn't this sense of *intuition* place the notion of material substance on a par with immaterial substance?" (cf. *DHP* 232–34).

No, this is not a problem. We are concerned with only *conceptual* necessity. As such, this does not entail existence. A *presumption* of conceptual necessity entails neither that the notion is significant nor that the notion is consistent (that there is a notion). Given Philonous' extensive criticisms of notions of material substance in the First Dialogue (see Chapter 5), we can understand his remark, "I say in the first place, that I do not deny the existence of material substance merely because I have no notion of it, but because the notion of it is inconsistent, or in other words, because it is repugnant that there should be a notion of it" (*DHP* 232).

Nor does the fact that intuition provides a nonempirical source of concepts tell against Berkeley's general program. Recall that in *Principles*, Part I, Section 18, Berkeley notes that knowledge is derived either from sense or reason. What does it mean to be known by reason? It is not clear that it would provide us with the notion of a mind as a thing that knows and acts by itself. But if we look back at the *New Theory of Vision*, we find a clue. There Berkeley *assumed* at the outset that distance is not directly perceived by sense. That presumption is not something that can be known by sense, at least not beyond the fact that we know by sense that other philosophers claimed it was true. But insofar as Berkeley's analysis is successful, it explains how it can be taken as true. Much the same can be said for the notions of an idea and a mind at the beginning of the *Principles*. They reflect the standard views of the time that ideas are known and minds are knowers. They are assumptions providing the basis for the analysis and are justified insofar as the analysis is successful (cf. *CSM* 1:150).

We can thus understand how Berkeley could claim to be directly aware of his own mind: by reflex act. We can also understand how he could claim to have a notion of the nature of mind by intuition. These "intuitions" reflect broad philosophical understandings. They function as the basis for inquiry and are justified only if the philosophical account of which they are a part is justified.

Your Mind and God's

Before closing, we need to look briefly at Berkeley's accounts of our knowledge of other minds and his arguments for the existence of God.

In both *Principles* Section 140 and the Third Dialogue passage sentence [8]—"However, taking the word *idea* in a large sense, my soul may be said to furnish me with an idea, that is, an image, or likeness of God, though indeed extremely inadequate"—Berkeley alludes to a "large sense" in which we may have an idea of mind. In both cases we use this "image" to understand other minds: the *Principles* passage concerns any minds, while the *Three Dialogues* passage concerns God. The notion of God is an expansion and perfection of the notion of oneself, a position that is standard fare among the empiricists (Locke, *Essay* 2.23.33; cf. Hobbes at CSM 2:131, Descartes at CSM 2:132). If my account of having intuitive knowledge of mind is correct, it seems implausible that we would *literally* have an image of mind. Berkeley's point seems to be that we conceive of other minds as analogous to our own, just as we conceive the ideas in other minds as resembling those in ours (*PHK* 140). This provides the basis for his argument for the existence of other finite spirits. In our own case we perceive certain ideas following our acts of will (*PHK* §28); for example, we perceive ideas of our arms moving when we will to move our arms. We have ideas of other bodies that resemble our bodies. We perceive ideas of moving arms that correspond to our ideas of our arms moving following acts of will. From like effects we infer like causes, and conclude that it is highly probable that there are other finite spirits (*PHK* 145).

Knowledge of the existence of God is a problem. Commentators are inclined to remark, "Berkeley was an Anglican bishop, and God occupies a central place in his metaphysics."[18] Both claims are true. It's the juxtaposition of the claims that should give us pause. Given Berkeley's *eventual* position in the Church of Ireland—he didn't become a bishop until 1734, twenty-four years after the original publication of the *Principles*—there might be a tendency to assume that there were religious motivations behind his writings. Indeed, such an assumption seems to be supported by the subtitle of the *Principles*: "Wherein the chief causes of error and difficulty in the Sciences, with the grounds of Scepticism, Atheism, and Irreligion, are inquired into." But does that mean that he simply imported a Judeo-Christian notion of God into his works?

In some places he does, but it does not appear he does so in all his works. In the *Three Dialogues*, Berkeley introduces "God" as the Being that perceives all the ideas we do not perceive and causes those ideas we ourselves do not cause. In *Alciphron*, the focus is on God-as-designer and the intelligibility of the Judeo-Christian notion of God. In *Siris* he argues for a strictly Christian (Trinitarian) notion of God. But there is some evidence that the Berkeley of the *Principles* was more cautious.[19]

Many people take *Principles*, Section 29, to present an argument for the existence of God.[20] The passage reads:

> But whatever power I may have over my own thoughts, I find the ideas actually perceived by sense have not a like dependence on my will. When in broad day-light I open my eyes, it is not in my power to choose whether I shall see or no, or to determine what particular objects shall present themselves to my view; and so likewise as to the hearing and other senses, the ideas imprinted on them are not creatures of my will. There is therefore some other will or spirit that produces them.

Notice that *if* this is an argument for the existence of God, it is peculiar insofar as it makes no mention of God. The argument concludes, "There is therefore some other will or spirit that produces them [those ideas I do not produce myself]." The word *some* is ambiguous between "exactly one thing" and "at least one thing." Given that this is part of a discussion that began in Section 26, a discussion that attempts to explain the "continual succession of ideas" that we experience, and given that Berkeley argued that we can explain only some of our ideas on the basis of the actions of our own minds, it is reasonable to suggest that he means "at least one thing" other than our own mind. This presumption can only be strengthened if we recognize that the account it *replaces* is one in which many material substances cause ideas in us: at the very least, it gives no reason to believe there is exactly one cause.

But those who contend that Section 29 contains an argument for the existence of God will reply that if we look at what follows, we can hardly doubt that Berkeley intended Section 29 to be understood as an argument for the existence of God, since in Section 30 the ambiguous "some other will or spirit" becomes the singular *Author*, and in Section 33 it becomes *the Author of Nature*. This Author is described as wise and benevolent (*PHK* §30), good (*PHK* §32), and "more powerful [than we are]" (*PHK* §33). Surely, they would claim, this shows that Berkeley intended this to be an argument for the existence of the Judeo-Christian God.

In reply we need to draw a distinction. Two things can be numerically identical (the same thing) even if we do not know that they are the same thing. The morning star is the same planet (Venus) as the evening star, but that was not always known, and you can still conceive of the evening star as the first "star" you see in the evening and conceive of the morning star as the last "star" you see in the morning. The morning star and the evening star are conceptually distinct, even though the two expressions pick out exactly one thing. I believe you confront a similar situation regarding the Author of Nature of Section 33, and the Judeo-Christian God of *Principles*, Section 146.

Between Sections 33 and 146, Berkeley raises objections to his position and replies to them, and then draws out some of the implications of his system. In Section 145, he presents his argument for the existence of finite minds distinct from his own: while some of his rhetoric had assumed the existence of other finite minds, this was the first time he presented an *argument* for the existence of other finite minds. After Section 145, "nature" is far more complex than it was in Section 29: it is now composed of ideas that are coordinated among indefinitely many finite minds. So the work of the Author of Nature is far more complex than it was earlier taken to be.

In Section 146, Berkeley takes this more complex world into account and expands the argument found in Section 29. He wrote:

> But though there be some things which convince us, humane agents are concerned in producing them; yet it is evident to every one, that those things which are called the works of Nature, that is, the far greater part of the ideas or sensations perceived by us, are not produced by, or dependent on the wills of men. There is therefore some other spirit that causes them, since it is repugnant that they should subsist by themselves. See *Sect.* 29. But if we attentively consider the constant regularity, order, and concatenation of natural things, the surprising magnificence, beauty, and perfection of the larger, and the exquisite contrivance of the smaller parts of the creation, together with the exact harmony and correspondence of the whole, but above all, the never enough admired laws of pain and pleasure, and the instincts or natural inclinations, appetites, and passions of animals; I say if we consider all these things, and at the same time attend to the meaning and import of the attributes, one, eternal, infinitely wise, good, and perfect, we shall clearly perceive that they belong to the aforesaid spirit, *who works all in all*, and *by whom all things consist*.

Notice that Berkeley takes the argument in Section 29 as the basis for this argument but expands upon it. The world is more complex than it was taken to be in Section 29, so the cause is not merely good, benevolent, and wise, it is "infinitely wise, good, and perfect," corresponding to the complexity of the world. If Berkeley was a careful philosopher, we would expect him to proportion his conclusions to the evidence. Insofar as he attributed "perfections" to the world, it was plausible to attribute perfections to the world's cause.

You will also notice that Berkeley's concept of God in Section 146 is *not* the typical philosophical notion of God expressed in omni-attributes. Indeed, it might be what one would expect from an Anglican bishop. The description of God parallels that in the First Article of the *Thirty-Nine Articles of Religion*, the basic doctrinal statement of the Churches of England and Ireland:

> There is but one living and true God, everlasting, without body, parts, or passions; of infinite power, wisdom, and goodness; the Maker, and Preserver of all things both visible and invisible.[21]

But some might object that my argument is implausible. Even if the verbiage in Sections 29–33 ascribes less-than-omni-attributes to the Author of Nature, the argument in Section 29 should still be understood as an argument for the existence of the Judeo-Christian God, for the rhetoric in *Principles*, Sections 57–107 *assumes* the existence of the Judeo-Christian God. For example, in Section 57 Berkeley writes that the "order and concatenation" of ideas is "an argument of the *greatest* [emphasis added] wisdom, power, and goodness in their Creator," which is plausible only if Berkeley assumed he had already proven the existence of God. So, even if it is enthymematic, the argument in Section 29 must be taken as an argument for the existence of the Judeo-Christian God.[22]

I do not find this objection persuasive. In *Principles*, Sections 34–107, Berkeley considers a number of objections to his philosophy, as well as the implications it has for specific issues. When discussing the *New Theory of Vision*, we saw that when Berkeley replies to objections, he incorporates elements of the critic's position into his discussion. For example, he includes light rays in his discussion of the moon illusion (*NTV* §§68–72). Since the critics to whom Berkeley is replying accept the existence of the Judeo-Christian God, it is consistent with his practice to accommodate his discussion to their views. In this case it is particularly unproblematic insofar as it is wholly consistent with his philosophy, as he later argues.

A Look Back; A Look Ahead

In this chapter we examined Berkeley's accounts of mind. We worked through the basic discussion of mind in the *Principles* before turning to the celebrated passage in Dialogue Three where Philonous claims to know the nature and existence of his own mind immediately and intuitively. Reflex acts provide immediate knowledge of the existence of mind. I argued that by *intuition* Berkeley was concerned with widely accepted philosophical concepts. The concepts do not entail existence. We are justified in accepting the notion of mind as that which perceives and acts only insofar as it is part of a broader philosophical account that is acceptable.

Insofar as this account explains both how we can have a notion of mind and how we can know that minds exist based on Berkeley's published works, it is unnecessary to examine the account of the mind as a congeries of ideas, an account that rests primarily on passages in the Notebooks. Our examination of the *Principles* showed that *if* you are given a notion of mind, it might be plausible to claim indirect knowledge of the mind. The *Principles* provide no account of how we obtain the notion. On the other hand, the *Three Dialogues* suggest that we can know our own minds directly by reflex acts and that we have a notion of mind by intuition.

We looked briefly at Berkeley's argument for the existence of other finite minds and concluded with an examination of the argument for the existence of God in the *Principles*.

Berkeley is best known for idealism and immaterialism, a discussion of which we have now finished. The *Principles*, as it has survived, is only the first part of what he envisioned as a multipart work. The Second Part was to have been on God and morals (*N* 508). Berkeley provides notes on morals in his Notebooks, and he discussed general moral issues in *Passive Obedience* and *Alciphron*. It is to those works that we now turn.

Further Reading

Talia Mae Bettcher (2007). *Berkeley's Philosophy of Spirit*. London: Continuum.
Stephen H. Daniel (2013). "Berkeley's Doctrine of Mind and the 'Black List Hypothesis': A Dialogue." *The Southern Journal of Philosophy* (51): 24–41.
Daniel E. Flage (1986b). *Berkeley's Doctrine of Notions: A Reconstruction Based on His Theory of Meaning*. London: Croom Helm.
Robert G. Muehlmann (1992). *Berkeley's Ontology*. Indianapolis: Hackett, especially pp. 107–10 and 170–204.

7

Moral Philosophy

Berkeley's moral philosophy—his theories of moral obligation and moral value—are presented in the *Mo* comments marked in his Notebooks, in *Passive Obedience*, in *Alciphron*, and in several essays he contributed to Richard Steele's *Guardian* (1713).

Most discussions of Berkeley's moral theory are historical. They focus on the classification of Berkeley's moral theory. Many scholars argue that Berkeley was a utilitarian.[1] Utilitarianism has evolved into an intricate web of moral theories since its original statement in the works of Jeremy Bentham (1748–1832) and John Stuart Mill (1806–1873). Once a scholar establishes to her satisfaction that Berkeley was a utilitarian, she spends considerable effort on discussing the nature of Berkeley's utilitarianism.

The primary alternative to a utilitarian interpretation places Berkeley in the natural law tradition. Natural law theory has roots in the philosophies of Plato and Aristotle. In the Christian tradition, it was championed by Thomas Aquinas (1225–1275) and had experienced a revival in the century preceding Berkeley's work. Unlike utilitarianism, natural law theory assumes either a robust metaphysics or the existence of God, or both.

The remarks on morals in the Notebooks focus on Locke's scattered remarks on morals. I believe it can be shown that the Locke of *An Essay concerning Human Understanding* was a sophisticated ethical egoist.[2] We might at least ask, then, whether Berkeley flirted with ethical egoism.[3]

Utilitarianism theories are very popular. Natural law theories are less popular due to their metaphysical or theological presuppositions.

Ethical egoism is popularly portrayed as little more than selfishness. Charitable interpreters tend to see the views they find most plausible in the works they interpret.

Our task is to discover Berkeley's own views. I shall argue that the Berkeley of the Notebooks was an ethical egoist, and this egoism evolved into the natural law theory presented in *Passive Obedience* and *Alciphron*. To understand the issues, we need to briefly examine the distinctions among these theories.

Moral Theories

If you take an ethics course, your instructor is likely to begin with a number of distinctions. She will distinguish between value and obligation. Concerns with values are concerns with good and evil. Obligations tell you what you should do and should refrain from doing.

In moral theory, values are of two sorts: there is natural goodness or evil and moral goodness or evil (virtue or vice). In the early eighteenth century, *natural goodness* was usually identified with pleasure or happiness, and *natural evil* was identified with pain (cf. Locke, *Essay* 2.21.55 and 1.3.3). By *pain* and *pleasure* moral philosophers meant at least pleasure and pain derived from sense experience. Natural goodness is generally distinguished from moral goodness or *virtue*. How is that done?

Eighteenth-century moral philosophers gave two answers. The traditional answer was that an action is morally virtuous if it falls under a law of obligation, often a divine law. For example, you find this in Locke:

> This [divine law] is the only true touchstone of *moral Rectitude*; and by comparing them to this Law, it is, that Men judge of the most considerable *Moral Good* or *Evil* of their Actions; that is, whether as *Duties, or Sins*, they are like to procure them happiness, or misery, from the hands of the ALMIGHTY.... Vertue and Vice are Names pretended, and supposed every where to stand for action in their own nature right and wrong: And as far as they really are so applied, they so far are co-incident with the *divine Law* above-mentioned. (Locke, *Essay* 2.28.8 and 10; cf. Locke, *Essay* 1.3.6)

On such a view, whether an action is virtuous or vicious depends upon whether it was done in compliance with or in opposition to a law of obligation. Here there is a clear sense in which laws of obligation are *prior* to considerations of virtue and vice, since it is only by compliance with such a law that an action is virtuous. But this was not the only putative source of our knowledge of virtue and vice.

In 1711, Anthony Ashley Cooper, Third Earl of Shaftesbury, published his *Characteristics of Men, Manners, Opinions, Times*, a book containing Shaftesbury's moral philosophy: a moral sense theory. According to Shaftesbury and his followers—who include Francis Hutcheson (1694–1746) and David Hume (1711–76)—the moral sense is effectively a sixth sense that allows us to judge the virtue or vice of an action or the motive for an action in much the same way that vision allows us to judge color. When attending to the moral sense, we experience a particular kind of pleasure or pain corresponding to moral virtue or vice. If the moral sense theorists proposed a theory of obligation, they held that moral virtue is prior to moral obligation: you are morally obligated to follow those laws that maximize moral virtue as known by the moral sense.

On the side of moral obligation, your ethics teacher is likely to draw a distinction between *consequentialist* (sometimes called *teleological*) and *nonconsequentialist* (*deontological*) moral theories. If she also introduces a divine command theory—you are obligated to do *x* because God says so—*knowing what your obligations are* could still follow either a consequentialist or nonconsequentialist model. *Typically* moral theories are understood in terms of laws or rules of obligation: an action is *right* or *wrong* insofar as it complies or fails to comply with a moral rule.[4] Nonconsequentialists include Immanuel Kant and W. D. Ross. Kant is an *indirect rule theorist*: he uses his categorical imperative to generate determinate moral rules. For example, if you can will that everyone keep her promises in all cases, then it is a moral rule that you ought to keep your promises. Ross, on the other hand, is a *direct rule theorist*: he holds that you know moral rules directly, although he claims they are rules of *prima facie* obligation, that is, they hold, all things being equal (there are exceptions).

The consequentialists claim that it is on the basis of the consequences of an action that we determine moral obligation. The *ethical egoist* claims that each actor ought to act in such a way that it furthers her own interest. The *utilitarian* claims that each actor ought to act in such a way that it furthers the interests of society (the morally relevant group or groups) as a whole. As with the nonconsequentialists, the egoist or utilitarian might be a direct rule theorist and apply her principle directly to actions (they are commonly known as act-egoists and act-utilitarians), or she may be an indirect rule theorist and use her principle to generate moral rules (rule-egoist, rule-utilitarian). In either case, the theory assumes that it is possible to calculate which actions will or most probably will yield the greatest (usually natural) good. The classical accounts of utilitarianism were presented by Jeremy Bentham and John Stuart Mill. In his *Principles of Morals and Legislation* (1789), Bentham was the first philosopher to *call* himself a utilitarian and describe the means for calculating the utility of an action. Both Bentham and Mill understood *goodness* to be natural goodness (pleasure, happiness), although Mill also suggested that intellectual pleasures are different from and more important than sensual pleasures.

A couple of comments should be made. First, I have characterized ethical egoism in terms of personal interests; the eighteenth-century philosophers call this *self-love*. A person who judges what she ought to do on the basis of her interests might recognize that long-term gains might require short-term losses: she might recognize that cooperating with others or contributing to charities or suffering through college classes might be the best means to her long-term end of a pleasant and secure life.

Second, while our taxonomy of moral theories complies closely with what you might expect to find in a contemporary ethics class, it is historically incomplete. *Natural law theory* is a theory of morality and politics that can trace its roots to Plato and Aristotle. In its classical (ancient) form, the natural lawyer holds that there are **ends** (or purposes) for each kind of thing; the end of human life was generally taken to be happiness. Plato and Aristotle grounded these ends in universal Forms. These Forms determine what something is *essentially*, and in so doing, they indicate what something *ought to be*, all things being equal. So, it's not merely that an acorn *does* grow into a magnificent oak (barring squirrels and disease), the oak is the end of the acorn: it *ought* to grow into an oak. Natural laws both *describe* how things develop and *prescribe* how they are to develop. Only humans can make choices. Thus only humans can act or fail to act according to the prescription of a natural law. Given this, we may divide natural laws into three kinds. *Primary* natural laws *describe* the end (purpose) of a thing: for example, the end of human beings is happiness. *Secondary* natural laws *prescribe* the means all human beings should follow to obtain their ends: for example, no human beings should murder other human beings. *Tertiary* natural laws *prescribe* additional means humans in a certain group should follow to obtain their ends: for example, no lawyer should reveal what her clients have told her in confidence.

Natural law entered the Christian philosophical tradition with Thomas Aquinas[5] when he synthesized Aristotelian philosophy with Christian theology: God became the creator of things having Aristotelian forms. Natural law theory experienced a revival in the late sixteenth and seventeenth centuries in the works of Richard Hooker (1524–1600), Hugo Grotius (1583–1645), Samuel Pufendorf (1632–1694), Richard Cumberland (1631–1718), and John Locke. The period between Aquinas and Berkeley saw a philosophical shift away from the realism of Thomistic Forms to the denial of universals in thirteenth-century nominalism. As we have seen, with the possible exception of the natures of minds and ideas as such, Berkeley appears to have been a nominalist (cf. *DHP* 192). Corresponding to the metaphysical shift was a theological shift: God is a designer who ascribes ends to individuals.

Natural law theory has interesting ties to ethical egoism. Both claim that each individual should seek what is in her best interest. Natural laws describe and prescribe the best means to that end. Some of these laws (secondary natural laws) are very general: murdering others is never in your best interest. Other laws (tertiary natural laws) pertain to persons at particular levels of society: the priest and the lawyer must maintain confidences under certain conditions. If they were ethical egoists, the priest and lawyer would conclude that those rules apply to them through a careful calculation of long-term interest; the natural lawyer prescribes the same rules as means to obtain happiness as parts of a carefully (divinely) integrated system. There is a sense in which natural law theories are universalized egoistic theories: each and every person ought to do what is in her long-term best interest.

There are also ties and contrasts to utilitarianism. Both natural lawyers and utilitarians express concerns regarding the general good of humankind. Does this mean one theory collapses into the other? No. The rule utilitarian calculates rules that tend to yield the greatest good for society as a whole. This is a *collective* sense of *all*. The natural lawyer calculates rules that tend to yield the greatest good for each and every member of society. This is the *distributive* sense of *all*. The difference between the utilitarian and the natural lawyer might be expressed this way:

Utilitarianism: What yields the greatest total amount of good for a society is a duty for each member.
Natural law: What yields the most good for each member of a society is a duty for all members.

Given these distinctions, we may turn to Berkeley's Notebooks.

The Egoistic Notebooks

Berkeley's 1707–1708 Notebooks contain thirty-nine entries marked *Mo*, entries concerning moral philosophy (*Works* 1:50). Many of his entries concern John Locke's moral theory in the *Essay concerning Human Understanding*. Berkeley could not adopt Locke's account of morals outright. Locke claimed that mixed modes provide the meanings of moral terms (Locke, *Essay* 2.22.12). Mixed modes are complex ideas we each create ourselves. They do not represent anything outside of themselves (Locke, *Essay* 2.31.3; see also 3.5.3–6). But insofar as mixed modes are *abstract* ideas, Berkeley could not accept the account as it stands. Indeed, at Notebooks 669 Berkeley might suggest that we have no ideas of moral properties: "We have no Ideas of vertues & vices, no Ideas of Moral Actions wherefore it may be Question'd whether we are capable of arriving at Demonstration about them, the morality consisting in the Volition chiefly." Does this mean that for Berkeley moral terms are meaningless? No, it means that he had no distinct and unique ideas that apply to moral terms. Moral terms obtain meaning by "piggybacking" on other terms: the idea that provides the meaning for *pleasure* also provides the meaning for *good*, and the idea that provides the meaning of *pain* also provides the meaning of *evil*. This kind of piggybacking is comparable to Locke's account of mixed modes, and it is consistent with Berkeley's later identification of the *summum bonum* with sensual pleasure (N 769).

As the passage above suggests, Berkeley was intrigued by Locke's claim that the truth of moral claims, like that of geometrical claims, is subject to demonstration (Locke, *Essay* 4.3.18, 4.4.7, 4.4.9, 4.12.8; N 669, 677, 683, 690, 697, 705, 732, 734, 739, 755, 804, 883; cf. 698, 728, 853). In working through this possibility, Berkeley concluded that demonstration in morals *is* possible, but then it is only a matter of the relations among the meanings of words: "To demonstrate Morality it seems one need only make a Dictionary of Words & see which included which. at least. This is the greatest part & bulk of the Work" (*N* 690). But, following Locke's remarks on mixed modes, the meanings of terms or signs "are perfectly arbitrary & in our power, made at pleasure" (*N* 732). This implies that the certainty obtained is purely verbal (*N* 804): like pure arithmetic, there is no guarantee that it is applicable to ordinary life.

But a concern with demonstration in morals is not the only theme that is found in Berkeley's early jottings on morals. Several entries on self-interest are among his earliest entries on morals:

> I allow not of the Distinction there is made twix't Profit & Pleasure. (*N* 541)

> I'd never blame a Man for acting upon Interest. he's a fool that acts on any other Principle. the not understanding these things has been of ill consequence in Morality. (*N* 542)

> I am glad the People I converse with are not all richer, wiser etc than I. This is agreeable to Reason, is no sin. Tis certain that if the Happyness of my Acquaintance encreases & mine not proportionably, mine much decrease. The not understanding this & the Doctrine about relative Good discuss'd with French, Madden etc to be noted as 2 Causes of mistake in Judging of moral Matters. (*N* 569)

These entries suggest that moral principles cannot be contrary to self-interest. Indeed, he goes further:

> Sensual Pleasure is the Summum Bonum. This the Great Principle of Morality. This once rightly understood all the Doctrines even the severest of the [Gospels] may cleerly be Demonstrated. (*N* 769)

> Sensual Pleasure qua Pleasure is Good & desirable. by a Wise Man. but if it be Contemptible tis not quâ pleasure but qua pain or Cause of pain. or (wch is the same thing) of loss of greater pleasure. (*N* 773)

These entries suggest that Berkeley was at least flirting with ethical egoism.

But someone might suggest that the identification of the *summum bonum* with sensual pleasure is ambiguous. She would claim, "Berkeley's remark should be understood as the factual claim that human beings are psychological hedonists, a claim that was fairly common at the time (cf. Locke, *Essay* 1.3.3). Even if one grants that Berkeley was concerned with a moral principle—as he suggests—it is ambiguous between the maximization of pleasure for an individual and the maximization of pleasure for a group. The former would suggest Berkeley's interests were egoistic; the latter would suggest his interests were utilitarian. So the passages do not establish that Berkeley was an ethical egoist."

There are several reasons why the passages in the Notebooks are more consistent with an egoistic reading than a utilitarian reading. First, egoism is consistent with the entries on self-interest and profit. Second, there is no entry in the Notebooks that is unequivocally concerned with the interests of society. Third, his 1708 sermon, "Of Immortality," takes the individual attainment of happiness to be the ultimate end of any action. To see what is entailed in ascribing ethical egoism to Berkeley, we must consider what constitutes a consistent form of ethical egoism, a position I believe is found in Locke's *Essay*.[6]

To be a consistent ethical egoist you must be concerned with what yields the greatest amount of pleasure in the long run, *not* immediately. Such a calculation will take the interests of other people into account. Berkeley acknowledges these points:

> One great Cause of Miscarriage in Men's affairs is that they too much regard the Present. (*N* 839)

> In Valuing Good we reckon too much on ye present & our own. (N 851)

The interests of others must be taken into account in calculating what is to your long-term advantage. People who engage in robbery, murder, adultery, lying, and so forth can expect various types of retaliation if discovered. So, to maximize your long-term self-interests, you need to attend to the interests of others and their probable reactions to your actions.

Further, while Berkeley might have concluded that a purely demonstrative ethic would yield nothing more than verbal truths, he suggested that "Morality may be Demonstrated as mixt Mathematics" (*N* 755; see also *N* 770). On the model of mixed mathematics, you apply a moral principle such as "Act in such a way that it maximizes your long-term self-interest (pleasure, happiness)" to individual cases or as the basis for formulating general rules of conduct. To do so, you would need to appeal to laws of probable behavior.[7] Such an ethical egoist is likely to conclude that she should accept general rules such as, "Do not kill," "Do not steal," "Do not commit adultery," "Do not bear false witness," and so on.[8]

Considerations of self-interest also point toward the kinds of pleasure that are best pursued. At Notebooks 787 Berkeley notes, "Mem. to excite men to the pleasures of the Eye & the Ear wch

Moral Philosophy

surfeit not, nor bring those evils after them as others." Later he remarked:

> There be two sorts of Pleasure the one is ordain'd as a spur or incitement to somewhat else & has a visible relation & subordination thereto, the other is not. Thus the pleasure of eating is of the former sort, of Musick is ye later sort. These may be used for recreation, those not but in order to their End. (N 852)

If the consistent ethical egoist focuses on sustainable pleasures, this focus on the pleasures of the eye and ear—art and music—is what one would expect. Gustatory pleasures are unsustainable; pleasures provided by the fine arts are indefinitely sustainable. Indeed, Berkeley suggests gustatory pleasures are little more than instrumental: the pleasures of the palate are merely a means to the attainment of health, which is a sustainable pleasure, even if it is a pleasure that is most noticed in its absence.[9] It is unclear how this passage would support a utilitarian reading of Berkeley, for on such a reading it seems to suggest that the good of society is more fully obtained by a focus on the fine arts than by a system that provides all members of society with at least the basic necessities of life. To the ethical egoist, however, it is little more than sage advice: the pleasures from the contemplation of art or music cannot be overdone nor do they result in subsequent pain; they are sustainable pleasures.

You might have noticed that I have had little to say about the future bishop's concern with the religious side of ethics. The reason is that the Berkeley of the Notebooks seldom ties his ethical concerns to religion. There are only two entries marked *Mo* that explicitly allude to God's role in moral obligation:[10]

> The 2 great Principles of Morality. the Being of a God & the Freedom of Man: these to be handled in the beginning of the Second Book. (N 508)

> God Ought to be worship'd. This Easily demonstrated when once we ascertain the signification of the word God, worship, ought. (N 705)

The allusion to free will in the first entry requires at least that we be capable of choices that can affect our actions (cf. N 145, 145a, 149, 166, 539, 626, 631, 816). How the Being of God, as such, plays a role in the moral considerations of a presumptive ethical egoist is less clear, but the second passage might shed some light on that issue.

Assume, as the future bishop certainly did,[11] that there is a God who has all the attributes theistic philosophers traditionally assign to God, that is, God is in some sense a person, all-powerful, unique, universal ruler, and so forth. If there were such a one, then it would be in our long-term best interest to recognize God's existence and to treat God with respect. Thus, just as a consideration of our long-term self-interests justify those claims regarding our duties to other human beings, duties that are summarized in the later commandments of the Decalogue, considerations regarding God with respect to our long-term interests are summarized in those commandments concerning God. Notice, this treats the commandments as nothing but implications of the egoistic principle: the best means to obtaining happiness is to act in accordance with God's commandments. If the will of God can be discerned either by reason or revelation,[12] then considerations based on the egoistic principle allow us to discern God's will by reason. Revelation reveals the same laws together with the threat of eternal punishment if you break them. An ethical egoist should thus conclude that long-term self-interest by itself justifies each of the commandments of the Decalogue. You are morally obligated on egoistic grounds to follow God's laws. And this is precisely what Berkeley argues in his sermon "Of Immortality."

The sermon "Of Immortality" comes from approximately the same period as the Notebooks: it was preached in Trinity College Chapel on Sunday evening, January 11, 1708. Focusing first on the question of the effect Christianity had on the world (*SER* 1:9), Berkeley suggests that promises of eternal bliss for living a virtuous life and eternal misery for living a vicious life gave reason to follow the path of virtue, that is, to follow divine laws (*SER* 1:10). Indeed, he presents a wager no less extreme than Pascal's famous wager. Pascal argued that even if the probability of life after death is small, given the enormity of the consequences of eternal rewards and punishments if there is eternal life, you should believe that God exists. Similarly, Berkeley contends that it is only rational to place the desires for eternal happiness above all others (*SER* 1:12–13). He concludes by explaining why humans do not focus on the eternal: we have no determinate idea of eternal pleasures and pains, and we assume that such eternal rewards and punishments are in the distant future (*SER* 1:13).

So Berkeley concludes that considerations of self-interest rationally oblige us to attend to our eternal interests, which are couched in terms of pleasure and pain. This suggests that we are morally obligated to follow God's laws *because* doing so yields an infinite increase in pleasure, while ignoring those laws yields an infinite increase in pain. This is precisely what one would expect from an ethical egoist. Further, this is wholly consistent with the remark at Notebooks 769 that "sensual Pleasure is the Summum Bonum. This the Great Principle of Morality. This once rightly understood all the Doctrines even the severest of the [Gospels] may cleerly be Demonstrated." Weighing our actions on a scale that includes eternal rewards and punishments, following "even the severest [doctrines] of the [Gospels]" is strictly a matter of self-interest. Berkeley's theology and philosophy of the period were consistent (see also *SER* 4:48n, *SER* 6:90, *SER* 9:115).

Do the views suggested by the Notebooks constitute Berkeley's mature views on morals? No. In *Passive Obedience* (1711) Berkeley identifies his position with natural law theory (subtitle and *PO* §§1, 2, 12). This does not mark, however, an abandonment of the position in the Notebooks.

Passive Obedience

Berkeley's stated objective in *Passive Obedience* was to show that loyalty to the supreme governmental power has the status of a natural law, a strict moral duty (*PO* §§1 and 3). He understood loyalty to be either following the laws of the sovereign or patiently accepting the punishments for transgressing those laws (*PO* §3). He bases his case on "the Principles of Reason common to mankind" (*PO* §2), lamenting the fact that previous attempts to discern natural laws by deductions of reason have "not, that I know, been anywhere distinctly explained, or treated of so fully as the importance of the subject doth deserve" (*PO* §4). Berkeley proposes to fill this lacuna by inquiring "into the origin, nature, and obligation of moral duties in general, and the criterions whereby they are to be known" (*PO* §4).

Berkeley's initial remarks focus on self-love. They at least point toward the assumption of a teleological metaphysics.[13] He wrote:

> Self-love being a principle of all others the most universal, and the most deeply engraven in our hearts, it is natural for us to regard things as they are fitted to augment or impair our own happiness; and accordingly we denominate them *good* or *evil*. Our judgment is ever employed in distinguishing between these two [good and evil,

happiness and unhappiness, pleasure and pain], and it is the whole business of our lives to endeavour, by a proper application of our faculties, to procure the one and avoid the other. (*PO* §5; cf. *DHP*, p. 262, *A* 2:13, 18)

The pairing of self-love with happiness suggests that Berkeley is concerned with the happiness of the individual. Up to this point, everything Berkeley says is consistent with ethical egoism. But we cannot ignore the fact that Berkeley *says* he's doing natural law theory. Tying this concern with self-love with natural law theory suggests that Berkeley accepted the principle, "Each and every human being seeks the maximization of her own happiness and the minimization of unhappiness," as a primary natural law, as a law describing the common end of a class of objects (humans). Happiness is a broad concept, a concept that subsumes numerous kinds of pleasure (cf. *PHK* §100, *Guardian* 49:193). So, one of the functions of judgment is to distinguish among different kinds of pleasure in an effort to determine the balance among those kinds of pleasure that constitute happiness. There is a natural development with respect to the kinds of pleasure one deems constitutive of happiness (cf. *Guardian* 62:203). Initially, we identify happiness with sensual pleasure. But as our experience increases, we discover that sensual pleasures are often impure:[14] pleasures often lead to greater pains, and pains sometimes lead to greater pleasures. "Besides," Berkeley writes,

> as the nobler faculties of the human soul begin to display themselves, they discover to us goods far more excellent than those which affect the senses. Hence an alteration is wrought in our judgments; we no longer comply with the first solicitations of sense, but stay to consider the remote consequences of an action, what good may be hoped, or what evil feared from it, according to the wonted course of things. This obliges us frequently to overlook present momentary enjoyments, when they come in competition with greater and more lasting goods, though too far off, or of too refined a nature, to affect our senses. (*PO* §5)

Does Berkeley, like Mill, maintain that some pleasures are inherently superior to others,[15] or is the quality of a pleasure determined by its sustainability or a combination of sustainability and purity? It seems to be the latter. As we have seen, this concern with "more excellent" pleasures is anticipated in the Notebooks, where Berkeley distinguishes between sensual pleasure and the pleasures of the arts (*N* 852). While the pain of hunger might be eliminated by the pleasure of eating, if that activity is carried beyond a certain point, it again results in pain (it is impure). The joys of music would seem to be both more sustainable and purer. Berkeley's concern with the remote consequences of actions in the passage above, and his concern with eternal interests in Section 6, both point toward sustainability and purity as the marks of superior happiness; that is, they both suggest that the total quantity of happiness marks its quality.

Passive Obedience Section 6 is important beyond its concern with the durability of pleasure (happiness), for it seems to draw a distinction between duty and self-interest. It is "evident by the light of nature, that there is a sovereign omniscient Spirit, who alone can make us for ever happy, or for ever miserable." This implies that it is to one's personal advantage to comply with the will of this Being. Like other natural lawyers of the time, Berkeley deemed God the legislator of natural laws (*PO* §6). This apparent distinction between duty and interest, however, is not a departure from his earlier discussion.

If we assume a teleological metaphysics (*PO* §5), there is a direct correlation between duty and self-interest. We naturally seek our end, and we ought to do so: it is in our interest insofar as it is self-affirming. Nonetheless, popular religion might not recognize the confluence of self-interest and duty found in teleological natural laws. In Section 6 Berkeley recognizes that some religious persons—and, presumably, some of the students in Berkeley's original audience—might hold that external sanctions (divine rewards and punishments) provide the only motive for following divine laws. To such people, divine laws differ little from positive civil laws: the differences are in the lawmaker and the sanctions. These are external motives. To the natural lawyer, the motive is internal and, while she might be concerned with eternal rewards and punishments, the effects of violating a law of nature are natural and relatively immediate.

Insofar as God is the legislator of natural law, Berkeley inquires into God's purposes. Noting that laws are "rules directive of the end intended by the legislator" (*PO* §7), he focuses on the ends God designs for human actions. Since God is perfect, these cannot be actions that are beneficial to God. God thus must be concerned with the good of his creatures. Since the actions of humans cannot affect higher intelligences (angels), God's legislation must concern actions among humans. Berkeley continues:

> But, as nothing in a natural state can entitle one man more than another to the favour of God, except only moral goodness; which, consisting in a conformity to the laws of God, doth presuppose the being of such laws, and law ever supposing an end, to which it guides our actions, it follows that, antecedent to the end proposed by God, no distinction can be conceived between men; that end therefore itself, or general design of Providence, is not determined or limited by any respect of persons. It is not therefore the private good of this or that man, nation, or age, but the general well-being of all men, of all nations, of all ages of the world, which God designs should be procured by the concurring actions of each individual. Having thus discovered the great end to which all moral obligations are subordinate, it remains that we inquire what methods are necessary for the obtaining that end. (*PO* §7)

Berkeley identifies moral goodness with compliance with the laws of God (laws of nature). This subordination of the moral goodness (virtue) of an action to compliance with a natural law is characteristic of natural law theory.[16] Laws presuppose an end. The divinely ordained end is independent of the end of any particular human. It is a common end: God does not show favorites to any individual or group of individuals. This common end is procured by each individual following God's laws.

What does this mean? Is it an end that is common to each individual, as I have argued one would expect in a natural law theory? Or is it an end of humankind as a whole? Before answering those questions we might notice what Berkeley says about these laws and the need for them.

There can be no question that Berkeley held that the laws of God maximize the "public good" (*PO* §8), and this is best obtained by "the observation of some determinate, established laws, which, if universally practised, have, from the nature of things, an essential fitness to procure the well-being of mankind" (*PO* §8; cf. *PO* §§9–10). A system of rules must then constitute the foundation of morality. These laws "have a necessary tendency to promote the well-being of the sum of mankind, taking in all nations and ages, from the beginning to the end of the world" (*PO* §10).

Berkeley's concern with the public good, "the well-being of the sum of mankind," however, does not imply commitment to some form of utilitarianism. If Berkeley was a natural lawyer, as he says he was (*PO* §§ 1, 2, 12), then the application of the law should yield goodness distributively, rather than collectively. If happiness is the God-given end of humans (*PO* §5),[17] then it is the end of each and every human being and the laws should maximize, or tend to maximize, the happiness of each and every human being. This conclusion can only be strengthened if one recalls Berkeley's salvific concerns in Section 6 and his commitment to an ontology composed solely of individuals. Indeed, the God-does-not-play-favorites argument in Section 7 also speaks against a utilitarian interpretation. To see this, let us examine what could be warranted by a utilitarian account of Berkeleian ethics.

We are concerned with laws that pertain to human beings as human beings. If we ask what those laws are, the answer drawn from Christian natural law tradition is that it is at least that portion of the Decalogue concerning human beings. Berkeley himself cites "Thou shalt not commit adultery" as an example of a natural law (*PO* §§3 and 15). Would the principle of utility sanction such a law? Perhaps, but there is no guarantee. The focus of utilitarianism is on what is best for society as a whole (collectively). For this to apply in Berkeley's case, "society" would need to be identified with "the sum of mankind, taking in all nations and ages, from the beginning to the end of the world" (*PO* §10). If one follows the dictum Mill attributes to Bentham, "everybody to count for one, nobody for more than one,"[18] it would be pragmatically impossible to construct the calculation for all past to present persons, and including future persons would be in principle impossible. The defender of the utilitarian interpretation of Berkeley would respond, "What is impossible for humans is possible for God. Given Berkeley's theistic assumptions, such practical considerations carry no weight." Very well, but on purely utilitarian grounds the greatest collective good *might* be obtained by something other than universal laws. It is consistent with utilitarian principles to divide humankind into various classes—a caste system—such that the topmost class obtains more happiness than that below, the second class more than the third, the third more than the fourth, and so forth down to some base, so long as the *total amount of happiness* is greater than on any other scheme. Indeed, on utilitarian grounds, if such an arrangement yielded the greatest amount of happiness overall, the utilitarian would seem morally obligated to accept such an arrangement. On such a scheme, none of the utilitarian laws that apply to one class need be—and almost certainly would not be—the same utilitarian laws that apply to any other class. But even if it is merely a matter of fact that such a caste system as this would yield the greatest total happiness, it would imply that God is procuring the greatest good of select groups of individuals at the cost of others, which would be inconsistent with the God-does-not-play-favorites-argument in Section 7.

The defender of utilitarianism might raise the following objection: "In Berkeley's time a social hierarchy was as much a fact of life as it is today, if not more so. You have contended that the natural law theorist is committed to natural laws concerning members of social classes. These become the rules that follow from the principle of utility, given the overall utilitarian superiority of the social system. So, either your objection carries no weight against the utilitarian interpretation, or natural law theory, as you have reconstructed it, collapses into utilitarianism."

The objection fails, for there is a fundamental difference between the hypothetical utilitarian justification of a caste system and the natural lawyer's concern with laws for people in particular places in a society. On the utilitarian account, the social arrangement, if it actually yields the greatest utility, carries moral weight. To the natural lawyer, society might evolve in any number of ways; the exact social structure that evolves is morally neutral. The natural lawyer claims only *given that* a certain social structure *has evolved*, a person within a certain stratum of the hierarchy will best maximize her happiness by way of the relevant tertiary natural laws.

But the utilitarian might raise yet another objection: "Berkeley was a theist. As a theist, he was certainly committed to the claim that God would not approve of the rather severe caste system you claim as a utilitarian possibility, indeed, God would not construct human beings in such a way that they could maximize the utility of society by such a scheme. So, you still have not shown that Berkeley eschewed utilitarianism. Indeed, Berkeley was a theological utilitarian, that is, he held that 'the happiness of mankind is the criterion of the will of God and should be the criterion of human will as well.'"[19] The objection misses the point. If Berkeleian natural laws are both utilitarian and divinely instituted, and if *as a matter of fact* a caste system yields the greatest overall utility, then divine law and utilitarian calculations must coincide. If *as a matter of fact* a caste system yields the greatest overall utility but God would disapprove of such a system, this would be sufficient to show that divine laws are not utilitarian. You cannot have it both ways.

Berkeley's laws of nature are universal: they apply to all human beings. They reflect what we naturally believe is right: "They are said to be *stamped on the mind*, to be *engraven on the tables of the heart*, because they are well known to mankind, and suggested and inculcated by conscience" (*PO* §12). They tend toward the well-being of

Moral Philosophy

all humans (*PO* §11), even if they do not yield the greatest happiness for each individual or group in every instance, since as they can be, "either by the unhappy concurrence of events, or more especially by the wickedness of perverse men who will not conform to them, made accidental causes of misery to those good men who do" (*PO* §13). In this respect they are comparable to purely descriptive natural laws, which, though they are "excellently suited to promote the general well-being of the creation" (*PO* §14; cf. *PHK* §§31, 146), will occasionally yield more pain than pleasure in sentient agents.

Continuing, Berkeley focuses explicitly on the contention "that loyalty is a moral virtue, and 'Thou shalt not resist the supreme power' a rule or law of nature, the least breach whereof hath the inherent stain of moral turpitude" (*PO* §15). He builds his case around 1. the importance of the law, 2. the universality of the law, 3. the impossibility that every individual is in a position to know what will preserve society, and 4. the fact that the lack of a principle of obedience would lead to the dissolution of society. Notice that the natural laws Berkeley has discussed thus far are *important* insofar as they specify a means to happiness, and *universal* insofar as they pertain to the happiness of each and every human being. The third and fourth considerations relate to the discussions of the general need for universal rules (*PO* §§8–9).

Berkeley stresses the need for general laws in his discussion of the origins of society. He writes:

> The miseries inseparable from a state of anarchy are easily imagined. So insufficient is the wit or strength of any single man, either to avert the evils, or procure the blessings of life, and so apt are the wills of different persons to contradict and thwart each other, that it is absolutely necessary several independent powers be combined together, under the direction (if I may so speak) of one and the same will, I mean the Law of the Society. Without this there is no politeness, no order, no peace, among men, but the world is one great heap of misery and confusion; the strong as well as the weak, the wise as well as the foolish, standing on all sides exposed to all those calamities which man can be liable to in a state where he has no other security than the not being possessed of any thing which may raise envy or desire in another. A state by so much more ineligible than that of brutes as a reasonable creature hath a greater reflexion and foresight of miseries than they. From all which it plainly follows, that Loyalty, or submission to the supreme civil authority, hath, if universally practised in conjunction with all other virtues, a necessary connexion with the well-being of the whole sum of mankind; and, by

consequence, if the criterion we have laid down be true, it is, strictly speaking, a moral duty, or branch of natural religion. (*PO* §16)

Berkeley's imaginative reconstruction of a state of nature is reminiscent of Hobbes. While, like Locke,[20] Berkeley maintains that the laws of nature apply in a state of nature insofar as they apply to all humans as humans, like Hobbes he maintains that the state of nature is not merely a pre-governmental state, it is also a pre-societal state.[21] Human beings are nearly equal in abilities and power, and, insofar as each naturally seeks her perceived self-interest, there will be conflicts among individuals. While Berkeley suggests that there is a natural evolution of those pleasures constituting happiness as a person matures (*PO* §5; *N* 852; *Guardian* 62:203), there must be a certain stability in order for that development to occur. Indeed, Berkeley says, "whoever considers the condition of man will scarce conceive it possible that the practice of any one moral virtue should obtain, in the naked, forlorn state of nature" (*PO* §16). Because societal stability is necessary for the attainment of happiness—it is necessary for the practice of most natural laws pertaining to all human beings—and because such stability can be obtained only by loyalty to a supreme power (the "Law of Society"), the principle "Thou shalt not resist the supreme power" should have the status of a law of nature.

Why should it count as a natural law? Berkeley gives four reasons. First, it is important enough to be a moral rule (*PO* §17). It yields the stability needed for the practice of moral rules. As Berkeley writes, "Government, I say, which is itself the principal source under heaven of those particular advantages for the procurement and conservation whereof several unquestionable moral rules were prescribed to men" (*PO* §17). Insofar as natural laws describe the best means to the happiness of all individuals, and insofar as happiness is the natural end of each human, following natural laws is the fundamental means to each person's end. The principal reason the law of obedience is important is that it provides the foundation of society, and society provides the context in which laws of nature can most easily be followed. Berkeley's quasi-Hobbesian state of nature is one in which each person seeks what she perceives to be in her best interest. Perceived interests can and often do conflict among agents. By imposing a societal-governmental structure there are restrictions on the means individuals can pursue to obtain their perceived interests. Thus it is a context in which it is easier to follow secondary natural laws, and thereby for each of us to obtain her natural end, namely, happiness.

Berkeley's second reason that the law of obedience should count as a natural law is that "obedience to government is a case universal enough to fall under the direction of a law of nature.... But what relation is there more extensive and universal than that of subject and law? This is confined to no particular age or climate, but universally obtains, at all times, and in all places, wherever men live in a state exalted above that of brutes" (*PO* §18). One of the marks of natural law is its universality. The fact that humans join together to form society and that those societies have a structural hierarchy that requires some obedience of those lower in the hierarchy to those who are higher implies that the law of obedience is natural. Thus, whether one examines a minimal society, such as a nuclear family, or a nation-state, *some* structure of obedience is found. Notice that this is no more than a factual claim, although it is a fact that is central to the naturalness of natural law.

Berkeley provides two additional reasons for deeming the law of obedience a natural law. Both of these are related, on one hand, to the question of *importance*, and, on the other, to Berkeley's argument in Section 9 that moral considerations must be based on a law rather than individual calculations of good. Berkeley writes, "Thirdly, there is another consideration which confirms the necessity of admitting this rule for a moral or natural law; namely, because the case it regards is of too nice and difficult a nature to be left to the judgment and determination of each private person" (*PO* §19). While individuals may make decisions that affect themselves and a few others, decisions that affect the good of a nation require someone with greater oversight. Questions of public interest or the need for modifying government structure "are points too arduous and intricate, and which require too great a degree of parts, leisure, and liberal education, as well as disinterestedness and thorough knowledge in the particular state of a kingdom, for every subject to take upon him the determination of them" (*PO* §19). Notice the parallels to the argument against act theories of morals in Section 9: in both cases the individual is portrayed as possessing too little wisdom and too little information to make an informed decision regarding the overall good that would be produced in a determinate situation. In the societal case, the sovereign is assumed to have the wisdom and the means to find the information necessary to make such judgments. So the rule of obedience provides the best means to obtaining what is in the general public interest and thereby the interest of each individual.

Finally, "It cannot be denied that right reason doth require some common stated rule or measure, whereby subjects ought to shape their submission to the Supreme Power. Since any clashing or disagreement in this point must unavoidably tend to weaken and dissolve the society" (PO §20). Again Berkeley's argument parallels that in Section 9. If we grant, as he argued in support of his first point, that society is necessary for the maximization of the happiness of its members, there must be a rule of obedience, for if the determination of societal actions were left to the individuals alone, there would be disagreements that would result in the dissolution of society. This rule of obedience must either prohibit resistance to the Supreme Power or be based upon considerations of the public good. But it cannot be based upon considerations of the public good undertaken by individuals or groups of individuals in society, for, again, this would result in disagreements that would result in the dissolution of society. Thus, the rule of obedience to the Supreme Power must have the status of natural law.

Before turning to the objections Berkeley poses for his position, we should notice that the kinds of considerations he raised were precisely those one would expect from a natural lawyer. The law of obedience is a means for maximizing the obedience to secondary natural laws, and thereby maximizing the happiness of each member of society. This suggests that the law of obedience should be understood as a tertiary natural law, since it specifies means necessary for the maximization of obedience to secondary natural laws. Further, as a natural law, the law of obedience reflects the universal tendency of humans to join together into societies. A supreme sovereign is in a better position than the individual members of a society to examine the interests of the society as a whole, and therefore to make civil laws governing the society. The law of obedience to the sovereign provides the best means to retain the benefits of society. Notice that at no point did Berkeley make the kind of move one would expect a utilitarian to make, namely, he never made an unequivocal appeal to the collective interests of society. Indeed, he eschewed appeals to the public good as grounds for determining whether one should obey societal laws.

Berkeley raises several possible objections to his position. The first is from something like a moral sense theory, namely, that the sense of horror regarding rebellion is not as great as that regarding other crimes against nature (PO §21). Berkeley replies by claiming that *some* beliefs are instilled by education (custom) and one develops a visceral response regarding some crimes that is indistinguishable from those for which one has a natural antipathy. Berkeley attributes this response to a lack of reflection on the crime of rebellion: "And if there be any who find they have a less abhorrence of Rebellion than of other villanies, all that can be inferred from it is that this part of their duty was not so much reflected on, or so early and frequently inculcated into their hearts, as it ought to have been" (PO §21).

Next he considers an objection based on contractual theories. These, he claims, are either absolute or conditional. Absolute contracts are "sacred and inviolable" (PO §22). Conditional contracts are implausible: they would "loosen the bands of civil society" (PO §24). A government based upon a conditional contract would be inherently unstable: rebellion would be warranted by the contract whenever any citizens judged that the government did not further the public good. The purpose of government is to form a society free of anarchy. Since there are no agreed criteria of public good (PO §9), such a contract would effectively warrant rebellion whenever any individual or group deems the actions of government contrary to the public good: it would fail to free the society from anarchy.

The final objection Berkeley considers is that "whereas civil polity is a thing entirely human in institution, it seems contrary to reason to make submission to it part of the law of nature, and not rather civil law" (PO §25). Berkeley replies, first, that even if government "depends upon the arbitrary humour of men" as to its form and existence, this is no different from most institutions governed by natural law. Property relations are based on agreements, even though theft is forbidden by natural law. Matrimony is based upon agreements, even though adultery is forbidden by natural law. Second, although the forms of government vary, the tendency of humans to join together into societies is natural and therefore subject to natural law. Finally, Berkeley remarks, "And surely that precept which enjoins obedience to civil laws cannot itself, with any propriety, be accounted a civil law; it must therefore either have no obligation at all on the conscience, or, if it hath, it must be derived from the universal voice of nature and reason" (PO §25). If obedience to civil law is itself based on a law, that law cannot be a civil law. It must be a law of a different kind, a law that is "above" and having authority over civil laws: it must be a natural law.

With the conclusion of Section 25, Berkeley has completed his argument that the principle of obedience to the sovereign power has the status of a natural law. We have seen how the natural law, as a teleological theory, dovetails with ethical egoism. Secondary and tertiary natural laws prescribe how all members of a society and members of particular social strata ought to act; these laws tend to yield the greatest good for each and every member of a society. Insofar as he is concerned with the welfare of each and every member of society, rather than society as a whole, Berkeley's theory falls within the natural law tradition, rather than the utilitarian tradition.

But even if the natural law theory of *Passive Obedience* might be seen as a development or generalization of the views in the Notebooks, it's still a view Berkeley held in his youth. Was he still a natural lawyer when he published the *Alciphron* more than twenty years later? I believe he was, and I conclude this chapter with some general remarks on *Alciphron*.

Alciphron

Alciphron is a dialogue. In it Berkeley's spokespersons, Euphranor and Crito, defend orthodox Christianity from the attacks of "free thinkers" (philosophical agnostics) such as Bernard Mandeville (1670–1733) and Shaftesbury, who are represented by Lysicles and Alciphron. As readers we are plagued with two problems. First, Euphranor's (Berkeley's) clearest statement of a moral position is in Dialogue 1, Section 16, and the language there is ambiguous between natural law theory and utilitarianism. Second, Dialogues 2 and 3 are fundamentally critical: Dialogue 2 is usually taken to be a criticism of Mandeville's *Fable of the Bees*, and Dialogue 3 is usually taken to be a criticism of Shaftesbury's moral sense theory. Insofar as they are criticisms, we can determine what Berkeley's theory is only by gleaning the assumptions that lie under the criticisms. In spite of these problems, I shall argue that the texts are more favorable to a natural law interpretation than they are to a utilitarian interpretation.

Alciphron, Dialogue 1, Section 16 is a reply to Euphranor's question "whether the notions of your minute philosophy are worth proving," that is, "whether they are of use and service to mankind" (*A* 1.16, p. 60). To someone raised in the utilitarian tradition, some of Euphranor's remarks sound familiar. In reply to Alciphron's shunning usefulness for truth, Euphranor asks, "But is not the general good of mankind to be regarded as a rule or measure of moral truths, of all such truths as direct or influence the moral actions of men?" (*A* 1.16, p. 60). Euphranor and Alciphron agree that wise people act for a good end, that the most excellent end is happiness (*A* 1.16, p. 61), and that "the general happiness of mankind [is] a greater good than the private happiness of one man, or of some certain men," indeed, it is "the most excellent happiness" (*A* 1.16, p. 61). So Euphranor concludes, "he who promotes the general well-being of mankind, by the proper necessary means, is truly wise, and acts upon wise grounds" (*A* 1.16, p. 61), and "those men are foolish who go about to unhinge such principles as have a necessary connexion with the general good of mankind" (*A* 1.16, p. 62). While concerns with "the general happiness of mankind" might sound utilitarian, we have already seen that the natural lawyer would understand them as concerns with the happiness of each and every person. Hence the opening remarks are ambiguous between natural law and utilitarianism.

Claiming to have granted a dubious premise, Alciphron rejects the claim: "the general happiness of mankind to be a greater good than the particular happiness of one man. For in fact the individual happiness of every man alone constitutes his own entire good. The happiness of other men, making no part of mine, is not with respect to me a good: I mean a true natural good" (*A* 1.16, p. 62). Interestingly, *if* Berkeley's speakers championed a natural law theory, Alciphron has unwittingly played into their hands, for, according to natural law theory, individual happiness is the proper end of each and every individual. So, the question for the natural lawyer is whether the happiness of others "makes a part of mine," or at least, whether the happiness of others is a necessary means to my own happiness.

Euphranor introduces a model that is found throughout the remainder of *Alciphron*: a whole-parts model. The natural world is like a vegetable body, in which the parts work together toward a common end. The same model is extended to the moral world (*A* 1.16, p. 63). On such a scheme, "a wise man should consider and pursue his private good, with regard to and in conjunction with that of other men" (*A* 1.16, 63–64), since there is an interdependence between the ends of the whole and the ends of its parts.

This kind of holistic structure is typically assumed by natural lawyers. The suggestion that Euphranor identifies with the natural law tradition can only be strengthened by his allusions to classical proponents of natural law: the Stoics (*A* 1.16, pp. 63 and 64), Marcus Aurelius (*A* 1.16, p. 63), the Platonists, the Peripatetics, and, to a lesser extent, the Christians (*A* 1.16, p. 64). Of course, this is inconclusive evidence.

The Second Dialogue presents a criticism of the claim that engaging in private vices, for example, drunkenness, yields public good: vices are "good for the economy," as we would say today. The position criticized—the position defended by Lysicles—can be seen as a type of utilitarianism,[22] and this comes through in the Dialogue.

Euphranor's initial criticism focuses on drunkenness and may be summarized as follows. Excessive drinking causes illness and death. Hence, a temperate drinker will, in the course of her lifetime, consume more alcohol and other goods than a drunkard. Since "money spent innocently doth . . . circulate as well as that spent upon vice" (*A* 2.7, p. 72), and since *in the long run* more money would be spent by the temperate drinker, it follows that Lysicles' factual premise that more public good comes from drunkenness than temperance is false.

At the beginning of Section 10 Euphranor asks "whether the public good doth not imply the particular good of individuals" (*A* 2.10, p. 79). In contrast, Lysicles says, "the sprightly excesses of vice inspire men with joy. And where particulars rejoice, the public, which is made up of particulars, must do so too: that is, the public must be happy" (*A* 2.13, p. 83). Notice the differences in focus. Euphranor infers the happiness of the parts from the happiness of the whole; Lysicles infers the happiness of the whole from the happiness of the parts. This is precisely what one would expect from a natural lawyer and a utilitarian respectively. For the natural lawyer a society is like a complex machine. If the whole works well, this tends to mean that each of the parts is fulfilling its end: the same laws that lead to the greatest happiness of the whole, also tend to yield the greatest happiness of each of its parts. Why? Because the parts of the whole are integrated. In contrast, Lysicles emphasizes that the happiness of the whole is nothing more than the sum of the happiness of its parts, as one would expect from a utilitarian.

Proposing an alternative to a life ruled by sensual pleasure, Euphranor later compares the intellectual life to gold, the life of imagination to silver, and the sensual life to copper (*A* 2.14, 85–86), an analogy that is reminiscent of Plato's discussion of the tripartite soul in the *Republic*.[23] When Euphranor suggests that the pleasure of reason is both more perfect than that of sense and the imagination and the proper end for humans to seek (*A* 2.14, p. 86), this parallels Plato's suggestion that reason is a governing principle. Reason allows us to judge on the basis of past experience. It gives foresight (*A* 2.14, p. 87; cf. *PHK* I §31), thereby allowing us to avoid pain. It allows us to calculate, to discover the best balance of pleasure over pain (*A* 2.18, p. 94). Reason allows us to discover and directs us to pursue long-term goods, rather than the immediate short-term goods of the senses or imagination.

The focus on reason and long-term interests is well within the natural law tradition. The holistic emphasis is common among natural lawyers. And given the citations of such classical natural lawyers as Plato and Aristotle, it is not unreasonable to place Euphranor and Crito, and therefore Berkeley, within the natural law tradition. Such an interpretation is bolstered by the fact they assume a more complicated metaphysics than is assumed by Lysicles (*A* 2.25, p. 107).

In Dialogue Three the critical focus is on moral sense theories. Alciphron is made the defender of a Shaftesburian theory of morals. Euphranor and Crito focus the discussion on human ends and the cause of this alleged sense. Can there be "a certain vital principle of beauty, order, and harmony, diffused throughout the world" (*A* 3.10, p. 128) without an intentional cause of the order? Berkeley answers no, Crito puts it this way:

> Either you suppose this principle intelligent, or not intelligent: if the latter, it is all one with chance or fate, which was just now argued against: if the former, let me entreat Alciphron to explain to me wherein consists the beauty of a moral system, with a supreme Intelligence at the head of it which neither protects the innocent, punishes the wicked, nor rewards the virtuous. (*A* 3.10, p. 129)

Indeed, if the world is structured by an intelligent being toward an end, it is properly

> a design to promote the common benefit of the whole, and conforming their actions to the established laws and order of the divine parental wisdom: wherein each particular agent shall not consider himself apart, but as the member of a great City, whose author and founder is God: in which the civil laws are no other than the rules of virtue and the duties of religion: and where every one's true interest is combined with his duty (*A* 3.10, p. 129).

Notice that this rings of Christian natural law theory. As elements of a design, the interests of the parts comply with the interests of the whole: each individual plays a distinctive part in advancing the end of the whole, and in so doing advances her own end: "wisdom and virtue are the same thing" (*A* 3.10. p. 129). In Crito's scheme, virtue is subordinate to duty.[24] Concerns with purely moral duties are conspicuously absent in the Shaftesburian scheme.[25]

Crito stresses reward and punishment, which is common in a system of natural law. Even purely descriptive natural laws allow us to avoid physical pain (*PHK* §§31 and 146). Alciphron, following Shaftesbury, stresses that virtue cannot arise from a fear of punishment,[26] that virtue is practiced solely for its own beauty (*A* 3.13, p. 133).

Granting that some of the ancients held that virtue is its own reward, Crito argues that these same philosophers did not reject concerns with reward and punishment. Aristotle, for example, held that what are vulgarly esteemed the greatest goods—riches, honor, power, and bodily perfections—can also be means to harm (*A* 3.13, p. 134). Virtue might be its own reward if one is sufficiently wise, but for most people the hope of reward and fear of punishment are a means to coax people into a virtuous life, and Aristotle would not have disagreed (*A* 3.13, p. 135).

It is important to notice that the moral position championed by Euphranor and Crito, and therefore Berkeley, was one that focused on ends. These ends were understood as relative to a system and the intentions of a conscious being. Since design as the effect of a conscious, intentional being was central to Berkeley's position, proving the existence of a designer—God—was of central concern for Berkeley's moral theory. Hence, proof of the existence of God and the intelligibility of religious claims—the focus in the later dialogues of *Alciphron*—was needed to support his moral theory. All this tends to show that Berkeley was a natural lawyer.

A Look Back; A Look Ahead

There is evidence, then, that places Berkeley in the Christian natural law tradition. The Notebooks appear to champion a sophisticated form of ethical egoism. Such a view focuses on long-term interests and recognizes the need to cooperate with others, to attend to the interests of others as a means of obtaining our own ends. Natural law theories can be understood as generalized versions of ethical egoism: each and every person ought to seek what is in her long-term self-interest. The most general prescriptive natural laws describe the best means for each and every person in a society to obtain happiness; less general laws describe the additional means for persons playing a particular role in society to obtain happiness. This is the kind of position Berkeley defends in *Passive Obedience*. While the discussions of moral philosophy in Dialogues Two and

Three of *Alciphron* are primarily critical, rather than constructive, the criticisms are based upon tenets consistent with natural law theory. Further, the discussions of the existence of God and the intelligibility of religious terms in the later dialogues can be seen as an outgrowth of one of the major assumptions of Christian natural lawyers, namely, that the world was designed, and every object in the world has a purpose comparable to that of a part in a cosmic machine.

If my account of utilitarianism is correct, these considerations also speak against a utilitarian interpretation of Berkeley. If Berkeley was a utilitarian, he was a rule utilitarian. A rule utilitarian holds that a moral rule is justified if and only if it tends to yield the greatest happiness to a society as a whole. A utilitarian theory requires neither interconnections among members of a society nor a divinity, although some utilitarianism theories incorporate the divinity. If our account is correct, both the interconnectedness of members of a society and a divine designer are essential to Berkeley's theory. Thus, the positions in *Passive Obedience* and *Alciphron* are consistent with natural law, rather than utilitarianism.

A philosopher's moral and social theories usually run in tandem. If Berkeley's moral theory is an instance of natural law theory, we might expect his social theory to follow similar lines. Berkeley's social theory focuses on the economic welfare of Ireland, and there we shall find the same kind of interactive holistic perspective that focuses on the role of the parts relative to the whole that we found in *Alciphron*.

Further Reading

Scott Breuninger (2010). *Recovering Bishop Berkeley: Virtue and Society in the Anglo-Irish Context*, Palgrave Studies in Culture and Intellectual History. New York: Palgrave Macmillan.

Stephen Darwell (2005). "Berkeley's Moral and Political Philosophy," in Winkler (2005). *The Cambridge Companion to Berkeley*. Cambridge: Cambridge University Press, pp. 311–38.

Matti Häyry and Heta Häyry (1994). "Obedience to Rules and Berkeley's Theological Utilitarianism." *Utilitas* 6:233–42.

Paul J. Olscamp (1970). *The Moral Philosophy of George Berkeley*. The Hague: Martinus Nijhoff.

8
Economics and the Irish Condition

Berkeley's contribution to social philosophy was in economic theory, particularly a theory of the nature and use of money. It was occasioned by economic crises in England and Ireland. His principal work, *The Querist*, was originally published anonymously in three parts in 1735, 1736, and 1737; a revised edition under Berkeley's name was published in 1750. It is a work composed entirely of rhetorical questions. As we shall see, there are conceptual connections between Berkeley's economic and moral theories.

Interest in Berkeley's theories in these areas is primarily historical. Some scholars place Berkeley's work within a broadly utilitarian framework.[1]

We begin this chapter with some remarks on the economic condition of Ireland in the early eighteenth century. Then we discuss the South Sea Bubble, and Berkeley's initial economic discussion, *An Essay towards preventing the Ruin of Great Britain*, in which he ties economic problems to the lack of industry (labor). Finally we examine the economic theory of money in *The Querist*.

Eighteenth-Century Ireland and the South Sea Bubble

In the eighteenth century, Ireland was a British colony. England controlled portions of Ireland beginning in 1171. Originally the English pale consisted of Dublin and surrounding areas. In response to unrest among the native Irish, English control expanded during the reigns of Queen Elizabeth I and King James I to cover the whole of Ireland. It was an uneasy relationship. After the Reformation, England was a Protestant country; Ireland was predominantly Roman Catholic. The seventeenth century was a period of civil unrest in England: there was the English Civil War in the 1640s, the Commonwealth, the Restoration of the monarchy in 1661, and the Glorious Revolution of 1688. After fleeing England, King James II attempted to retain his control of Ireland by granting expanded rights to the Catholics. James and his followers were defeated, which resulted in greater restrictions on the Catholics. Most of the same restrictions applied to Protestants who were not members of the Anglican Church of Ireland, that is, the Dissenters (mostly Presbyterians in Ulster).

The early eighteenth century is known as the period of the Protestant Ascendency. The rights of Catholics were severely limited. With few exceptions, Catholics were not allowed to own land: more than 85 percent of Irish land was owned by Protestants. Large estates were sublet several times, ultimately to Irish farmers who typically cultivated only a few acres. Catholics were banned from attending the University of Dublin. They were not allowed to serve in the Irish Parliament. Further, the rights of the Irish Parliament were severely limited: the Irish Parliament could propose laws, but they could be ratified only by the British Parliament. In 1720, the British House of Lords became the supreme court of Ireland.

This system resulted in a wide split between the rich and the poor. The landowners became such either by inheritance or royal favor: some of the British military who served in Ireland were granted estates. The landowners were not always educated. They lived on the proceeds of their rents, often enjoying a life of luxury. Many of these luxuries were imported, for example, French wines and continental fashions. The tenant farmers, on the other hand, often subsisted on potatoes (Q 169), and when the potato crops failed, many starved. Insofar as there was a middle class, it was composed of government officials, artisans, and merchants.

This was the age of **mercantilism**, which was based on two fundamental principles: national wealth is based on international trade, and money is understood as **specie**, that is, gold or silver. These two elements were intimately related. If a country bought more products than it sold—if there was an unfavorable balance of trade—the balance was paid in gold. Since Ireland was a colony of Great Britain, Britain controlled Irish trade. For example, raw wool could be exported only to Great Britain, and wool products manufactured in Ireland could be sold only in Ireland. There were similar restrictions on the sale of beef and dairy products.

This was also the era of large stock companies. These companies were distinct from the government, but in a mercantilist society, their interests and the interests of the government corresponded. The East India Company dominated the English spice trade in the seventeenth century: when ships made a successful voyage, the profits were substantial. Another company, the South Sea Company, was established in 1711 to trade with Spanish America. A large portion of its business was to be in the slave trade. The South Sea Company guaranteed a return of 6 percent on its stock, and its first voyage in 1717 was moderately successful. In 1718, King George I became governor of the company, which significantly increased investor confidence. Interest paid on the stock rose to a rate of 100 percent of its par (original) value.

In 1720, the South Sea Company took over the British national debt of £50,000,000. It financed the debt through additional stock issues. In January 1720, company stock sold for £128½ per share. The Company issued stock in April for £300 per share, and in August for £1,000 per share. In August, the stock reached its peak of £1,050 per share. Much of the stock was sold on margin, that is, investors paid only a certain percentage of the buying price with a promise to pay the balance at a certain point in the future. With stock prices rising, this was a perfect situation for profit-taking. In September the markets collapsed. By December, South Sea stock was selling for only £124 per share.[2] This market collapse was known as the South Sea Bubble, since it was primarily caused by fluctuations in the value of South Sea Company stock.

An Essay towards Preventing of the Ruin of Great Britain

In 1721, Berkeley provided an analysis of causes of the South Sea Bubble. His *Essay towards preventing the Ruin of Great Britain* is his first economic essay, and it sounds themes that are developed further in *The Querist*. He appeals to "old-fashioned trite maxims concerning religion, industry, frugality, and public spirit" (*RGB* 69). These themes are consistent with his moral philosophy.

The *Essay* was written eight years after the *Guardian* essays and eleven years before *Alciphron*, but his first theme is consistent with both: the consequences of "free-thinking" (agnosticism) are detrimental to society. The remarks on religion are brief: religion is necessary for conscience, and conscience is necessary for virtue (*RGB* 69). The free-thinker confuses license with liberty, and short-term satisfaction with genuine self-interest (*RGB* 70). Genuine self-interest is long-term self-interest. Religion promotes constraint, and therefore public safety. Public safety thus justifies governmental suppression of free-thinking.

Berkeley's second theme is that industry (labor, work) is essential to a viable economy, a theme that comes to the fore in *The Querist*. He writes:

> Industry is the natural sure way to wealth. This is so true that it is impossible an industrious free people should want the necessaries and comforts of life, or an idle enjoy them under any form of government. Money is so far useful to the public as it promoteth industry, and credit having the same effect is of the same value with money; but money or credit circulating through a nation from hand to hand without producing labour and industry in the inhabitants, is direct gaming. (*RGB* 71)

Industry is a means to obtaining the necessities of life, that is, those goods that are necessary for health, and therefore, for happiness. Industry—working to obtain goods—is a major theme in Berkeley's economic works. Even as late as his *Word to the Wise* (1749), Church of Ireland Bishop Berkeley encourages the Roman Catholic clergy to do what they can to instill their parishioners with greater industry.[3]

How is the presumption that industry is the natural and best way to wealth relevant to the South Sea Bubble? Stock speculation is like poker. It can be a means to substantial monetary gain without labor. But there is no guarantee of gain by gambling, and there is at least an equal chance of loss. This possibility of income without labor "encourage[s] them to despise the slow moderate gains that are to be made by an honest industry" (*RGB* 71). Industry is necessary for sustained prosperity. Berkeley's commitment to labor as the means to self-subsistence is extended to the poor. He was no opponent of workhouses, in which the poor would be required to labor. He sketched a tax scheme to finance workhouses and to force the unemployed to work on roads and waterways as a way of taking them off the public dole. He even included childbearing under *industry*, since it would both provide needed workers and encourage their parents to work. This would allow domestic manufacture to replace many of the goods that had been obtained through international trade.

Frugality complements industry and opposes luxury. If prosperity is obtained by industry, it is conserved and increased by frugality. Frugality "is the nourishment and strength of bodies politic. It is that by which they grow and subsist" (*RGB* 72). The frugal person reinvests the fruits of industry into honest commerce (*RGB* 74). Reinvestment provides increased capital for manufacture, trade, and employment. Ultimately, frugality increases the common good.

Berkeley contrasts frugality with luxury. Under *luxuries* Berkeley includes fancy clothing and entertainments such as opera and masquerades. Did Berkeley believe these to be inherently evil? Maybe. He cites a passage from Isaiah 3:16–24 as evidence for the evil of extravagant dress (*RGB* 75–76), and he suggests that luxury bears other evils—"faction, ambition, envy, avarice, and . . . penury"—in its wake. He favors sumptuary laws (luxury taxes, *RGB* 76, 77; cf. *Works* 6:185) to limit expenditures on luxury items. He argues that expenditures on luxuries limit the domestic circulation of money. As we shall see when examining *The Querist*, Berkeley considered money valuable only insofar as it circulated broadly within a society. Luxuries do not yield broad circulation of money. In Berkeley's era, most luxury goods were imported, meaning that the local labor force gained nothing from the tendencies of some members of society to purchase luxury goods. While frugality promotes industry by reinvestment, purchasing luxury goods has the opposite effect.

Berkeley's fourth theme is public spirit. Berkeley ties this with religion (*RGB* 79). Here he shifts to considerations of governmental actions, that is, public expenditures. He proposes building "monuments of public services [that] have in former times been found great incentives to virtue and magnanimity, and would probably have the same effects on Englishmen which they have had on Greeks and Romans" (*RGB* 79), pillars of infamy condemning those that have committed crimes against society (*RGB* 79–80), public buildings (*RGB* 80–81), and an academy to compile a history of Great Britain (*RGB* 81). Why is this important? It would have two effects. On the one hand, it would be a public endorsement of the moral virtues Berkeley deems necessary for the greater good of society. On the other hand, it would foster industry: artisans, artists, and scholars would be employed, which would further the circulation of money.

So, how do these four elements fit together to explain the South Sea Bubble and prescribe a means for avoiding such catastrophes in the future? It is closely tied to Berkeley's theory of natural law. Religious duties are described and prescribed by the laws of nature, and virtues follow from them. While a purely rational person with sufficient information would be able to discover all those laws on the basis of reasoning—she would be able to calculate what is in the long-term self-interest of the individual as a member of a society with a certain structure, and therefore in the long-term interest of the society as a whole—most people would accept them only on religious authority. Following the laws of nature is the minimum condition for being public spirited. Industry and frugality in conjunction with the laws of nature are the best means to the general good of society and of each of its members.

Berkeley summarizes the situation in *Maxims concerning Patriotism* (1750), Section 27: "The patriot aims at his private good in the public. The knave makes the public subservient to his private interest. The former considers himself as part of a whole, the latter considers himself as the whole" (*Works* 6:254).

The Querist

The economic situation in early eighteenth century Ireland was far from ideal. For the Irish Catholic majority it was dire. *The Querist* proposes solutions to these economic problems. It does *not* propose a system for the redistribution of wealth, that is, it does not propose a system of taxation that would provide for the basic needs of the poor. Rather, *The Querist* presents a program for the generation of wealth. Its focus is on the Irish situation. Its program is consistent with the *Essay towards preventing of the Ruin of Great Britain*, but there is a difference in emphasis. While the *Essay* says little about the nature of money beyond, "Money is so far useful to the public as it promoteth industry, and credit having the same effect is of the same value with money; but money or credit circulating through a nation from hand to hand without producing labour and industry in the inhabitants, is direct gaming" (*RGB* 71), the nature of money comes to the fore in *The Querist*. Berkeley proposes a national bank that would issue paper currency not backed by specie (gold and silver). He emphasizes the development of a domestic Irish economy, while working within the constraints of British mercantile interests. In addition and related to this are concerns with the lack of frugality among the landed gentry and the lack of industry among the native Irish. I begin this discussion with some remarks on the monetary crisis in Ireland in the 1720s and 1730s. Then we shall turn to *The Querist*.

The Irish monetary system was based on the Irish pound, a monetary unit that was worth less than the British pound sterling. The typical rate of exchange was 13 Irish pounds to 12 pounds sterling, that is, £108 6s 8d Irish were equal to £100 pounds sterling.[4] No coins had been minted in Ireland since 1475, and in the early eighteenth century there was a monetary crisis. Many foreign coins circulated in Ireland. The value of money was determined by the value of the metal of which it was composed: one British pound sterling was equal to one troy pound of pure silver. The foreign coins that circulated in Ireland varied in purity of the gold or silver of which they were composed. So, commerce was hampered by the many rates of exchange of the circulating coins.[5] But most daily commerce required small-denomination coins, and of those there were few. Merchants resorted to promissory notes. Some banks printed paper money, but since all banks were privately owned and subject to failure, accepting bank notes was risky.

The British were not deaf to Irish calls for small coin. In 1722, William Wood was contracted by the British government to mint £100,800 Irish in copper coins over a period of fourteen years. The agreement was to mint no more than 30 pence of coins per pound of copper. At the time, copper sold for 12 pence per pound: the coins could have been undervalued. Further, the coins were not marked as legal tender, so there was no guarantee that they would be accepted at face value. There were protests. The coins were never distributed.

We may now turn to *The Querist*.

As in the *Essay*, the Berkeley of *The Querist* identifies industry as the source of prosperity (Q 1). In an industrious society, everyone should have ample means to meet her basic necessities (Q 2), and governments should do what they can to encourage industry (Q 3). The circulation of money is useful insofar as it is a means of increasing industry (Q 5–6), and even the natural tendency of humans to seek power (Q 7) is a desire to direct industry (Q 35).

What causes people to be industrious? Berkeley suggests it is a matter of fashion (Q 10). Fashion creates appetites, which result in actions, that is, industry (Q 9). So, if fashion were to change, there would be a comparable change in the direction of industry. This had implications for both the top and bottom economic tiers of society. The Anglo-Irish gentry lived well and imported many luxuries from continental Europe. The Irish tenant farmers lived poorly and subsisted on little more than potatoes. Berkeley proposed a change of fashion. Regarding the poor Berkeley asked, "Whether the creating of wants be not the likeliest way to produce industry in a people? And whether, if our peasants were accustomed to eat beef and wear shoes, they would not be more industrious?" (Q 20). Berkeley's focus, however, was on the gentry.

The gentry imported wine from France. Their clothing imported from the continent was the mark of fashion. Their homes were built with wood imported from Norway. Many were absentee landlords, and those who lived in Ireland but imported most of their goods differed little from absentee landlords (Q 104). None of those actions supported the Irish economy. Further, given the restrictions on the woolen trade and the profitability of exporting raw wool, there was a shift from renting land for tillage to sheep grazing, which yielded greater profits by requiring less labor. So the landlords, who gained the most from Irish labor while engaging in no labor themselves, did almost nothing to further the Irish economy. This is another manifestation of the problem of "luxury" Berkeley condemned in the *Essay*.

Berkeley's proposed solution was to develop a largely closed, self-sufficient Irish economy. His approach took several tacks. He suggested that fashions could and should be changed. He proposed a monetary system that would be for the Irish and nearly worthless outside of Ireland. He suggested loosening laws that limited the economic opportunities of the Roman Catholics. The system would be overseen and directed by the government, since those governing are in the best position to understand the needs of the whole (cf. *PO* §19). This could work, however, only if those eligible for public office were well-educated (Q 15, 185, 195, 203, 330).

The concern with fashion focused largely on the practices of the Anglo-Irish gentry. He asked, "How far the vanity of our ladies in dressing, and of our gentlemen in drinking, contributes to the general misery of the people?" (Q 102). He answered this question by detailing the imports that typified gentry life: Their houses were built from Norwegian fir (Q 117). The ladies identified fashion with French silk and lace from Flanders (Q 144). If such fashions were changed, the whole of Ireland could flourish. What did Berkeley have in mind? It was *not* a matter of taxing the rich to support the poor—he was critical of the English tax to support the poor (Q 376)—although Berkeley did favor sumptuary laws (luxury taxes) on imported goods (Q 103, 422; cf. *Works* 6:175). He proposed a change in fashion from dress to housing, and the construction of that housing from native materials—resulting in houses that would be both warmer and safer than houses built from imported softwoods (Q 118). If the houses were then furnished with goods made in Ireland, and if there were well-tended gardens, Irish hands would be employed both in the building and maintaining of the estate, thereby furthering the Irish economy. He put the question this way:

> Whether larger houses, better built and furnished, a greater train of servants, the difference with regard to equipage and table between finer and coarser, more and less elegant, may not be sufficient to feed a reasonable share of vanity, or support all proper distinctions? And whether all these may not be procured by domestic industry out of the four elements, without ransacking the four quarters of the globe? (Q 119; cf. Q 123, 201, 398–405, 413–14)

Such estates would be comparable to Italian palaces, which were constructed and maintained without foreign trade (Q 120). Similarly, if the gentry shifted from drinking French claret to drinking Irish mead and cider, this would encourage Irish industry (Q 123, 538, cf. Q 152). In short, Berkeley's purpose was neither to deprive the gentry of their estates nor to require them to work nor to restructure society in any significant way. It was rather to change the fashion: by shifting the gentry's interests from imported goods to native goods, more of the Irish would be employed and the Irish economy could be expected to flourish.

Berkeley was also concerned with changing the fashions at the bottom of the economy, that is, changing the desires of the native Irish. Berkeley's remarks on the native Irish are anything but complimentary (see Q 19, 132, 357, 512). He believed that if their tastes changed, there would be more industry, and therefore more prosperity. He asks, "Whether the creating of wants be not the likeliest way to produce industry in a people? And whether, if our peasants were accustomed to eat beef and wear shoes, they would not be more industrious?" (Q 20; cf. Q 112, 169, 353). If Irish peasants were better fed and clothed, they would be healthier and, therefore, happier. He takes industry to be the sole basis for obtaining goods. Desire inspires industry. So, he concludes, changing the desires of peasants would make the native Irish more industrious.

The focus is on industry. Even if the top economic echelon remains committed to luxury, which is essentially nonproductive, the shift from imported goods to domestic goods would employ more Irish workers and would require the increased domestic manufacture of goods. Similarly, if the peasants' desires for food and clothing were upgraded, this would increase Irish manufacture. Berkeley believed, then, that shifts in the "fashions" desired by those at the top and the bottom of the economy would stimulate the economy as a whole.

We should notice that Berkeley was committed to the principle that each person should earn her own way. While the good bishop could have quoted the biblical injunction "If any one will not work, let him not eat" (2 Thessalonians 3:10), Berkeley the querist points in much the same direction when asking, "Whether it be true that in the Dutch workhouses things are so managed that a child four years old may earn its own livelihood?" (*Q* 373). He suggested that criminals should be used to construct public works (*Q* 53, 387, 389), and beggars might be enslaved for the same purpose for a period of years (*Q* 384–387). Presumably, the latter practice would encourage beggars to find gainful employment.

But what should be done to encourage industry? Berkeley answers this in terms of the relationship between money and industry, a theory of money as credit, and a proposal for a national bank.

Some of Berkeley's early queries suggest that money and the circulation of money produce industry. He asked, "Whether money be not only so far useful, as it stirreth up industry, enabling men mutually to participate the fruits of each other's labour? Whether any other means, equally conducing to excite and circulate the industry of mankind, may not be as useful as money. Whether the real end and aim of men be not power? And whether he who could have everything else at his wish or will would value money?" (*Q* 5–7). Industry is the means to a prosperous nation (*Q* 1). Money is a means to increase industry. It is a means by which we can acquire those goods we desire. So, money is valuable only insofar as it allows us to obtain those goods we desire; if there were no desires, money would have no value (cf. *Q* 35). Wealth itself is not understood in monetary terms; rather, as Berkeley already suggested in the *Essay*, it is found in industry, frugality, the size of the population, and the interrelations of those factors (*Q* 217–18; cf. *Q* 423). Nor is money as such a means to industry and prosperity; it is primarily the circulation of money that yields industry and prosperity. For this reason, currency in small denominations does more to promote industry than large-denomination currency, since it circulates more readily (*Q* 468–82). The shortage of small coins in Berkeley's own day restricted domestic commerce. Those considerations are addressed by Berkeley's theory of money and a national bank.

Theories of money in the early eighteenth century were based upon specie; that is, the value of a piece of currency was either equal to the value of the precious metal of which it was composed or it was a token that represented a certain amount of that metal. Berkeley asks whether money-as-metal is intrinsically valuable: "Whether money is to be considered as having an intrinsic value, or as being a commodity, a standard, a measure, or a pledge, as is variously suggested by writers? And whether the true idea of money, as such, be not altogether that of a ticket or counter?" (Q 23). If precious metals were inherently valuable, then countries with unmined gold reserves would be deemed wealthy, but they are not (Q 29; cf. Q 283–87). If the "value or price of things be not a compounded proportion, directly as the demand, and reciprocally as the plenty" (Q 24), then "the terms crown, livre, pound sterling, etc., . . . [may] be considered as exponents or denominations of such proportion," that is, they function only as counters marking proportions (Q 25). But if currency does nothing more than mark proportions, there is no inherent reason that those counters need to be made of or backed by precious metals. Berkeley was aware that Rhode Islanders had devised a form of paper money to fulfill that function. Indeed, because of the shortage of coins in Ireland, merchants had recourse to promissory notes, and private banks had issued paper money. Money is fundamentally credit. At a basic level, it is no more than marks on a ledger sheet, and currency consists of tokens representing such marks.

In Rhode Island, the currency was backed by land: it was issued as loans on land. Banking practices in Rhode Island were inflationary, a problem Berkeley traced to self-serving legislators (Q 247). But the Rhode Island scheme was instructive. Berkeley proposed a system of Irish paper money and monetary tokens backed by a national bank.

In the original edition of *The Querist*, considerable space was devoted to the national bank; by the 1750 edition the question of forming an Irish national bank was moot, and *The Querist* was pared of many of its earlier entries. Berkeley proposed forming a government-owned and -controlled bank. It would engage in normal savings and loan activities, but it would also issue paper money and coins (tokens) minted in Ireland (cf. Q 94, 485, 573, 575). This was not to be money backed by specie; it was to be legal tender backed solely by the reputation of the Irish government. Profits were to go to the government. It was to be overseen by a committee of twenty-one government officials, "one third of these persons in great office for the time being, the rest members of either House of Parliament, some whereof to go out by lot and as many to come in by ballot once in two years" (*Works* 6:186). The initial fund for this bank was to be raised by a combination of taxes on wine, the mortgage of land, and funds from the Irish government (*Works* 6:185). A fundamental function of the bank would be to issue a sufficient amount of currency to fuel the industry of the Irish. He asked, "Whether a national bank be not the true philosopher's stone in a State?" (Q 459).

Berkeley's queries address certain objections. He takes the Bank of Amsterdam as a model of the efficiency and success of a publicly owned bank that issues paper money and conducts banking by check (Q 44, 221, 230, 241–43, 250, 293–302). Given this precedent, his potential critics should grant the plausibility of his scheme. Should anyone suggest that an Irish mint issuing money strictly for Ireland is contrary to broader British interests, he notes that similar schemes were undertaken in Sicily and Naples while they were colonies of the Spanish and Austrians without untoward consequences (Q 94, 575).

While his theory of money and his proposal for a national bank stand at the center of his discussion in *The Querist*—proposals that he believed would stimulate the Irish economy once the "fashions" favored by the gentry and the native Irish shifted—they were not his only proposals. He suggests that Catholics might be granted certain property rights if they denied the temporal authority of the pope in favor of the king: "Whether a scheme for the welfare of this nation should not take in the whole inhabitants? And whether it be not a vain attempt, to project the flourishing of our Protestant gentry, exclusive of the bulk of the natives? Whether an oath, testifying allegiance to the king, and disclaiming the pope's authority in temporals, may not be justly required of the Roman Catholics? . . . Whether there is any such thing as a body of inhabitants, in any Roman Catholic country under the sun, that profess an absolute submission to the pope's orders in matters of an indifferent nature, or that in such points do not think it their duty to obey the civil government?" (Q 255–57). "And whether the suffering Roman Catholics to purchase forfeited lands would not be good policy, as tending to unite their interest with that of the government?" (Q 265). After suggesting that Ireland should have a second college (Q 187–190), he also suggested that Roman Catholics should be given broader educational rights, although such a proposal is not without economic and political considerations: "Whether, in imitation of the

Jesuits at Paris, who admit Protestants to study in their colleges, it may not be right for us also to admit Roman Catholics into our college, without obliging them to attend chapel duties, or catechisms, or divinity lectures? And whether this might not keep money in the kingdom, and prevent the prejudices of a foreign education?" (Q 191).

Thus, Berkeley's social philosophy focuses on developing conditions that would improve the economic well-being of Ireland as a whole and would tend to improve the economic status of each Irishman. Since a philosopher's social philosophy typically reflects her moral philosophy, this is the approach one would expect from a natural lawyer. By refocusing the tastes of both the gentry and the native Irish, Berkeley suggests that Ireland could develop a relatively independent domestic economy. This economic independence would be furthered by an Irish currency not backed by specie, a currency that could be produced in denominations that would meet the needs of the Irish economy. But because this currency would not be backed by specie, it effectively would be of value only in Ireland, furthering domestic industry and discouraging international commerce.

Berkeley's economic scheme failed in the sense that it had no impact on Irish policy: no Irish national bank was established during Berkeley's lifetime, no Irish paper currency was introduced, and both the gentry and the native Irish continued to follow the "fashions" prevalent at the beginning of the century. On the other hand, within the past century, his proposal to separate currency from metallic specie has become standard monetary policy throughout most of the world.[6]

Further Reading

Constantine George Caffentizis (2000). *Exciting the Industry of Mankind: George Berkeley's Philosophy of Money*. Dordrecht: Kluwer Academic Publishers.
Joseph Johnston (1970). *Bishop Berkeley's Querist in Historical Perspective*. Dunkirk: Dundalgan Press.
Patrick Kelly (2005). "Berkeley's Economic Writings," in Winkler (2005), pp. 339–68.

9

Concluding Remarks

Our journey through Berkeley's philosophical writings is now complete. I have attempted to present a philosophically plausible and textually charitable reading of Berkeley's works. The goal was to find coherent readings of the individual works and conceptual ties among his works. We examined the works in the order in which they were written. Since Berkeley engaged in philosophical contemplation for a period of more than forty years, this approach does not assume that Berkeley held the same views throughout his philosophical career.

After a brief discussion of Berkeley's life and works, we turned to a discussion of the *New Theory of Vision*. Taking our cue from a remark in the *Theory of Vision . . . Vindicated*, that Berkeley used the method of analysis in *New Theory of Vision* (*TVV* §38), we began by sketching an account of an analytic method. Analysis, as it was understood in the seventeenth and early eighteenth centuries, is a search for explanatory principles. It is comparable to what later philosophers called *abduction* or *argument to the best explanation*. We showed that Berkeley criticized the standard geometrical account of visual perception and championed an empirical account. Both accounts are found in Descartes's *Optics*, although Berkeley's account goes far beyond its Cartesian roots. He shows how a correlation of aspects of visual ideas with tactile ideas explains how we can see distance and magnitude, even though both distance and magnitude are properly ideas of touch. He showed that one of the implications of considering Molyneux's blind-man-made-to-see is—as Locke failed to recognize—that the objects of sight and touch are distinct from one another.

We examined Berkeley's criticisms of abstract ideas in Chapter 3. Although his focus was on Locke's account, his criticisms cut across ancient, medieval, and modern traditions. Nor are all his distinctions found in Locke's account. He argued that he could not, in fact, form an abstract idea by separation of ideas and that the abstractionists were committed to an inconsistent triad of principles. He argued that abstract ideas are not needed to ground the meanings of general terms. And he argued that even the best account of abstraction—Locke's—entails that abstract ideas are inconsistent and, therefore, cannot be formed.

Turning to the body of the *Principles* in Chapter 4, we noted that many scholars believe Berkeley's most basic arguments for idealism and immaterialism fail, and, therefore, that the edifice he builds upon them is unsound. I believe that if an important philosopher appears to give poor arguments, it is incumbent upon us to explore the assumptions upon which the philosopher builds those arguments. Since the nominal topic of the *Principles* is knowledge, we explored the possibility that Berkeley, like Descartes, built his ontology on epistemic foundations. Our approach to the texts was minimalist: conclusions we attributed to Berkeley were no stronger than his arguments warranted. I argued that the first seven sections of the *Principles* show that ordinary objects are composed of *at least* ideas and that the only kind of substance is mental, although there is no analysis of the nature of mental substance. Sections 8–24 show that material substance cannot be known and, therefore, there is no reason to include material substance in our ontology. Sections 25–33 show that there are at least two minds and that ordinary objects are composed solely of ideas of sense. But the critic might contend that none of this is plausible since Berkeley provides no explicit argument for the existence of ideas, a claim upon which his entire metaphysics is built. Coming to the *Principles* after the *New Theory of Vision*, we noted that the Berkeley of the *Principles* did exactly what one would expect if he followed the method of analysis: he *assumed* the existence of ideas as objects of knowledge and took that assumption to be justified only if the philosophical system he developed on that basis is cogent.

The *Three Dialogues between Hylas and Philonous* is often treated as little more than a popular restatement of the case for idealism and immaterialism. Here Berkeley focuses on immaterialism. While he builds his ontology on epistemic foundations, the approach is different from that found in the *Principles*. The *Three Dialogues* defends immaterialism by drawing out the skeptical consequences of the doctrine of material substance, showing that none of those skeptical consequences apply to immaterialism, and that the only skeptical attacks to which immaterialism is subject also apply to the doctrine of material substance.

Chapter 6 focuses on knowledge of mind. In the *Principles* it is assumed that we have a notion of mind as that which perceives ideas and acts (*PHK* §2). His remarks there do not commit Berkeley to the claim that we have special access to our own minds; they are consistent with holding that all minds are known indirectly on the basis of the perceptual and causal relations in which they stand. While it is a recurrent theme that we have no ideas of minds and their acts, the *Principles* provide no clue to the source of our notion of mind. In the Third Dialogue, however, Berkeley says, "I know what I mean by the terms *I* and *myself*; and I know this immediately, or intuitively, though I do not perceive it as I perceive a triangle, a colour, or a sound" (*DHP* 232). His remarks on reflex acts explain how we might have direct access to our own minds, but they do not explain how we have a notion of mind as that which perceives and acts. Thus we asked whether we might know the notion by intuition. I argued that the most plausible sense of *intuition* takes it to consist of assumptions common across philosophical traditions. These are putative claims of conceptual necessity, and as such they entail no existence claims. They can be taken to imply existence only if they provide the basis for a cogent analysis.

Turning to Berkeley's moral philosophy in Chapter 7, we saw how the egoistic musings in the Notebooks were developed into a full-blown natural law theory in *Passive Obedience* and *Alciphron*. A natural law theory of ethics is consistent with his early metaphysics. I argued that it is more plausible to place his account in the natural law tradition than in the utilitarian tradition insofar as Berkeley stressed that the good of the whole society is based on laws that tend to benefit each and every individual in a society.

We concluded with a brief review of Berkeley's economic theories in Chapter 8. I showed that his economic theories are consistent with a natural law theory of morality.

So, as we reach the end of this book are you in a position to say that you know what Berkeley held? No. First, we have not examined all of Berkeley's works. I have said nothing about his works in mathematics and natural science, since I claim little expertise in either of those disciplines or their histories.[1] Nor have I discussed Berkeley's final philosophical work, *Siris*, which appears to develop a metaphysical position that is inconsistent with the idealism and immaterialism of his early works.[2] Since this is an introduction to Berkeley's philosophy, and since introductory studies focus on the *Principles* and the *Three Dialogues*, I saw no reason to muddy the waters by attempting to provide an account of the philosophy in *Siris*.

Second, I always tell my history of philosophy students that all interpretations of significant philosophical works are wrong, at least in detail. For this reason, they should not place confidence in secondary sources. There is no reason to believe my work is an exception to that principle. You might not find some of my arguments persuasive. For example, if my account of our knowledge of our own minds leaves you with questions, you should read other interpretations. Or if you find reason to believe that my distinction between utilitarianism and natural law theory is problematic, you will need to revisit the discussion of Berkeley's moral theory. But any secondary source only gives one person's attempt to make sense of the texts. The only way you can know what *Berkeley* held is to read Berkeley's works. The only way you can understand Berkeley's philosophy is to think very hard about what he wrote and develop philosophical models for understanding those writings. And as your philosophical acumen increases, your understanding of what Berkeley held and how he defended his views is likely to change.

In this book I have followed the first half of Berkeley's recommendation to his American correspondent Samuel Johnson:

> I could wish that all the things I have published on these philosophical subjects were read in the order wherein I published them, once, to take in the design and connection of them, and a second time with a critical eye, adding your own thought and observation upon every part as you went along. (B-J 4 §3; *Cor.* 319)

Berkeley's suggestion that one can understand "the design and connection" of his works in a single reading was optimistic. I've been studying the works of Berkeley and his contemporaries for nearly forty years, and I regularly notice elements of the texts, connections among the texts, and connections between Berkeley and the works of his contemporaries that I had not seen before.

I have not focused on Berkeley's call for criticism. As a *historian* of philosophy, I believe it is my duty to provide a consistent and plausible interpretation of the texts. Berkeley writes well. But as many discussions show, it is easy to raise criticisms. *Fair* criticism

Concluding Remarks

requires an understanding of his arguments and his methods of inquiry. I hope this book has furthered that understanding.

Of course, *you* are a budding philosopher. *Your* interests in Berkeley might not be the same as mine. If you're interested in contemporary philosophical issues, what can you gain by studying Berkeley?

The dominant metaphysical position in the early twenty-first century is metaphysical materialism, the view that every existent is either material or depends upon matter for its existence. Metaphysical materialism and metaphysical (Berkeley's) idealism stand in diametric opposition. *Some* materialists might simply assume the existence of matter—just as Hylas did—and develop their theories from there. Careful philosophers worry about their most basic assumptions. So careful materialists must at least show that arguments against the existence of matter—Berkeley's arguments—fail.

"But," you might contend, "Berkeley builds his account on an archaic theory of ideas. Nobody still takes ideas or their philosophical heirs, sense-data, seriously. So, it should be easy to show that Berkeley's arguments fail."

But it's not that easy. Assume you can develop a coherent theory of the nature of matter. Assume you can show that your theory of matter can explain all phenomena in the natural world, including brain-states. Assume, further, that by explaining brain-states materialistically, you do away with any basis for claiming the independent existence of mental states. Given the method of analysis—Berkeley's method—this would be sufficient to show that all existents are material. What exists depends upon your theory of what there is; in W. V. Quine's famous words, "to be the value of a [bound] variable."[3] But a theory is a mental construction, even if that mind itself is material. So, your materialism is rooted in idealism.

Can't you imagine Berkeley smiling?

Endnotes

Chapter 1

1 Most of the details about Berkeley's life are taken from Luce (1949), Gaustad (1979), and Berman (1994).
2 As we shall see, Berkeley uses the word *materialism* differently. He calls anyone a *materialist* who claims that matter exists, even if she *also* holds that minds exist.
3 Stephens (1982), p. 27.
4 Quoted in Luce (1949), p. 142.
5 Armstrong (1960), pp. 2–9.

Chapter 2

1 Pitcher (1977), pp. 5–20; see also Armstrong (1960), pp. 9–15.
2 Pitcher (1977), pp. 38–41.
3 Atherton (1990), p. 7.
4 Atherton (1990), pp. 16–57.
5 Atherton (1990), pp. 177–83.
6 Atherton (1990), pp. 183–94.
7 Hight (2008), p. 239; cf. Pitcher (1977), p. 57.
8 Hight (2008), p. 237.
9 Turbayne (1963), p. vii.
10 Turbayne (1970), pp. 28–53.
11 Kant (1977), p. 23n.
12 See Flage and Bonnen (1999).

Notes to pages 24–55

13 Galilei (1967), p. 51; Newton (1952), pp. 404–5; cf. Newton (1966), pp. 398–400; Boyle (no date).
14 See Arnauld and Nicole (1996), pp. 233–39; Watts (1996), pp. 330–32; Hutcheson (2006), p. 54.
15 See Peirce (1940); Lipton (1991); Hanson (1961). For a more complete discussion of the method of analysis, see Randall (1940); Turbayne (1970), pp. 28–53, Flage and Bonnen (1999), pp. 13–71; Flage (2011).
16 Atherton (1990), p. 80.
17 Malebranche (1980), pp. 34–35, and 41–44.
18 Molyneux (1709), pp. 103–4.
19 Barrow (1669).
20 Cf. Molyneux (1709), p. 104; Malebranche (1980), pp. 44–45.
21 Molyneux (1709), p. 104, Malebranche (1980), pp. 44–45.
22 Cummins (1987).
23 Cf. Molyneux (1709), pp. 103ff.
24 Hume (2000), 1.2.1, ¶ 4, p. 24.
25 Hume (1999), p. 135.
26 Descartes, *CSM* 2:50, 54; Locke, *Essay* 2.13.26, 2.14.26, 2.27.1, Hume (2000), 1.2.2 ¶9, p. 26.
27 See, for example, Tipton (1974); Pitcher (1977); Bennett (1971); Roberts (2007).
28 See also *TVV* §11; Intro. §22; *PHK* §1.

Chapter 3

1 Craig (1968); Pitcher (1977), pp. 62–90; Tipton (1974), pp. 133–52; cf. Bennett (1971), pp. 35–39.
2 See Pappas (2000), pp. 31–32; Fields (2011), pp. 117–47.
3 Aaron (1967), pp. 18–66.
4 Weinberg (1967); Muehlmann (1992), pp. 7–76.
5 Mackie (1976), pp. 115–16.
6 Plato, *Phaedo*, 72e–92e; *Meno* 81c–98a.
7 See St. Thomas Aquinas, *Summa Theologica*, Part I, Question 40, Article 3, body, ¶1; Part I, Question 44, Article 3, Reply 3; Part I, Question 79, Article 4, body, ¶2; Question 85, Article 1, body, ¶1; Part I, Question 85, Article 1, Replies 1 and 2; Part I, Question 88, Article 2, body.
8 Pappas (2000), pp. 73–79.
9 *Works* 2:125; see also Berkeley (1987), pp. 74–75.
10 Cf. Craig (1968).
11 Wittgenstein (1958).
12 Cf. Locke, *Essay* 4.3.30, 4.4.17; Hume (1999), p. 99.
13 See, for example, Craig (1968); Pitcher (1977), pp. 62–90.
14 Arnauld and Nicole (1996), pp. 35–36.

Chapter 4

1 Muehlmann (1995b), p. 1.
2 Dicker (2011), pp. 68–69 and 83.
3 Dicker (2011), pp. 73–75; cf. Bennett (1971), pp. 31–35.
4 Pitcher (1977), p. 93.
5 Pitcher (1977), p. 94.
6 Dicker (2011), pp. 70–71 and 73–75.
7 I argue below that Section 5 is an explanation of an error.
8 Dicker (2011), pp. 79–80.
9 Allaire (1963); cf. Hausman and Hausman (1995), p. 53.
10 See, for example, T. E. Jessop's comments in *Works* 2:8–9, and 2:41n1; Luce (1945), pp. 39–40; Ayers (1975), p. 89n; Grayling (1986), p. 50; Berman (1994), p. 21.
11 On ideas of reflection, see Flage (2006).
12 Cf. Luce (1963), p. 30.
13 Yolton (1984), p. 135; cf. Winkler (1989), p. 172.
14 See Hight (2008), pp. 11–22, 138–176 *passim*.
15 Hume (1999), p. 203n.
16 Berkeley claims intuitive knowledge of the existence of his own soul in much the same way that Locke does. See *N* 563, *A* 4.5, p. 147; cf. Locke, *Essay* 4.9. We discuss this further in Chapter 6.
17 Cf. Kant (1977), p. 36–37.
18 On the primary/secondary qualities distinction, see also Boyle (1666).
19 See, for example, Winkler (1989), pp. 30–31, and Doney (1983).
20 Suarez (1994), Disputation 18, §7, pp. 131–77, and Disputation 17, Introductory Remarks, p. 3.
21 For a more detailed discussion of this point, see Flage (2003).
22 Locke (1963), p. 21; cf. Locke (1963), p. 42.
23 I discuss relative ideas and notions in greater detail in Chapter 6.
24 For example, Nicholas Malebranche wrote, "A true cause as I understand it is one such that the mind perceives a necessary connection between it and its effect." Malebranche (1980), p. 450; cf. Locke, *Essay* 2.31.6.
25 Winkler (1989), p. 184. Cf. Muehlmann (1995b), pp. 4–5; J. O. Urmson, *Berkeley*, p. 45; Prior (1955); Williams (1973), p. 27; Tipton (1974), pp. 158–78; Pitcher (1977), pp. 113–15.
26 Cummins (1990).
27 Berkeley explicitly avoids the use of *person* (*N* 713), in part, perhaps, because of Locke's distinction between person and substance in *Essay* 2.21.
28 Luce (1945), pp. 99–102; Fogelin (2001), p. 68; Dancy (1987), p. 43; Pitcher (1977), p. 133; Muehlmann (1992), pp. 249–50; Umbaugh (2000), pp. 50–51; Tipton (1974), pp. 316–29; Bettcher (2008), pp. 122–29; Jones

(2009), pp.112–15; Fields (2011), pp. 201–9. Cf. Bennett (1971), p. 165, Berman (1994), pp. 45ff; Johnston (1965), p. 194.
29 Dicker (2011), pp. 73–75.
30 *Hamlet* Act 5, Scene 1.
31 Cf. Dicker (2011), p. 69.
32 Bracken (1974), pp. 42–43.

Chapter 5

1 Dicker (2011), pp. 84–145.
2 Cf. Hausman and Hausman (1995).
3 Exceptions are Stoneman (2002) and Garrett (2008).
4 See Bayle (1965), s.v. "Pyrrho," p. 195.
5 Sextus Empiricus (1933), Book I, Section 19, p. 15. Further references to the *Outlines of Pyrrhonism* (*OP*) will be made parenthetically by book and section numbers.
6 Popkin (2003), pp. 3–43.
7 Notice that this is a special sense of the word *materialism*. Most people who discuss materialism hold that only material objects exist, or that if immaterial objects exist, they depend for their existence on material objects.
8 See, for example, Pappas (2000), pp. 209–34; Bordner (2011).
9 Cf. *OP* I, §124. In his representation of the sixth mode, Diogenes Laertius explicitly alludes to mixtures with heat. See Diogenes Laertius (1925), 2:497.
10 On color see *OP* I, §§44, 46, 105, 120, 125.
11 On theoretical virtues, see Schick and Vaughn (1999), pp. 161–70; cf. Flage (2004b), pp. 294–308. See also the discussion of abstraction in Chapter 2. In addition to the purely theoretical reasons for the discussion, Berkeley probably wanted to distinguish his theory from those of Malebranche and others, since some of his critics suggested there were similarities to Malebranche and Norris. See the letter from Percival of 30 October 1710, *Cor.* 47–48.
12 Cf. Suarez (1994), Disputation 18, §7, pp. 131–77, and Disputation 17, Introductory Remarks, p. 3; Fourth Objections (Arnauld) in *CSM* 2:146–48.
13 One might believe that Berkeley would hold to one of the standard accounts of the relation, for example, inherence, but all references to inherence in the *Dialogues* are made with respect to an alleged material substance (see DHP_1 176, 180, 181, 183, 185, 186, 188, 189, 190, 192; DHP_3 230, 234).
14 Cf. Sextus Empiricus (1936), Book I, Sections 162–66.
15 Hume (2000), I.iv.6, pp. 164–71.

Chapter 6

1 Hume (2000), 1.4.6 ¶4, cf. 1.4.2 ¶39.
2 Muehlmann (1978); Muehlmann (1992), pp. 107–10 and 170–204; Muehlmann (1995c); Daniel (2008b); Daniel (2013).
3 Flage (1986a); Flage (1986b), especially pp. 133–72.
4 Reid (1969), p. 7.
5 See also Locke (1963), 4:21; Hume (2000), 2.6.9, p. 49, 4.5.19, p. 158; Hume (1999), p. 146n; compare the discussion of *determinations* in Arnauld and Nicole (1996), pp. 45, 89–94.
6 Aristotle (1984), *Metaphysics*, 1017^{b}23–25.
7 Aristotle (1984), *Metaphysics*, 1017^{b}15–17.
8 See *PHK* §78 where the identification is explicit. It also follows from his discussion of primary and secondary qualities, *PHK* §§9–15.
9 Which is not to say the critics of the doctrine of substance were unwilling to do so. See David Hume's (satirical?) discussion of substance at Hume (2000) I.iv.5, ¶¶ 17–28, pp. 157–61.
10 See Cummins (1982).
11 Obviously this is a sketch in very broad strokes. For more details on Locke, see Odegard (1969). A more complete account would need to distinguish between relations and connections, the latter which might obtain between ideas, or between substances, or between ideas and substances.
12 Luce (1945); see also Jessop's footnote to Berkeley's *Works* 2:41n1; Johnston (1965), Cornman (1975), p. 104; Grayling (1986), p. 50; Berman (1994), p. 21; Ayers (1975), p. 89n1; Adams (1979), p. xxiv; and McGowan (1982), p. 232. This position is not universally granted. See Hicks (1932), p. 108; Urmson (1992), p. 109; Pappas (2000), p. 106; Flage (2006); Dicker (2011), p. 68.
13 See, for example, Bettcher (2007).
14 And it is an open question whether he did. See Winkler (1989), pp. 53–75.
15 At *Essay* 2.9.2 Locke claims to have intuitive knowledge of his own existence, and his argument in 2.9.3 is reminiscent of Descartes's *Cogito*.
16 Sextus Empiricus (1933), Book I, Section 19, p. 15.
17 See Chapter 2.
18 Dicker (2011), p. 230.
19 If my arguments regarding the *Principles* are cogent, then an analogous case can be made regarding the Author of Nature in the *New Theory of Vision*.
20 See, for example, Luce (1945), pp. 99–102; Fogelin (2001), p. 68; Dancy (1987), p. 43; Pitcher (1977), p. 133; Muehlmann (1992), pp. 249–50; Umbaugh (2000), pp. 50–51; Tipton (1974), pp. 316–29; Bettcher (2008), pp. 122–29; Jones (2009), pp.112–15; Fields (2011), pp. 201–9; Bennett (1971), p. 165, although Bennett acknowledges that "the argument's

Notes to pages 133–147

conclusion falls short of theism, let alone Christian monotheism." Cf. Berman (1994), pp. 45ff; Johnston (1965), p. 194.
21 *Thirty–Nine Articles of Religion*, Article 1, Sentence 1. For a more extensive examination of Berkeley's argument for the existence of God in the *Principles*, see Ksenjek and Flage (2012).
22 I wish to thank Sam Rickless for this objection, personal correspondence, 23 July 2012.

Chapter 7

1 See, for example, Copleston (1964), pp. 57–61; Olscamp, (1968); Olscamp (1970); Häyry (1994), pp. 27–28; Häyry and Häyry (1994); Berman (1994), pp. 87–88; Berman (2005), p. 155; Darwell (2005); cf. Clark, (2005). Opponents of utilitarian interpretation include Orange (1890); Hicks (1932), pp. 185–86; Pitcher (1977), pp. 228–54; Jakapi (2007).
2 Flage (2000).
3 See Flage (2008b) and below.
4 There are also *act deontologists*, that is, moral philosophers who hold that there is a method that, if followed, allows us to determine whether a particular action in a particular set of circumstances is morally obligatory or morally forbidden without appealing to rules. See Rosen (1976). Since this is clearly *not* Berkeley's view, we may ignore it.
5 Some people might find foreshadowings of it in Romans 2:15.
6 Flage (2000).
7 See *PHK* 31 and *N* 817. The latter alludes to Locke, *Essay* 4.17.4.
8 See also *Guardian* 126, where Berkeley comments, "because the good of the whole is inseparable from that of the parts; in promoting therefore the common good, every one doth at the same time promote his own private interest" (*Works* 7:227–28).
9 Sustaining health would seem to depend on "excellent rules [descriptive natural laws] about exercise, air, and diet" (*A* 6:28).
10 *N* 734 might be considered a third passage, but the issue there is moral demonstration, alluding to "some principle of Nature which is the effect of God's will and we know not how soon it may be changed." A fourth is *N* 769, where Berkeley claims that sensual pleasure is the *summum bonum*, claiming "This once rightly understood all the Doctrines even the severest of the [Gospels] may cleerly be Demonstrated." I discuss *N* 769 below.
11 This will become clear when we look at the sermon "Of Immortality."
12 *SER* 10:130; cf. Locke (1999), p. 149, where Locke claims even pagan philosophers, upon hearing Christian laws of morality, "found them agreeable to reason; and such as can be by no means contradicted."
13 Teleologists, following Aristotle, often refer to ends as final causes. Throughout his philosophical career, Berkeley embraced final causes.

See *PHK* §§60–61, 107; *Alciphron*, 3.1, p. 113; *Analyst* §11, *Works* 4:71; *Siris* §§231 and 251.
14. In his hedonistic calculus, Bentham defines "purity" as "the chance it has of *not* being followed by sensations of the *opposite* kind: that is, pains if it is pleasure; pleasures, if it be a pain." Bentham (2000), Chapter 4, §3.
15. Olscamp (1970) p. 83.
16. Locke, *Essay* 2.28.10–11; Cumberland (2005), p. 463.
17. Cf. *Guardian* 83:214.
18. Mill (2001), p. 90.
19. Fiering (1981), pp. 299–300.
20. Locke (1960), Book 2, Chapter 2, §6. This seems to reflect the view in the natural law tradition that the formation of society was a natural outcome of human nature: see *PO* §25, Grotius (2005), pp. 79–81.
21. See Hobbes (1991), Chapters 13 and 18. See also Pufendorf (2003), p. 190; Pufendorf (2009), pp. 126–28, 146–48, and 268–70.
22. See Kaye (1924), pp. lviii–lxi.
23. Plato, *Republic*, 414^b–415^e.
24. Cf. Cumberland (2005), p. 463; Locke, *Essay* 2.28.10–11.
25. Shaftesbury's references to duty in the *Inquiry* are few and often unfavorable. See Shaftesbury (1999), pp. 196, 199, 207, 214, 225.
26. Shaftesbury (1999), p. 183.

Chapter 8

1. Caffentzis (2000), p. 344.
2. For more details on the South Sea Bubble and the Mississippi Bubble, which occurred concurrently in France, see Caffentzis (2000), pp. 21–31 and 53–58.
3. On Berkeley's views of the native Irish see *Q* 19–20, 132, 357.
4. Johnston (1970), p. 65.
5. Johnston (1970), pp. 52–71.
6. For a more thorough introduction to Berkeley's economic theory, see Kelly (2005).

Chapter 9

1. See Brook (1973) and Jesseph (1993).
2. See Moked (1988).
3. Quine (1948), p. 34.

Bibliography

Aaron, Richard I. (1967). *The Problem of Universals*, 2nd edition. Oxford: Clarendon Press.
Adams, Robert Merrihew (1979). "Introduction," in Berkeley (1979).
Allaire, Edwin (1963). "Berkeley's Idealism." *Theoria: A Swedish Journal of Philosophy* 29: 229–44.
Allaire, Edwin (1995). "Berkeley's Idealism: Yet Another Visit," in Muehlmann (1995a), pp. 23–37.
Armstrong, D. M. (1960). *Berkeley's Theory of Vision: A Critical Examination of Berkeley's Essay towards a New Theory of Vision*. Parkville: Melbourne University Press.
Aquinas, St. Thomas (1920–1942). *Summa Theologica*, translated by the Fathers of the English Dominican Province, London: Burns, Oates & Washburn. References are by part, question, article, body/reply, and paragraph.
Aristotle (1984). *The Complete Works of Aristotle*. Revised Oxford Translation. Edited by Jonathan Barnes. 2 vols. Princeton: Princeton University Press. References to individual works are by standard (Bekker) page numbers, that are found in the margins of many editions.
Arnauld, Antoine, and Nicole, Pierre (1996). *Logic or the Art of Thinking*, translated by Jill Vance Buroker, Cambridge Texts in the History of Philosophy. Cambridge: Cambridge University Press.
Atherton, Margaret (1990). *Berkeley's Revolution in Vision*. Ithaca: Cornell University Press.
Ayers, M. R. (1975). "Introduction" and notes to Berkeley (1975).
Barrow, Isaac (1669). *Eighteen Lectures*. London.
Bayle, Pierre (1965). *Historical and Critical Dictionary, Selections*, translated by Richard H. Popkin. Indianapolis: Bobbs-Merrill, Library of Liberal Arts.

Bennett, Jonathan (1971). *Locke, Berkeley, Hume: Central Themes*. Oxford: Clarendon Press.
Bentham, Jeremy (2000). *An Introduction to the Principles of Morals and Legislation*. Ontario: Batoche Books.
Berkeley, George (1948–1957). *The Works of George Berkeley*, 9 vols, edited A. A. Luce and T. E. Jessop. London: Thomas Nelson.
Berkeley, George (1975). *Philosophical Works: Including the Works on Vision*, edited Michael R. Ayers. London: Dent.
Berkeley, George (1979). *Three Dialogues between Hylas and Philonous*, edited Robert Merrihew Adams. Indianapolis: Hackett.
Berkeley, George (1987). *George Berkeley's Manuscript Introduction: An edition diplomatica*, transcribed and edited by Bertil Belfrage. Oxford: Doxa (Oxford). Ltd.
Berkeley, George (2013). *The Correspondence of George Berkeley*, edited Marc A. Hight. Cambridge: Cambridge University Press.
Berman, David (1994). *George Berkeley: Idealism and the Man*. Oxford: Clarendon Press.
Berman, David (2005). *Berkeley and Irish Philosophy*, Continuum Studies in British Philosophy. London: Continuum.
Bettcher, Talia Mae (2007). *Berkeley's Philosophy of Spirit: Consciousness, Ontology and the Elusive Subject*, Continuum Studies in British Philosophy. London: Continuum.
Bettcher, Talia Mae (2008). *Berkeley: A Guide for the Perplexed*. London: Continuum.
Bordner, S. Seth (2011). "Berkeley's Defense of Commonsense." *Journal of the History of Philosophy* 49.3: 315–38.
Boyle, Robert (no date), "MS Notes on a Good and an Excellent Hypothesis," in Boyle (1979), p. 119.
Boyle, Robert (1666). "The Origin of Forms and Qualities According to the Corpuscular Philosophy," in Boyle, (1979), pp. 1–96.
Boyle, Robert (1979). *Selected Philosophical Papers of Robert Boyle*, edited M. A. Stuart, Philosophical Classics. Manchester: Manchester University Press.
Bracken, Harry M. (1974). *Berkeley*, Philosophers in Perspective. New York: St. Martin's Press.
Breuninger, Scott (2010). *Recovering Bishop Berkeley: Virtue and Society in the Anglo-Irish Context*, Palgrave Studies in Culture and Intellectual History. New York: Palgrave Macmillan.
Brook, Richard J. (1973). *Berkeley's Philosophy of Science*, International Archives of the History of Ideas 65. The Hague: Martinus Nijhoff.
Caffentzis, Constantine George (2000). *Exciting the Industry of Mankind: George Berkeley's Philosophy of Money*, International Archives of the History of Ideas 170. Dordrecht: Kluwer Academic Publications.
Clark, Stephen R. L. (2005). "Berkeley on Religion," in Winkler (2005), pp. 369–404 .

Bibliography

Copleston, Frederick (1964). *A History of Philosophy*, Volume 5, *Modern Philosophy: The British Philosophers*, Part 2. Garden City: Doubleday Image Books.

Cornman, James W. (1975). *Perception, Common Sense, and Science*. New Haven: Yale University Press.

Craig, E. J. (1968). "Berkeley's Attack on Abstract Ideas." *Philosophical Review* 77: 425–37.

Cumberland, Richard (2005). *A Treatise of the Laws of Nature*, translated by John Maxfield (1727), edited by Jon Parkin. Indianapolis: Liberty Fund.

Cummins, Phillip (1982). "Hylas' Parity Argument," in Turbayne (1982), pp. 283–94.

Cummins, Phillip D. (1987). "The Status of Visibles in Berkeley's New Theory of Vision," in Sosa (1987), pp. 165–94.

Cummins, Phillip D. (1990). "Berkeley's Manifest Qualities Thesis." *Journal of the History of Philosophy* 28 (3): 385–401.

Dancy, Jonathan (1987). *Berkeley: An Introduction*. New York: Basil Blackwell.

Daniel, Stephen H. (2008a). *New Interpretations of Berkeley's Thought*. Journal of the History of Philosophy Books. New York: Humanity Books.

Daniel, Stephen H. (2008b). "Berkeley's Stoic Notion of Spiritual Substance," in Daniel (2008a), pp. 203–30.

Daniel, Stephen H. (2013). "Berkeley's Doctrine of Mind and the 'Black List Hypothesis': A Dialogue." *The Southern Journal of Philosophy* (51): 24–41.

Darwell, Stephen (2005). "Berkeley's Moral and Political Philosophy," in Winkler (2005), pp. 311–38.

Descartes, René (1984–85). *The Philosophical Writings of Descartes*, 2 vols., translated by John Cottingham, Robert Stoothoff, and Dugald Murdoch. Cambridge: Cambridge University Press.

Dicker, Georges (2011). *Berkeley's Idealism: A Critical Examination*. New York: Oxford University Press.

Diogenes Laertius (1925). *Lives of Eminent Philosophers*, translated by R. D. Hicks, Loeb Classical Library, 2 vols. Cambridge: Harvard University Press.

Doney, Willis (1983). "Berkeley's Argument Against Abstract Ideas," in *Midwest Studies in Philosophy VIII: Contemporary Perspectives on the History of Philosophy*, edited by Peter A. French, Theodore E. Uehling, Jr., and Howard K. Wettstein. Minneapolis: University of Minnesota Press, pp. 295–308.

Fields, Keota (2011). *Berkeley: Ideas, Immaterialism, and Objective Presence*. Lanham, Md: Lexington Books.

Fiering, Norman (1981). *Moral Philosophy at Seventeenth-Century Harvard: A Discipline in Transition*, Published for the Institute of Early American History and Culture at Williamsburg. Chapel Hill: University of North Carolina Press.

Flage, Daniel E. (1985). "Berkeley's Notions." *Philosophy and Phenomenological Research* 45: 407–25.
Flage, Daniel E. (1986a). "Berkeley on Abstraction." *Journal of the History of Philosophy* 24: 483–501.
Flage, Daniel E. (1986b). *Berkeley's Doctrine of Notions: A Reconstruction Based on His Theory of Meaning*. London: Croom Helm.
Flage, Daniel E. (2000). "Locke and Natural Law." *Dialogue: Canadian Philosophical Review* 39: 437–460.
Flage, Daniel E. (2003). "Berkeley's Principles, Section 10." *Journal of the History of Philosophy* 40: 543–551.
Flage, Daniel E. (2004a). "Berkeley's Epistemic Ontology: *The Principles*." *Canadian Journal of Philosophy* 34 (2004): 25–60.
Flage, Daniel E. (2004b). *The Art of Questioning*. Upper Saddle River, N.J.: Pearson.
Flage, Daniel E. (2006). "Berkeley's Ideas of Reflection." *Berkeley Newsletter* 17: 7–13; http://people.hsc.edu/berkeleynews/issues/BN%20No%20017/BNL_017_Flage_Article.pdf.
Flage, Daniel E. (2008a). "Berkeley's Epistemic Ontology: The *Three Dialogues*," in Daniel (2008a), pp. 45–75.
Flage, Daniel E. (2008b). "Was Berkeley an Ethical Egoist?" *Berkeley Studies* 19 (2008): 3–18; http://people.hsc.edu/berkeleystudies/issues/BS%20No%20019/BS_019_Flage_Article.pdf.
Flage, Daniel E. (2011). "Analysis in Berkeley's Theory of Vision," in *Berkeley's Lasting Legacy: 300 Years Later*, edited by Tim Airaksinen and Bertil Belfrage. Newcastle upon Tyne: Cambridge Scholars Publishing, pp. 35–53.
Flage, Daniel E. and Clarence A. Bonnen (1999). *Descartes and Method: A Search for a Method in Meditations*. London: Routledge.
Fogelin, Robert (2001). *Berkeley and the Principles of Human Knowledge*. London: Routledge.
Galilei, Galileo (1967). *Dialogue Concerning the Two Chief World Systems*, translated by S. Drake, 2nd revised edition. Berkeley: University of California Press.
Garrett, Aaron (2008). *Berkeley's Three Dialogues: A Reader's Guide*. London: Continuum.
Gaustad, Edwin S. (1979). *George Berkeley in America*. New Haven: Yale University Press.
Grayling, A. C. (1986). *Berkeley: The Central Arguments*. LaSalle: Open Court.
Grotius, Hugo (2005). *The Rights of War and Peace*, 3 volumes, edited by Richard Tuck. Indianapolis: Liberty Fund.
Hanson, Norwood Russell (1961). *Patterns of Discovery: An Inquiry into the Conceptual Foundations of Science*. Cambridge: Cambridge University Press.
Hausman, Alan and Hausman, David (1995). "A New Approach to Berkeley's Ideal Reality," in Muehlmann (1995a), pp. 47–65.

Häyry, Matti (1994). *Liberal Utilitarianism and Applied Ethics*. London and New York: Routledge.
Häyry, Matti and Häyry, Heta (1994). "Obedience to Rules and Berkeley's Theological Utilitarianism." *Utilitas* 6: 233–42.
Hicks, G. Dawes (1932). *Berkeley*. New York: Russell & Russell.
Hight, Marc A. (2008). *Idea and Ontology: An Essay in Early Modern Metaphysics of Ideas*. University Park: The Pennsylvania State University Press.
Hobbes, Thomas (1991). *Leviathan*, edited Richard Tuck. Cambridge: Cambridge University Press.
Hume, David (1999). *An Enquiry concerning Human Understanding*, edited by Tom L. Beauchamp, Oxford Philosophical Texts. Oxford: Oxford University Press.
Hume, David (2000). *A Treatise of Human Nature*, edited by David Fate Norton and Mary Norton, Oxford Philosophical Texts. Oxford: Oxford University Press.
Hutcheson, Francis (2006). *Logic, Metaphysics, and the Sociability of Mankind*, edited by James Moore and Michael Silverthorne. Indianapolis: Liberty Fund.
Jakapi, Roomet (2007). "Was Berkeley a Utilitarian?" in Lemitti (2007), pp. 53–68.
Jesseph, Douglas M. (1993). *Berkeley's Philosophy of Mathematics*. Chicago: University of Chicago Press.
Johnston, G. A. (1965). *The Development of Berkeley's Philosophy*. 1923; reprint New York: Russell & Russell.
Johnston, Joseph (1970). *Bishop Berkeley's Querist in Historical Perspective*. Dunkirk: Dundalgan Press.
Jones, Nick (2009). *Starting with Berkeley*. London: Continuum.
Kant, Immanuel (1977). *Prolegomena to Any Future Metaphysics*. Revised from Carus translation by James W. Eddington. Indianapolis: Hackett.
Kaye, F. B. (1924). "Introduction" to Mandeville (1924), 1:xvii–cxlvi.
Kelly, Patrick (2005). "Berkeley's Economic Writings," in Winkler, (2005), pp. 339–68.
Ksenjek, Ekaterina Y., and Daniel E. Flage (2012). "Berkeley, the Author of Nature, and the Judeo-Christian God." *History of Philosophy Quarterly* 29 (3): 281–99.
Lemetti, Juhana, ed. (2007). *Human Nature As the Basis of Morality and Society in Early Modern Philosophy*. Helsinki: Philosophy Society of Finland.
Lipton, Peter (1991). *Inference to the Best Explanation*. London: Routledge.
Locke, John (1960). *Two Treatises of Government*, edited by Peter Laslett. New York: Mentor Books.
Locke, John (1963). *The Works of John Locke*. London, 1823; reprint edition Darmstadt: Scientia Verlag Aalen.
Locke, John (1975). *An Essay concerning Human Understanding*, edited by P. H. Nidditch. Oxford: Clarendon Press.

Locke, John (1999). *The Reasonableness of Christianity*, edited by John C. Higgins-Biddle. The Clarendon Edition of the Works of John Locke. Oxford: Clarendon Press.

Luce, A. A. (1945). *Berkeley's Immaterialism*. Oxford: Clarendon Press.

Luce, A. A. (1949). *The Life of George Berkeley, Bishop of Cloyne*. London: Thomas Nelson and Sons.

Luce, A. A. (1963). *The Dialectic of Immaterialism*. London: Hodder and Stroughton.

Mackie, J. L. (1976). *Problems from Locke*. Oxford: Clarendon Press.

Malebranche, Nicholas (1980). *The Search After Truth*, translated T. Lennon and P. J. Olscamp, and *Elucidations of the Search After Truth*, translated T. Lennon. Columbus: Ohio State University Press.

Mandeville, Bernard (1924). *Fable of the Bees, Or Private Vices, Publick Benefits*, 2 vols., edited by F. B. Kaye. Oxford University Press; reprint Indianapolis: Liberty Fund.

McGowan, William (1982). "Berkeley's Doctrine of Signs," in Turbayne (1982), pp. 211–46.

Mill, John Stuart (2001). *Utilitarianism*. London: Electric Book Company.

Moked, Gabriel (1988). *Particles and Ideas: Bishop Berkeley's Corpuscularian Philosophy*. Oxford: Clarendon Press.

Molyneux, William (1709). *Dioptrica nova. A treatise of dioptricks, in two parts. Wherein the various effects and appearances of spherick glasses, both convex and concave, single and combined, in telescopes and microscopes, together with their usefulness in many concerns of humane life, are explained*. London: Benj. Tooke.

Muehlmann, Robert (1978). "Berkeley's Ontology and the Epistemology of Idealism." *Canadian Journal of Philosophy* 8: 89–111.

Muehlmann, Robert (1992). *Berkeley's Ontology*. Indianapolis: Hackett.

Muehlmann, Robert, ed. (1995a). *Berkeley's Metaphysics: Structural, Interpretive, and Critical Essays*. University Park: The Pennsylvania State University Press.

Muehlmann, Robert (1995b). "Introduction," in Muehlmann (1995a), pp. 1–19.

Muehlmann, Robert (1995c). "The Substance of Berkeley's Philosophy," in Muehlmann (1995a), pp. 89–105.

Newton, Isaac (1952). *Optics, or A Treatise of the Reflections, Refractions, Inflections & Colours of Light*, based on the 4th edition London [1730]. New York: Dover.

Newton, Isaac (1966). *Mathematical Principles: Of Natural Philosophy and His System of the World*, 2 volumes, translated A. Mott, revised F. Cajori. Berkeley: University of California Press.

Odegard, Douglas (1969). "John Locke and the Unreality of Relations." *Theoria* 35: 147–52.

Olscamp, Paul J. (1968). "Some Suggestions About the Moral Philosophy of George Berkeley." *Journal of the History of Philosophy* 6: 147–56.

Olscamp, Paul J. (1970). *The Moral Philosophy of George Berkeley*. The Hague: Martinus Nijhoff.

Orange, Hugh W. (1890). "Berkeley as a Moral Philosopher." *Mind* 15: 514–523.
Pappas, George (2000). *Berkeley's Thought*. Ithaca: Cornell University Press.
Peirce, Charles Sanders (1940). "Abduction and Induction." In *Philosophical Writings of Peirce*, Justus Buchler (ed.). New York: Dover, pp. 150–55.
Pitcher, George (1977). *Berkeley*. The Arguments of the Philosophers. London: Routledge.
Prior, A. N. (1955). "Berkeley in Logical Form." *Theoria* 21: 117–22.
Plato (1961). *Plato: The Collected Dialogues*, edited Edith Hamilton and Huntington Cairns. Princeton, N.J.: Princeton University Press. References to individual works are by standard (Stephanus) page numbers that are found in the margins of many editions.
Popkin, Richard H. (2003). *The History of Scepticism from Savonarola to Bayle*. Oxford: Oxford University Press.
Pufendorf, Samuel (2003). *The Whole Duty of Man, According to the Law of Nature*, translated Andrew Took, edited Ian Hunter and David Saunders. Indianapolis: Liberty Fund.
Pufendorf, Samuel (2009). *Two Books of the Universal Jurisprudence*, translated by William Abbott Oldfather, translation revised Thomas Behme. Indianapolis: Liberty Fund.
Quine, Willard V. (1948). "On What There Is." *Review of Metaphysics* 2 (#5): 21–38.
Randall, John Hermann (1940). "The Development of Scientific Method in the School of Padua." *Journal of the History of Ideas* 1, pp. 177–206.
Reid, Thomas (1969). *Essays on the Active Powers of the Human Mind*, edited Baruch Brody, Cambridge: M.I.T. Press.
Roberts, John Russell (2007). *A Metaphysics for the Mob*. New York: Oxford University Press.
Rosen, Bernard (1976). *Strategies of Ethics*. Boston: Houghton Mifflin.
Schick, Theodore, Jr. and Lewis Vaughn (1999). *How to Think About Weird Things*, 2nd edition. Mountain View, Calif.: Mayfield.
Sextus Empiricus (1933). *Outlines of Pyrrhonism*, translated R. G. Bury, Loeb Classical Library #273. Cambridge: Harvard University Press.
Sextus Empiricus (1936). *Against the Physicists and Against the Ethicists*, trans. R. G. Bury, Loeb Classical Library #311. Cambridge: Harvard University Press.
Shaftesbury, Anthony Ashley Cooper, Third Earl (1999). *Characteristics of Men, Manners, Opinions, Times*, edited Lawrence E. Klein, Cambridge Texts in the History of Philosophy. Cambridge: Cambridge University Press.
Sosa, Ernest, ed. (1987). *Essays on the Philosophy of George Berkeley*. Dordrecht: Reidel.
Stephens, John Calhoun (1982). "Introduction," in Richard Steele, *The Guardian*, John Calhoun Stephens (ed.). Lexington: University of Kentucky Press.

Stoneham, Tom (2002). *Berkeley's World: An Examination of the Three Dialogues*. Oxford: Oxford University Press.
Suarez, Francesco (1994). *On Efficient Causality: Metaphysical Disputations 17, 18, and 19*. Translated by Alfred Freddoso. New Haven: Yale University Press.
Thirty-Nine Articles of Religion, http://anglicansonline.org/basics/thirty-nine_articles.html.
Tipton, I. C. (1974). *Berkeley: The Philosophy of Immaterialism*. London: Methuen.
Turbayne, Colin M. (1963). "Editor's Commentary" to George Berkeley, *Works on Vision*, Library of Liberal Arts. Indianapolis: Bobbs-Merrill.
Turbayne, Colin M. (1970). *The Myth of Metaphor*, Columbia: University of South Carolina Press.
Turbayne, Colin M., ed. (1982). *Berkeley: Critical and Interpretive Essays*. Minneapolis: University of Minnesota Press.
Umbaugh, Bruce (2000). *On Berkeley*, Wadsworth Philosophers Series. Belmont, Calif.: Wadsworth.
Urmson, J. O. (1992). Berkeley, in John Dunn, J. O. Urmson, and A. J. Ayer (1992), *The British Empiricists*, Past Masters Series. Oxford: Oxford University Press.
Watts, Isaac (1996). *Logic, or The Right Use of Reason in the Inquiry After Truth with a Variety of Rules to Guard Against Error in the Affairs of Religion and Human Life, as well as the Sciences* [1724]. Morgan, Penn.: Soli Deo Gloria Publications.
Weinberg, Julius R. (1965). "The Nominalism of Berkeley and Hume," in his *Abstraction, Relation, and Induction: Three Essays in the History of Thought*. Madison: University of Wisconsin Press, pp. 3–60.
Williams, Bernard (1973). "Imagination and the Self," reprinted in his *Problems of the Self*. Cambridge: Cambridge University Press.
Wilson, Fred (1995). "On the Hausmans' 'A New Approach'," in Muehlmann (1995a), pp. 67–88.
Winkler, Kenneth W. (1989). *Berkeley, An Interpretation*. Oxford: Clarendon Press.
Winkler, Kenneth W., ed. (2005). *The Cambridge Companion to Berkeley*. Cambridge: Cambridge University Press.
Wittgenstein, Ludwig (1958). *Philosophical Investigations*, translated by G. E. M. Anscombe. New York: Macmillan.
Yolton, John W. (1984). *Perceptual Acquaintance: from Descartes to Reid*. Minneapolis: University of Minnesota Press.

Index

abduction 24–5; *see also* analysis
abstract ideas 18, 23, 37, 42–55, 57, 66–7, 77, 82, 84, 123, 142, 178
abstraction 42–55
  principle of abstraction 48
  selective attention model 43, 45–7, 51, 53
  separation model 43, 45–8, 50, 53, 178
Addison, Joseph 4
Advice to the Tories who have Taken the Oath 5
Alciphron, or the Minute Philosopher 4, 12–13, 19, 49, 50, 61, 92, 114, 130, 132–3, 137, 138, 158–62, 163, 166, 179
analysis, method of 18, 23–6, 39–40, 95, 129–31, 177, 178, 179, 180
Analyst, or a Discourse Addressed to an Infidel Mathematician 13
Aquinas, Thomas 2, 44, 45, 137, 141
argument to the best explanation 24–5 *see also* analysis
Aristotle 2, 43, 44, 54, 71, 77, 98, 118, 137, 140, 161, 162

Armstrong, D. M. 20
Arnauld, Antoine 55, 76
Atherton, Margaret 22–3, 25

Barrow, Isaac 25, 28
Bayle, Pierre 99
Bentham, Jeremy 2, 137, 140, 151
Berkeley, California 12
Bermuda Project 7–12
Boyle, Robert 71
Bray, Thomas 11
bundle theory of mind 115
Byrd, William 11

categories of existents 62, 85
causality 76, 106, 187n.13
  efficient causality 76–7
  final causality 187n.13
common sense 97–113
conceivability 18, 35, 49–50, 53, 66–7, 72, 84–5; *see also* possibility
conceptualism 44
congeries theory of mind 115, 136
consequentialism *see* ethical egoism; utilitarianism
contradictions 70, 73

corpuscles 71, 87, 109
corpuscular hypothesis 71
criterion of ontological commitment 62
Cumberland, Richard 141
Cummins, Phillip 29, 87

Daniel, Stephen 115
Defense of Free-thinking in Mathematics 13
Democritus 71
deontological theories of ethics 139
Descartes, René 3, 20, 21, 23, 24–8, 33, 34, 39, 46–7, 54, 58, 59, 61, 62, 65, 69, 70, 76, 79, 93, 95, 99, 102–3, 118, 120, 129, 130, 132, 177, 178
descriptive laws of nature 110, 153, 162
distance perception 4, 23–35, 39–40, 95, 102, 103–5, 111, 131, 177
duty *see* obligation

efficient causality 76, 106
ends 140–1, 149, 159, 161, 162, 187n.13; *see also* final causes
epistemology 56–113
Essay towards a New Theory of Vision 4, 13, 18, 22–3, 29, 31, 38, 39, 40, 41, 47, 49, 51, 52, 55, 60, 92, 95, 121, 131, 135, 177, 178
Essay towards Preventing the Ruin of Great Britain 8, 20, 164, 166–9
esse is *percipi* 57, 62–4, 66, 69, 94
essence 52, 61, 93, 106, 108–9, 129
  nominal 52, 93, 108–9, 111
  real 108–9, 129
ethical egoism 19, 137–47, 148, 157, 162
  and natural law theory 141
ethics 137–63

Farther Thoughts on Tar-Water 15
form 42, 43–5, 54, 118, 140–1; *see also* universals

Foster, Anne 10
Fraser, Alexander Campbell 21
free-thinking 4, 13, 166–7

Gibson, Edmund 10
God 17, 68, 70, 76, 90, 91, 100, 106–8, 109–10, 112, 113, 116, 118, 120, 125–6, 127, 130, 132–5, 137, 139, 141, 145–7, 149–52, 161–2, 163
  Judeo-Christian 17, 132–5
  knowledge of the existence 19, 106, 132–5
  natural law theories of morality 137, 139, 141, 149–52, 161–2, 163
Grotius, Hugo 141
Guardian 4, 13, 19, 137, 148, 154, 166

Harvard University 11, 12, 17
heterogeneity thesis 22, 23, 33–9, 110
Hight, Marc 23
Hobbes, Thomas 132, 154
Honeyman, James 10
Hooker, Richard 141
Hume, David 1, 31, 34, 65, 83, 87, 111, 115, 139
Hutcheson, Francis 139

idealism 2, 6, 17, 19, 56–70, 94–5, 97, 136, 178, 179, 181
ideas
  objects of knowledge 54–5, 115–16
  of reflection 59, 124–5
identity 66, 111–12, 125
immaterialism 4, 5, 6, 7, 17, 19, 20, 22, 69, 70–86, 94–5, 97–8, 100, 108–12, 178–9, 180
impossibility 72–3, 153; *see also* possibility
  criteria for 72–3
  epistemic 104–5
  kinds of 73–4
  logical 104

Index

inconceivability 50, 53, 67, 73, 75, 76, 77, 82, 84, 104
  conceptual 73
  criterion or impossibility 67, 72–3
  epistemic 73
  logical 73
inherence 81, 102–3, 119
intuition 129–31, 136, 179

Johnson, Samuel 6, 10, 21, 114, 180

Kant, Immanuel 24, 70, 139
Kepler, Johannes 25

Ladies Library 4
language 36–9, 43, 45, 52, 53–4
  divine 13, 92
  natural 53–4
  visual 36–9
law of nature 24, 91–3, 110, 149–57, 169
likeness principle 71–5, 78, 88, 105, 111, 124, 126
Locke, John 1, 3, 18, 34, 37, 38, 40, 42, 55, 59, 60, 65, 69, 71, 74, 75, 78, 79, 80, 82, 84, 87, 137
  abstraction 43–53
  intuitive knowledge 129
  language 111
  laws of nature 154
  moral theory 138, 141, 142–3, 144
  nominal essences 93, 108–9, 111
  qualities 118
  real essences 108–9
  relations 123
  representative realism 93
  substance 103, 109, 115, 118, 120
Logic or the Art of Thinking 55
Luce, A. A. 21, 125

magnitude 22, 26, 29, 31–3, 35, 37, 39, 40, 177
Malebranche, Nicholas 3, 5, 20, 23, 25, 106–7

Mandeville, Bernard 13, 158
Manifest Qualities Thesis 87
master argument 84–6, 104–5
materialism
  21st-century use 2, 181
  Berkeley's use 98, 100, 108, 110, 112
matter 2, 4, 19, 56, 70–86, 88, 90, 94, 97, 99–105, 107, 126, 130, 181
  as individuator Aristotle 44–5
Maxims concerning Patriotism 169
meaning 48–54
  as use 54
  extensional (denotative) theory 50–1, 128, 130
  intentional (connotative) theory 51
means (to an end) 140–1, 145, 146, 153, 154–6, 159, 162. 167, 168–9, 170, 173
mercantilism 165, 169
metaphysics 15, 19, 34, 50, 56, 57, 58, 62, 98, 107, 120, 132, 137, 147, 149, 161, 178, 179
  Aristotle 118
  relation to epistemology in Berkeley 56–113
microscope 102, 110–11
Mill, John Stuart 2, 137, 140, 148, 151
mind 114–32
  knowledge of other minds 131–2
  knowledge of your own 114–31
minimum tangibles 31–2
minimum visibles 31–2, 127
mode 48, 50, 62, 67, 73, 80, 109, 118–20
Molyneux, William 3, 25, 29
Molyneux Problem 3, 29, 33, 35, 38
  Molyneux man 29, 33, 35, 38
moon illusion 32–3
moral evil *see* vice

moral goodness *see* virtue
moral sense theory 139, 156, 158, 161–2
Muehlmann, Robert 56, 115

national bank 169, 173–6
natural evil 138; *see also* pain
natural goodness 138, 140
natural law theory of ethics 2, 19, 137–8, 140–2, 147–62, 169, 172
  primary natural laws 140
  secondary natural laws 140–1, 156, 157–8
  tertiary natural laws 141, 156, 157–8
new science 1, 71, 79; *see also* primary qualities
New Theory of Vision see Essay towards a New Theory of Vision
Newman, Henry 10
Newport, Rhode Island 10–11, 17
Newton, Isaac 1, 13, 28
Nicole, Pierre 55
nominal essence 52, 93, 109, 111
nominalism 44, 46, 129, 141
Notebooks 4, 6, 18, 19, 21, 52, 114–15, 136, 137, 138, 142–7, 148, 158, 162, 179
notions 13, 18, 19, 49, 55, 57, 58, 59, 60, 66, 74, 77–86, 88–9, 95, 107, 109, 114–36, 179
  of material substance 77–86, 107
  of mind 88–9, 95, 109, 114–36, 179
  of relations 123–4
  relative notions 115

objects of human knowledge 58–60, 116–17, 123
obligation 16, 137, 138–9, 146, 147, 150, 157
Ockham, William of 44
Ockham's Razor 44; *see also* parsimony

ontology 56, 68, 76, 79, 83, 85, 104, 109, 151, 178; *see also* metaphysics

pain 101, 110, 138, 139, 142, 143, 145–9, 153, 160–2
Pappas, George 47
Pappus of Alexandria 24
parity argument 109, 120, 125, 127
parsimony, principle of 44, 45, 106, 107–8, 120
Pascal, Blaise 146
Passive Obedience 4, 5, 19, 114, 136, 137, 138, 147–58, 162, 163, 179
Percival, John 3, 5, 6, 7, 8, 9
Philosophical Commentaries see Notebooks
Pitcher, George 22, 40, 57
Plato 43–4, 45, 98, 137, 140, 159, 160, 161
pleasure 89, 101, 134, 138–40, 142–9, 153, 154, 160
Pope, Alexander 4
Popkin, Richard 98
possibility 18, 35, 49–50, 53, 66–7, 72, 84–5
  conceivability 18, 35, 49–50, 53, 66–7, 72, 84–5
  conceptual 73
  epistemic 73, 104–5
  inconceivability 72–3
  logical 73, 104
possibility, conceivability criterion of (*CCP*)
prescriptive laws 140–1, 162; *see also* means
primary qualities 34–6, 38, 71, 74–9, 87, 94, 103–4, 107
Primary Visitation Charge 13
Principles of Human Knowledge see Treatise concerning the Principles of Human Knowledge
Prior, Thomas 3, 5, 10, 12, 14, 15
Proposal for the Better Supplying of Churches in our Foreign Plantations 8

psychology 22, 26
Pufendorf, Samuel 141
Pyrrho of Elis 98

qualities
  Locke 118
  see also primary qualities or secondary qualities
Querist 14, 20, 164, 167, 168, 169–76

real essence 108–9, 129
real things 91–3
realism
  metaphysical 44
  representative 64, 69, 74
Reasons for Not Replying to Mr. Walton's Full Answer 13
Reid, Thomas 115
relations 123–4
relative ideas 115
relative notions 115
representative realism 64, 69, 74
Rhode Island 10–13, 174
Ross, W. D. 139

Scholasticism 43, 44, 54, 55, 76, 129
Seabury, Samuel 17
secondary qualities 34–6, 71, 74–9, 103–4
self-love 140, 147, 148
Sextus Empiricus 98
Shaftesbury, Anthony Ashley Cooper, Third Earl of 13, 139, 158, 162
Siris: A Chain of Philosophical Reflexions and Inquiries concerning the Virtues of Tar-water and divers other Subjects connected together and arising One from Another 14–15, 18, 133, 179–80
Skinner, John 17
skepticism 19, 97–113
  Pyrrhonian 98–9

Society for the Promotion of Christian Knowledge 9
Society for the Propagation of the Gospel 9
Society of Colonial Dames of Rhode Island 11
South Sea Bubble 8, 164–6, 167, 168
specie 165, 169, 174, 176
spirit *see* mind
Steele, Richard 4, 5, 137
Stuart, Charles Edward 15
Stuart, James Edward 5
Suarez, Francesco 76
substance 1, 2, 19, 48, 50, 57, 58, 60, 62–3, 67, 69, 70, 90, 92, 94–5, 118–19, 178
  immaterial 1, 70, 88–9, 90, 91, 99–112, 114–35
  independence model of 62
  inherence model 81, 102–3, 119
  material 1, 2, 19, 53, 59, 70–86, 88, 90, 91, 97, 99–112, 179
  mental *see* mind; substance, immaterial
  modes of substance 50, 62–3, 67
  spiritual *see* mind; substance, immaterial
substratum 69, 71, 79–82, 85, 94, 104, 109, 118, 119
Swift, Jonathan 3, 4
synthesis, method of 23–4

teleological 139, 147, 149, 157
Theory of Vision, or Visual Language shewing the immediate Presence and Providence of a Deity Vindicated and Explained 13, 18, 23, 40, 177
Three Dialogues between Hylas and Philonous 2, 4, 13, 18, 19, 22, 92, 95, 97–113, 114, 116–17, 119, 124–31, 132, 136, 178, 180
Tory Party 5

Treatise concerning the Principles of Human Knowledge 4, 6, 7, 13, 18, 19, 22, 41, 42–95, 97, 98, 105, 112, 113, 114–24, 125, 127–36, 178, 179, 180
Trinity College Dublin 3–4, 7, 9, 146
Turbayne, Colin 23

universalia ante rem 44
universalia in re 44
universals 46, 141
　problem of 43–5,
utilitarianism 2, 137, 140–2, 144–5, 150–2, 156, 158–9, 160, 163–4, 179, 180
　theological 139

Van Homrigh, Hester 9
vice 138–9, 142, 160
virtue
　moral 138–9, 146, 150, 153, 154, 161–2, 167, 168, 169
　theoretical 98, 106
vision 22–41
visual inversion 22, 33

Walpole, Richard 11
Whitehall 10, 11
Winkler, Kenneth 85
Wittgenstein, Ludwig 54
Word to the Wise 20, 167

Yale University 10, 11–12, 17